MW01487203

"Canales's work . . . offers a cl
official teachings on homose_____, _____ _____ ___
teachings as unjust and potentially dangerous. His theological and pastoral
responses to LGBTQ youth and young adults are valuable for Catholic congregations, bringing this urgent discussion to ministers in a manner that is
both reflective and resourceful."

—THERESA O'KEEFE
School of Theology and Ministry, Boston College

"A must-read . . . Canales writes in language that we can all understand. A
great resource to be referred to over and over again. You cannot read this
book without coming away with new knowledge, perspective, insights, and
appreciation for LGBTQ youth, and how to better understand and appreciate them, especially those who are Christian/Catholic."

—ROSLYN A. KARABAN
St. Bernard's School of Theology and Ministry, retired

"Grounded in the best of the Christian tradition yet sufficiently comfortable
to ask critical and necessary questions, Canales has written a must-read
work for anyone engaged in ministry with LGBTQ youth and young adults.
If reading this book makes you uncomfortable and calls you to reassess
common biases and misunderstandings, then you understood it. Accept
the invitation; take a risk, as the author did."

—HOSFFMAN OSPINO
School of Theology and Ministry, Boston College

"The church desperately needs work like this . . . Canales implores us to
follow the example of Jesus' message and ministry and to embrace our LG-
BTQ+ brothers and sisters without hesitation and without judgement. He
does all of this in an approachable manner, using sound theology, biblical
examination, and discussion questions for self-reflection and community
dialogue. This is a truly timely and necessary work for our church."

—PAUL GRIFFITH
Jesuit High School

"I welcome this publication by Arthur Canales. This is an extremely important topic . . . I recommend that all our bishops, priests, and pastoral leaders read and study this book. It is well structured, with some very challenging questions for discussion and refection at the end of each chapter. Don't just buy the book. Read it!"

—GERARD GALLAGHER
Pastoral Coordinator, Archdiocese of Dublin

"This is the most exhaustive and practical text I know of on one of our most current and controversial issues for our society and church. I think it should be in the library of every church and Christian organization . . . Whatever your and your church's perspective, I urge you to consider this challenging text."

—DEAN BORGMAN
Gordon-Conwell Theological Seminary, emeritus

"Canales provides powerful support to youth ministers, seminary professors, and faithful allies to the sexually marginalized in families, communities and congregations. Grounded in liberation theology, including a careful exegesis of frequently cited antigay biblical 'texts of terror,' as well as practical suggestions for youth leaders, Canales ends each chapter with questions for discussion, making this an effective teaching resource fully in accord with Christian principles of *imago Dei*—that of God in everyone."

—FELICITY KELCOURSE
Christian Theological Seminary

Pastoral Care to and Ministry with LGBTQ Youth and Young Adults

Pastoral Care to and Ministry with LGBTQ Youth and Young Adults

Arthur David Canales

WIPF *&* STOCK · Eugene, Oregon

PASTORAL CARE TO AND MINISTRY WITH LGBTQ YOUTH AND YOUNG
ADULTS

Copyright © 2022 Arthur David Canales. All rights reserved. Except for brief quota-
tions in critical publications or reviews, no part of this book may be reproduced in
any manner without prior written permission from the publisher. Write: Permis-
sions, Wipf and Stock Publishers, 199 W. 8th Ave., Suite 3, Eugene, OR 97401.

Wipf & Stock
An Imprint of Wipf and Stock Publishers
199 W. 8th Ave., Suite 3
Eugene, OR 97401

www.wipfandstock.com

PAPERBACK ISBN: 978-1-6667-1932-1
HARDCOVER ISBN: 978-1-6667-1933-8
EBOOK ISBN: 978-1-6667-1934-5

06/10/22

To my brothers, Patrick & Michael,

and

to all the LGBTQ youth and young adults

Contents

Figures and Tables

Figures

Tables

Acknowledgments

PASTORAL CARE TO AND *Ministry with LGBTQ Youth and Young Adults* has been a journey to write and has been an enjoyable process, but not without some bumps along the way. LGBTQ issues is a topic that does not always elicit positive interest. However, I am excited to get this book into people's hands. I think this book will be a staple for youth and young adult ministers, for youth and young adult ministry educators, and for a variety of ministers and pastors who work with young people.

I did not set out to write a book on this topic. Someone suggested that I research on LGBTQ youth back in 2014, so I thought about it for a while, researched the topic, and decided to write my first article on the subject. Some of that article appears in this book. It was not until I began to immerse myself into this topic that I realized I had a real love and concern for LGBTQ young people. Through this process, I discovered I was an LGBTQ ally. It was also the first time I began to consider myself a liberation theologian and the first time I began to see myself as a theologian who did his theological work from the margins. These insights were a bit of an epiphany for me and I continued to embrace the new theological ideas I was encountering. Consequently, this process has been an illuminating journey and I hope the content of this book also will be enlightening for the reader.

Before I thank a few people who have helped me with this book, I need to make sure a few journals and their editors receive mention. Three chapters in this book have been rewritten, redacted, and lengthened here: chapter 5 was originally published in *New Theology Review*; chapter 6 was originally published in the *Journal of Pastoral Care & Counseling*; and chapter 7 was originally published in the *Journal of Youth & Theology*. I am grateful to the following editors for allowing the reworking and reprinting of those original articles into this book: Dawn Nothwehr, Terry R. Bard, and David F. White.

This is not my first book and conventional wisdom dictates that no book writes itself; this book is no different. There are several people whom I am appreciative of for their suggestions and insightful guidance along the way. First and foremost, my wife, Tanya, for her unwavering support of my ideas and my scholarship. She always encourages and supports me to look at different perspectives than my own.

Second, I am indebted to my employer, Marian University in Indianapolis, Indiana. I am provided with a beautiful office, computer, and the opportunity to teach, research, and write—a tremendous privilege that I do not take for granted. Moreover, I am grateful for the support I receive from the administration of the university, especially when writing and publishing on such a sensitive and electric topic within Christianity in general, and Catholicism in particular. One administrator specifically, Dr. William Mirola, former Dean of the College of Arts & Sciences, has been a true supporter and encourager of my research.

Third, my friends and colleagues within the Department of Theology & Philosophy at Marian University merit gratitude for their encouragement and reassurance as we have had plenty of theological, moral, and pastoral conversations regarding ideas and strategies pertaining to LGBTQ folks. I am thankful to Mark Reasoner and Domenic D'Ettore for their challenging, and oftentimes opposite points of view, which have made me think critically about my own position and beliefs on certain points. I am even more grateful to Matthew Sherman and John T. Noble for insights and editing two chapters in this book and for helping me work through some of my thoughts on certain issues.

Fourth, a "shout-out" of praise must go to the library staff, especially Lynnē Colbert at Marian University, predominantly for helping me gather books through interlibrary loans, collecting articles from various journals, and always being ready to help when I asked.

Fifth and finally, warm and sincere appreciation goes out to many youth and young adult LGBTQ folks and to many students (present and past) who have encouraged me to keep writing on this subject even when it seemed bleak. So many people have been supportive of me researching and writing on this topic even though traditional Christians and Catholics may be reticent to engage the topic.

Introduction
Getting an Understanding of Things

It is my desire that, in this our time, by acknowledging the dignity of each human person, we can contribute to the rebirth of a universal aspiration to fraternity. Brotherhood [and sisterhood] between all men and women . . . We must put human dignity back at the center and on that pillar build the alternative social structures we need.

—POPE FRANCIS
Fratelli Tutti, §8 & 168

MOST PEOPLE WHEN THEY extend their hand in greeting to shake another person's hand usually do not say, "Hi, my name is such-and-such. I am a heterosexual and cisgender." However, with this book, perhaps there is a need for some personal introductory comments. I am a male. I am heterosexual, cisgender (explained below), married, middle-aged, white and Mexican American, with three beautiful children. I am a practicing Catholic. I live in Indianapolis, Indiana. I, like most Americans, know someone who is very close to me, be it a family member, relative, close friend, or coworker, who is either lesbian, gay, bisexual, transgender, or questioning their sexuality (LGBTQ).

In large part, this book comes about because I have a family member, good friends, close associates, and great professors who I have had the

1

privilege of knowing over the years that are lesbian or gay and part of the LGBTQ community. Yet, this book really has grown out of my love and admiration for young people. For most of my adult and professional life, I have been involved to some degree or another in Catholic youth and young adult ministry. I have worked for over thirty years with teenagers and college students, and adult catechists who work with young people. In fact, I consider myself an adolescent and young adult ministry scholar; that is, a person who has been academically prepared and professionally trained as a theologian, and who advances the pastoral discipline of Christian youth and young adult ministry. Over the years in working with thousands of Catholic teenagers, emerging adults, and young adults, I have encountered scores of young people who have struggled with their innate birth sex and inherent sexual identity. These young people struggled because their personal experience did not mesh with the historical and traditional Christian teaching on homosexuality.

This book is not necessarily concerned with presenting the same old message that the LGBTQ community is used to hearing—namely, pray, abstain, and obey. Of course, I am not opposed to those three areas of Christian life (and encourage them with young people), but my concern comes out of an advocacy approach and pastoral care model, which promotes equality, respect, and dignity for the human person. Perhaps most importantly, a ministry of advocacy and pastoral care is interested in catering to the spiritual, developmental, and emotional needs of the LGBTQ young person and desires to help them to grow as a young person in their respective Christian churches and denominations without fear, prejudice, repercussion, and/or persecution.

I am a Hispanic, Catholic, pastoral, and liberation theologian who specializes in youth and young adult ministry. I have been working in fields of youth and young adult ministry for over thirty years as both a pastoral practitioner and as a scholar. For the past eight years most of my research agenda has concentrated on advocating for and ministering with lesbian, gay, bisexual, transgender, and questioning youth and young adults. I am also an LGBTQ ally and I am proud of this fact! Being an LGBTQ ally is extremely important to me as a Christian. It is important because as a liberation theologian, I maintain that theology must be done on the margins and in cultural contexts. The context that I work from is youth and young adult ministry, which is a subculture of the larger society, and LGBTQ young people, which is a sexual minority group. Therefore, claiming to be an LGBTQ ally has significance with me, and by writing this book, "I put my money where my mouth is," so to speak.

My sincere hope is that this book, *Pastoral Care to and Ministry with LGBTQ Youth and Young Adults* , will encourage youth and young adult ministers to embrace LGBTQ young people with openness and affirmation. It is also my desire that this book will be a helpful tool in advancing the study and field of Christian youth and young adult ministry in all denominations: Orthodox, Catholic, Protestant, and Evangelical Christianity. As stated above, I am Catholic, but my beliefs and my work are ecumenical, interfaith, and open-minded. This will *not* be a Catholic book per se, but a book that addresses a real, urgent, pastoral need for LGBTQ young people.

This book is concerned with providing competent pastoral care to and ministering with members of the LGBTQ community who are youth or adolescents (ages 13–18), emerging adults (ages 19–25), and young adults (ages 26–35).[1] Therefore, this book is applicable to and offers insights for all Christian youth and young adult ministers. It is with optimism that this book will help to contribute to creating more competent and effective youth and young adult ministers working in the field.

Finally, this book will chart a new course that nudges forward that which is possible within Christian youth and young adult ministry. The topics in this book may not be for everyone, but youth and young adult ministry *is* open to everyone, including LGBTQ folks who are on the margins of society and the church. There is an absolute *need* for this book in the Christian churches today, and youth and young adult ministers would be wise to read it, integrate the ideas and implement some of the strategies that are contained inside, and discover the joy of providing pastoral care to and ministering with the LGBTQ community.

Some Preliminaries regarding LGBTQ Terminology

Before getting into the core of this conversation and book, it is worthwhile to review some terminology that pertains to the LGBTQ community. It may seem simplistic for the readers of this book; however, it is beneficial for a Christian audience, and for youth and young adult ministers, and parents for that matter, to learn the basic terminology for this pastoral and ministry conversation. The language will also give a general Christian audience common ground to speak from, as well as and the proper understanding

1. Canales, *Models & Methods*, 6–10.

of the terminology, which can be incorporated into future discussions and perhaps documents.

LGBT is an acronym that refers to individuals who consider themselves as either lesbian, gay, bisexual, or transgender. All children, adolescents, and young adults (and adults too for that matter) who claim the LGBT sexual status are considered "sexual minorities" by the American Academy of Pediatrics.[2] In recent literature surrounding LGBT youth, the letter "Q" has been added to young people who refers to the word *questioning*, and can be added at times to the acronym LGBT to read LGBTQ. Questioning refers to an young person who is still discerning their sexual orientation and/or struggling with their sexual identity. The letter *Q* can also represent the word *queer*, which has become more popular in homosexual and bisexual literature and in queer theory (explained briefly below and in greater detail later in the book). Therefore, it is not uncommon to see the acronym LGBTQQ, which includes a second *Q* to represent queer understanding. The second Q will *not* be part of the parameters of this work. Sometimes there may appear a plus sign (+) after the acronym LGBT, which reads LGBTQ+ and is supposed to refer to all the other letters that represent a sexual minority group. For example, the acronym LGBTQQIA can be understood to represent: lesbian, gay, bisexual, transgender, questioning, queer, intersex, and asexual or ally, but such an acronym is too clumsy, so some people simply use LGBT+. I may use the LGBT+ term in this book from time to time, but I use the acronym LGBTQ as an all-encompassing term for all sexual and gender minorities. I will also use the word queer throughout this book as a *positive* term that embraces and respects all LGBTQ people.

Another term that I will use throughout this book is *young people*. The term is meant to be a term that encapsulates all ages from 14–35. Pope Francis uses the phrase "young people" and considers this group to be from 16–29 years of age, which is a fourteen-year age span.[3] In this book, however, I will use the entire range of developmental periods: early adolescence, adolescence, emerging adults, and young adults. Ages twenty-nine and above may seem old to be considered "young people"; nevertheless, most young adult ministry scholars note that "young adulthood is typically seen as ages 26–35, which seems old enough to be considered an adult, rather than *young* adult. However, since the period of adolescence is extending,

2. Levine et al., "Office-Based Care," 198–99.
3. Francis, *Christus Vivit*, §68.

it only makes sense that young adulthood is also extended."[4] Unless specifically stated otherwise, the term *young people* in this book will consist of ages 14–35, a nineteen-year span.

The following is a list of commonly used terms that you may have heard or encountered in professional settings or in popular situations regarding sexual orientation and gender identity. This list is not exhaustive, but it is an attempt to keep language current with new terminology being invented every year within the LGBTQ community. It is also important for pastoral workers to be knowledgeable of the trends and changes in definitions that come about within the LGBTQ community, because inevitably a pastoral encounter will take place between someone in ministry and an LGBTQ person, whether one realizes it or not. Therefore, this list of terms and definitions should serve pastoral practitioners well.

LGBTQ Gender & Sexuality Terminology

Abjection: The term literally means "to cast out." Abjection is often associated with transgender folks because their appearance can upset the traditional, dominant, cisgender and heterosexual mindset.

Affectional orientation: Affectional orientation stresses the romantic feelings and emotions that a person has toward another person. Sometimes the term used in place of "sexual orientation."

Ally: The designation given to heterosexual or "straight" and/or gender-conforming people who support, advocate, and carry out social justice actions for those who are LGBTQ.

Androgynes/Androgynous: Someone who displays both feminine and masculine characteristics; partly female and male in appearance, although not necessarily in equal parts. Some androgynes feel they are a blended gender, neither feminine nor masculine.

Asexual: someone who does not experience sexual attraction.

Agender: Someone who does not identify with any gender or gender identity; this person would be considered gender neutral.

Assigned sex at birth: This is also called "natal sex." This is the sex—female, male, or intersex—designation made by medical professionals regarding

---

4. Canales, *Models & Methods*, 9.

a person's sex based on a visual examination of an infant's genitalia at birth. If genitalia is ambiguous, then further investigations and assessments are conducted. Sex assignment is often incorrectly conflated with a person's identity in our society, and one's sex assignment at birth is not always descriptive of a person's gender identity throughout life.

Bigender: Someone who identifies with two different genders or gender identities; these identities can be held simultaneously or they may shift at different times. Sometimes called "multigender" too.

Bisexual: Someone who experiences sexual and physical attraction to both women and men.

Butch: This term is used to label a lesbian who has masculine characteristics in identity and expression. Butches tend to dress in stereotypically masculine ways.

Celibate/Chaste/"Third Way": A person who voluntarily choices to abstain from any and all sexual activity, it is more of a lifestyle; people who choose this lifestyle are not indicating that they are asexual, but are selecting to live their lives according to a philosophical or spiritual mindset that they believe affords them a different way, a "third way" to live, which is through prayer, self-sacrifice, and abstinence.

Cisgender: This is a term used to distinguish from transgender and to signify that a person's psychological and emotional experience of gender identity is congruent or consistent with their natal sex or biological sex and bodily presentation of gender.

Closeted: A word used to designate someone who is actively hiding one's true sexual identity and affectional orientation and/or gender identity from others, particularly family and friends.

Coming out: A phrase used to define a person's process of opening up or coming out to self-acceptance regarding one's sexual orientation or gender identity; often this corresponds with making one's sexual orientation or gender identity known to others.

Coming home: A more affable term that is akin to "coming out," and refers to a person's experience of fully embracing their identity: it is coming home to themselves; a coming home to their family, perhaps for the very first time; and a coming home to God too in some cases.

Congruence: The experience of people having all dimensions of their gender aligned; for example, women who identify as women in both their physical appearance and their internal disposition, and who are attracted to men and vice versa.

Conversion therapy: Sometimes referred to as "reparative therapy." This is an extremely abusive and outdated form of pseudoscientific treatment and practice of trying to change an individual's sexual orientation from homosexuality or bisexual, or someone experiencing gender dysphoria using psychological and/or spiritual interventions, and sometimes physical restraints. Such practices have been rejected by every mainstream medical and mental health organization for decades, but due to continuing discrimination and societal bias against LGBTQ people, some practitioners continue to conduct conversion therapy. Minors are especially vulnerable, and conversion therapy can lead to depression, anxiety, drug use, homelessness, and suicide. In short, there is clear evidence that conversion therapy does not work, and some significant evidence that it is also harmful to LGBTQ people.

Cross-dresser: Someone who wears clothing or adopts the presentation of the opposite gender. However, it is inappropriate to use the term "cross-dresser" when referring to a transgender person. Typically, a cisgender male would wear clothing or present himself as a woman. Cross-dressing is done for a variety of reasons; for instance, "drag shows," fun, party or celebration, entertainment, and personal choice.

Demi-gender: The word "demi" means "half." Someone who identifies *partially* with one or more genders. This person feels a partial, but not a full, connection to a particular gender identity or just to the concept of gender. Most demigender folks self-identify as nonbinary. Demigender people feel a partial connection to a "third gender," that possibly cannot be described by the term "agender" or the absence of gender. For example, a female adolescent who partially identifies as a girl, but does not feel she is all girl, is called a "demigirl."

Demi-sexual: This word describes someone who tends *not* to exhibit strong sexual attractions or has limited sexual attractions with anyone unless there is a strong emotional connection or bond. The demisexual person always creates significant emotional intimacy as a primary component above other factors like physical chemistry, spiritual attraction, or common interests.

Down-low: This phrase is used explicitly in the African American communities, and is used to designate men who present themselves as straight (heterosexual) in public, but whose sexual practices and predilections are gay (homosexual).

Drag: This term is used to describe a person who is typically cisgender and who wears clothing of the other gender or presents themselves as another gender, and sometimes flamboyantly. For example, a cisgender man who wears woman's clothing and makeup, and would be referred to as a "drag queen."

Dyke: Typically, a derogatory word used to label a homosexual female. Sometimes the term is used to harass, humiliate, and subjugate females who have a sexual attraction to other women. The term is considered quite offensive in the lesbian community.

Faggot: A derogatory word used to label homosexual males. The term is used to harass, humiliate, and subjugate males who have a sexual attraction to other men. The term is considered quite offensive in the gay community.

Femme: A term used to describe a lesbian whose feminine expression, gender identity, or gender role are stereotypically feminine, and such a person stereotypically dresses in feminine ways.

Female-to-Male (FtM): A child, adolescent, or adult whose natal sex was female, but experiences a male gender identity and has or is in the process of adopting a male presentation and masculine identifies. So, this person is transitioning to male.

Gay: In the strict sense, the term is associated with homosexual men (and boys) or men who have sexual tendencies, overtures, and attraction toward other men; a male that experiences same-sex attraction. However, the term has become common and inclusive, so the general public refers to every sexual minority as "gay."

Gender: This word encompasses more than biology of male and female binary, it is a complex interrelationship between three elements: (1) *the body* (one's experience of her/his physical body, as well as the way society genders people's bodies and interacts with people based on one's body and perceived sex); (2) *identity* (internal disposition and sense of self as female, male, neither, a blend of both, or something else; whom a person privately know to be her/himself); and (3) *expression*

8

(the ways a person present their own gender to others, and the way society, culture, community, and family perceive, interact with, and try to shape one's gender). The interdependence and connection between these three areas comprises a person's gender.

Genderism: This is a term of prejudice; it is a pejorative term aimed at those who live their lives against the female and male binary or against the feminine-masculine dyad (consisting of two parts).

Gender Confirming Surgeries (GCS): Also known as Gender Affirming Surgeries (GAS). These are medical procedures which are available to transgender and gender nonconforming people. Gender confirmation surgeries are performed by multispecialty physicians that typically include board-certified plastic surgeons. The goal is to give transgender individuals the physical appearance and functional abilities of the gender they know themselves to be since birth so their exterior characteristics corresponds with their interior disposition. There are several gender confirming procedures for transwomen (MtF) and transmen (FtM) to aid in their journey: facial feminization surgery, transfeminine top surgery, transfeminine bottom surgery, facial masculinization surgery, transmasculine top surgery, and transmasculine bottom surgery. The phrase Sexual Reassignment Surgery has fallen out of favor in recent years with the medical and transgender communities.

Gender bender: Someone who intentionally crosses or bends gender roles and expressions.

Gender dysphoria: Someone who experiences some sort of discomfort and/or distress associated with the incongruence (not compatible, out of place, or not the same) when one's psychological and emotional gender identity does not match one's natal or biological sex. For example, when a teenage boy feels that his internal disposition and material makeup does not correspond to his exterior appearance and demeanor and natal sex; therefore, he is experiencing an incongruity, which can be a significant source of ongoing pain, anxiety, and impairment.

Gender expression: The public (and private) signals and symbols that a person uses to communicate to the world a gendered presentation, including such things as behavior, dress, clothing, mannerisms, hairstyle, voice, communication styles, and other forms of presentation. A person's gender expression or gender presentation may not match the person's gender identity that is congruent with a person's gender assigned at birth. Gender expression is related to gender roles and the way society uses these roles to try and enforce conformity to current cultural and gender norms. Everyone expresses gender in some way.

Gender fluid: The term that describes a person who wants to convey that their experience of gender is not fixed or static as either female or male, but fluctuates along a spectrum of gender qualities. Gender fluid people move between genders as something dynamic and fluid, they go with the flow in regards to their gender experiences.

Gender flux: This is a similar identity and expression to gender fluid; however, the movement between specific genders—binary, nonbinary, agender—or possibly one gender is fixed, while the other part is in flux. For example, a gender flux person will typically move from one gender identity or expression from home to school, from school to work, and from work to gym or going out.

Gender identity: This refers to a person's social, psychological, spiritual, and behavioral expression and experience; the innermost core of a person's concept of self and *gender*, and can include female, male, both, or neither. Gender identity is the way a person perceives themselves and call themselves, and this identity may evolve or shift over time.

Genderqueer: Those people who intentionally live counter-culturally to female and male social categories. A person who identifies as genderqueer challenges the construction of binary gender and dyad sexual orientation.

Gender nonconforming: The gender that a person has and self-identifies with that does not comply with ecclesial, familiar, communal, cultural, and/or societal expectations of gender.

Gender normative: This term describes a person whose presentation or behavior ascribes to culturally assigned norms for living out as female and male gender.

Gender spectrum: This refers to gender as not a static binary or standard categories of gender, but rather is viewed as a spectrum of multiple, intersecting dimensions, and falls outside of the dominant social norms of a person's assigned sex at birth.

Heterosexual: People who experience congruence. Persons who experience their sexual and emotional attraction directed toward persons of the presumed opposite gender.

Heterosexism: The discrimination against sexual minorities on the assumption that heterosexuality is the normal and superior sexual orientation. An example of heterosexism is US government agencies continuing a ban against LGBT military personnel.

Homophobia: The illogical and irrational fear of and prejudice against lesbian, bisexual, and gay persons.

Homosexual: A person who has romantic and physical attraction to or engages in sexual behavior with members of the same sex and gender.

Intersex: This term describes people whose physical anatomy, chromosomal, or hormonal characteristics assigned at birth do not fit nice and neat categories of either female or male, but are ambiguous at birth.

Lesbian: A woman (or girl) who self-identifies as a person who has sexual tendencies, overtures, and attraction toward other females; their sexual, emotional, and spiritual attraction is directed toward other women.

Male-to-Female (MtF): A child, adolescent, or adult whose natal sex was male, but experiences a female gender identity and has or is in the process of adopting a female presentation and feminine identifies. So, this person is transitioning to female.

Misgender: The act of incorrectly labeling a person's gender.

Pangender: Someone who resonates and reflects multiple genders identities and gender expressions. Some people use it to indicate that they are all genders or omnigender.

Pansexual: Someone who experiences sexual attraction or romantic intimacy to any and all genders; typically, people who self-resonate with this term reject the notion of binary gender division between female and male, and view gender as a more multifaceted or unsolidified experience.

Polysexual: The sexual attraction to some, but *not* all multiple genders. Sometimes people in the bisexual community use this term. However, I have never met anyone who self-identified as polysexual.

Queer: The *Oxford English Online Dictionary* defines *queer* as "strange, odd, peculiar, eccentric," as well as "relating to homosexuals or homosexuality." The term *queer* is the "inside" and *preferred* word used within the LGBTQ community, and terms such as "homosexual" and "homosexuality" are used more from those people, organizations, and institutions that desire to keep queer people and queer theology away from mainstream society, culture, and church. Therefore, *queer* has a negative connotation, and is a derogatory term, but has been turned positive, an insult reclaimed for power. *Queer* is an inclusive or all-encompassing term for all sexual minorities: gay, lesbian, bisexual, transgender persons. Queer refers to anyone who lives outside of or beyond heterosexual and gender-conforming norms of society and culture; for example, a young adult woman might refer to herself as pansexual. The word "queer" can also include straight and cisgender "allies" who do not self-identify as lesbian, gay, bisexual, transgender, intersex, or questioning, but stand in unity and solidarity with queer people in hopes of cultivating a more just and equitable church, society, and world with respect to sexuality and gender identity. Queer is also used in academic literature and is understood from a dynamic, inquisitive, and research-based manner in several disciplines, such as anthropology, biology, feminism, women's studies, gender studies, historical criticism, sociology, queer theory, and theology.

Same gender loving: A phrase that is more commonly expressed in the African American contexts and communities; it is a phrase that is sometimes used in place of the terms "gay" or "lesbian."

Sex: This term usually refers to one's biological gender assigned at birth: female, male, or intersex. Typically, sex is equated with gender, but it is separate, because gender encompasses factors beyond biology.

Sex assigned at birth: See assigned sex at birth.

Sexual identity: This term defines one's own self-identification in terms of affectional orientation and attraction.

Sexual orientation: This term describes a person's primary sexual, emotional, and physical attraction. It can be used as a synonymous term with "affectional orientation" and "sexual intimacy."

Straight: A colloquial expression for someone who self-identifies as heterosexual and cisgender.

Transgender/Trans: This term is an umbrella and inclusive word that covers a wide range of expressions and experiences, but it is certainly bound by culture and context. Those who self-identify as trans (abbreviation for transgender) may consider themselves homosexual, heterosexual, or bisexual. It is possible that some might consider themselves pansexual, polysexual, or asexual. Thus, being trans does not imply any specific sexual orientation. People who consider themselves transgender may also include transsexuals, cross-dressers, drag queens, intersex folks, and straight people. Being transgender is not necessarily a reflection of affectional and sexual orientation. Today, most people who are transgender prefer to use the abbreviated term *trans* to self-identify.

Transition: This is when a person is in the process of changing or altering from one's natal sex to align with one's gender identity. The transitioning process can be long and arduous, and it may include an assortment of procedures and processes, including switching one's gender expression through mannerisms, choice of dress, behaviors, and one's name. The term *transition* is preferred over the term *sex change* in the transgender community.

Transphobia: The term means the dislike *of*, or fear *of*, and prejudice *against* transgender people.

Transsexual: *All* transsexuals are transgender, but not all transgender people are transsexual. Many transsexual persons are in transition—either from hormone therapy and/or cosmetic surgery—to live in a gender role of choice, and to better align their exterior appearance with their interior disposition. Some transsexual folks have not undergone Sexual Reassignment Surgery (SRS), and perhaps never will for both personal and health reasons. Today, however, most people in the transgender community prefer the phrase Gender Confirming Surgery (GCS) or Gender Affirming Surgery (GAS) as distinct from SRS.

Transvestite: This term is an out-of-date and undesirable term within the transgender community. For most heterosexual and cisgender people, the term refers to those who cross-dress.

Two-spirit: The term used by US Native Americans to define transgender, intersex, and gender nonconforming folks, whose gender identities are ambiguous.

This not an exhaustive list of LGBTQ+ terms, there are more terms for sure; but it does provide a greater understanding of the breadth and depth of queer religious literacy. Hopefully, such a glossary of terms will allow scholars and practitioners alike to come to a more open and affirming propensity which will lead to greater positive engagement and sensitivity.

It is important for youth and young adult ministers to keep up with sexuality and gender terminology and language skills. The object is not to be perfect or to know every term, acronym, or definition, but to have some basic familiarity with the sexuality and gender terminology. The goal is to simply not say the *wrong* word that might be offensive to someone or to remain *silent*, because a youth or young adult minister's silence might not be well received or might be misperceived as uncaring or judgmental, which is the exact opposite of a minister's intent. Like all good youth and young adult ministry, systematic and intentional planning and attentiveness goes a long way.

Chapter 1

A Pastoral Framework at the Service of Sexual Minorities

See, all we do is talk about loving one another as Christ has loved the Church,
but what good is talking? What does it really look like to model Jesus loving
others, to truly love those young people who identify as LGBTQ?

—ANONYMOUS CATHOLIC YOUTH MINISTER

Opening Comments

MINISTRY TO SEXUAL MINORITIES can make level-headed lay ministers
and ordained ministers a bit nervous and cautious due to their particular
denominational affiliation and/or their personal theology. For over eight
years now, I have been researching and writing about LGBTQ youth,
emerging adults, and young adults. Moreover, I have presented at several
local, regional, and national conferences on this topic.

This topic is near and dear to me precisely because I, like many other
Catholics, have family members, relatives, or close friends who self-identify
as LGBTQ. Sexual identity and gender expression is a subject that is continually evolving in our country and world. Today's young people are growing
up in a much different secular context than people who grew up just twenty
years ago. The United States, Canada, and Europe have gradually paved the

way for full acceptance, inclusion, and affirmation of sexual minorities.[1] For young people today, then, the religious context is no different. Sexual minorities have become a topic of discernment and discussion over the past five to ten years with much regularity. The skillful youth, campus, and young adult minister will have to have knowledge and wisdom to navigate through these different and difficult times.

Discussing sexual minorities is an important aspect of ministry with young people and merits dialogue and discernment. The topic is significant because this group of people have been marginalized and ostracized by many within churches and feel like they have no voice or place within the church.[2] For example, and to further exacerbate the situation, many Catholic or Christian LGBTQ young people will not even darken the door of a church because they have preconceived notions that sexual minorities are not welcome in this particular denomination of Christianity. Of course, nothing could be further from the truth in the majority of Christian churches. Perhaps with a new focus and perspective, pastoral ministers can provide quality pastoral care, advocacy, and support for this incredible and gifted group of people, and begin to tear down the walls of sexism and genderism, and avoid the attitude of the primacy of heterosexualism.

The intent of this chapter is to offer a new method and model for providing quality pastoral care to and ministry with sexual minorities in Christian churches. My hope is that the approach in this chapter will be beneficial to all those ministers, regardless of denomination and affiliation, who work with or are open to working with LGBTQ young people.

The Hermeneutical Circle for Pastoral Ministry

As a Hispanic pastoral theologian who engages in liberation theology and ethics, one model that I enjoy is the "hermeneutical circle," a process that relies on introspection and reflection. Many theologians, especially from South America, utilize the hermeneutical circle because it is a model that is "motivated by a passion to establish justice-based relationships from which love can flow."[3] The hermeneutical circle of pastoral ministry begins with the lived experience of oppressive social situations (seeing); then proceeds by working out a concept (judging); next a plan of action is implemented

1. Sanders, *Brief Guide*, 1.
2. Canales, "Ministry to Catholic LGBTQ Youth," 69–70.
3. De La Torre, *Doing Christian Ethics*, 47.

that dismantles the mechanisms that cause persecution (acting).[4] Hence, there is a threefold framework at play: seeing, judging, and acting. These three actions are the main components of the hermeneutical circle.

This threefold framework originated with South American liberation theologians' understanding of eradicating marginalization and oppressive social sins. This same framework is also employed by the Catholic Church's Second Vatican II document *Gaudium et Spes* (1965)[5] and Pope Paul VI's apostolic letter *Octogesima Adveniens* (1971).[6] Both documents can be seen as a "call to action" for the people and parishes in modern society regarding the pastoral activity of the Catholic Church. The main goal of the hermeneutical circle is to formulate a praxis—a system of Christian pastoral ministry that reflects on practice—which ultimately tries to change the harsh reality of people who face living in disenfranchised and marginalized ways daily.

In this chapter, the hermeneutical circle will move slightly beyond the threefold framework of South American theologians to a five-step model that Cuban American Protestant moral theologian Miguel A. De La Torre embraces in this book *Doing Ethics from the Margins*. The five-step model is: (1) observing, (2) reflecting, (3) praying, (4), acting, and (5) reassessing, and De La Torre's model will be used in this book as a tool for doing pastoral theology with LGBTQ folks.[7] How does this pastoral circle work? It helps pastoral theologians and pastoral ministers to make better decisions about human actions and social approaches to certain situations. Typically, people need to be connected to an issue to become personally invested in it or impacted by it in some way. Moreover, people need to comprehend an issue well enough to be able to formulate an opinion and before they make their response. Furthermore, people usually need a sense of direction and hope in order to shape a larger problem into a manageable framework.[8] It might be advantageous to examine each of these five steps of the hermeneutical circle for pastoral ministry before using this model of pastoral care with LGBTQ youth and young adults. Figure 1 below illustrates the hermeneutical circle for pastoral ministry.

---

4. De La Torre, *Doing Christian Ethics*, 47.

5. *Gaudium et Spes*, 903–1001.

6. Paul VI, *Octogesima Adveniens*, 1971.

7. De La Torre, *Doing Christian Ethics*, 56.

8. Holland and Henriot, *Social Analysis*, 9–11.

Figure 1

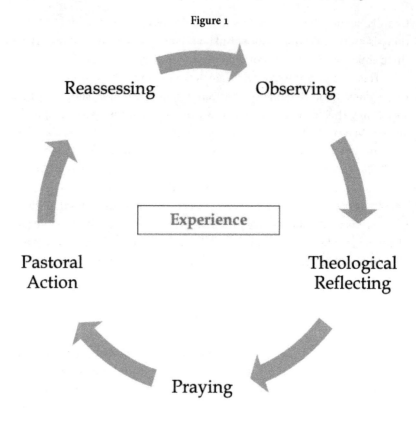

Step 1: Observing—the Initial Analysis

This is the most important step in the process. Observation is a more in-depth form of seeing. Observing is a form of analyzing; it looks critically and constructively at something, usually an object or a person, for the purposes of intellectually gathering and assimilating information. In her book *Franciscan Prayer*, Franciscan theologian Ilia Delio describes the "power of gazing" that may help to understand the process of observing. Delio writes, "Gazing is not simply physical sight like other physical senses that help situate oneself in an environment. Rather, gazing is of the heart by which the heart 'opens its arms,' so to speak, to allow the Spirit of God's love to enter."[9] Gazing requires a space within the heart to receive the object or persons that we see and to embrace what might be different or foreign. Christians cannot afford to be seen as prejudiced, racist, or xenophobic!

9. Delio, *Franciscan Prayer*, 78.

Seeing and observing LGBTQ young people may open once hardened hearts. If our observation recognizes the *imago Dei* within each LGBTQ young person, then Christians will view LGBTQ teenagers and young adults with dignity and respect. If a particular denomination views LGBTQ people with disdain, then they will be viewed as objects. De La Torre notes, "Probably the worst consequences to befall persons who are viewed as 'objects' is that they see themselves through the eyes of their oppressors, as inferior, and lacking power."[10] LGBTQ people appear different or foreign to the dominant Euro-American culture, which tends to be white, and defines reality for those on the periphery or margins.

To seek the voices of the marginalized is to observe the marginalized through the lenses of the poor, oppressed, disenfranchised, and powerless. Observing with the eyes of the marginalized is considered *observing from below*.[11] Observing from below has positive benefits, because observing LGBTQ young people from below allows the first step in the hermeneutical circle to be examined and analyzed from the perspective of those who are not in power or who are not part of the dominant culture.

Political writer Frantz Fanon reminds us that "official" history is always written by the colonizer and is devoid of the voices of the disenfranchised.[12] Observing from below cannot ignore the past because it gives rise to the present and future circumstance. Therefore, the history of sexual minorities, like all marginalized people, in the United States is rarely told because history is written by the dominant power. Post-colonial theorist Homi K. Bhabha has coined the phrase "syntax of forgetting," which does not remember the defeated Other, but usually only recognizes heroic figures and triumphant battles of the hegemonic culture, while it suppresses sexual differences, racial divisions, and class conflicts.[13] Eventually, dominant culture becomes fixed, normalizes its power, and becomes part of the national fabric.

Croatian theologian Miloslav Volf describes a "phenomenology of embrace" that may be useful in remembering the voices of those neglected; to acknowledge the exploitation of the oppressors and greet it with "open arms" is the real embrace of Triune love.[14] For Volf, *embrace* is concerned

10. De La Torre, *Doing Christian Ethics*, 47–48.

11. De La Torre, *Doing Christian Ethics*, 48.

12. Fanor, *Wretched of the Earth*, 51.

13. Bhabha, *Location of Culture*, 160–61.

14. Volf, *Exclusion and Embrace*, 141–42.

with justice, self-boundaries, and liberation, because the Other cannot be entirely obliterated. The challenge of embrace becomes one of reconciliation. Reconciliation in contexts of persisting enmity in which no clear line can be drawn between victims (marginalized) and perpetrators (dominant culture) is part of the observing that needs to take place for evocative embrace to flourish.[15]

LGBTQ young people's lives matter and need to be woven into the fabric of Christian youth and young adult ministry in some meaningful way, to help shape and form ministry with queer people. Doing ministry from the margins requires that white, heterosexual, congregational ministry does not forget about young people and their sexual, racial, economic, and racial oppression while trying to normalize today's understanding of liberation and emancipation. Thus, youth and young adult ministry from below must be done in the margins and as a contextual enterprise; a method that seeks to gaze and observe the work of God through the lens of liberation with its eyes on the disenfranchised, the poor (physical and spiritual), and those who struggle to overcome race, sex, class, sexual orientation, and gender expression. Observing LGBTQ young people, naturally leads to the next step in the pastoral circle—reflecting.

Step 2: Reflecting—Social Analysis

Before structures and systems can change, social analysis is needed to utilize the tools of social sciences. As a Hispanic and pastoral theologian, social sciences such as political theory, history, economics, anthropology, sociology, and psychology help to ground my understanding of social analysis. Theological reflection and introspection are part of pastoral practice that helps to illuminate marginalized systems and structures.

Being aware of oppressive systems and structures and advocating for change is a human and Christian enterprise. Liberation from oppressive systems and structures is a pastoral and human initiative. To engage in the process of introspection and self-liberation is needed for social analysis. By claiming one's own deficient reality, and to point out the social, political, and economic mechanisms that are at work in societies, and perhaps in Christianity as well, is to reveal and disrupt institutional oppression.[16]

15. Volf, *Exclusion and Embrace*, 144, 220.
16. De La Torre, *Doing Christian Ethics*, 50.

Reflecting on social analysis will help Christianity to eradicate unjust social issues that oppress and dominate certain groups of people.

Sex and sexuality have endured oppressive social stigmas over the centuries; oppressive social structures, rooted in a two-thousand-year-old misunderstanding of Christian sexuality, prevents the church from a more just social order.[17] Social analysis, just like biblical interpretation, can never be totally objective, and is incapable of being fully neutral and unbiased.[18] Such subjectivity has been coined the *epistemological privilege* and is observed and stressed more with the disenfranchised and marginalized. Christianity maintains a preferential option for the poor, and obligation to protect the dignity and well-being of the less fortunate, and a responsibility to see everyone as created in *imago Dei*. Every human person is created in *imago Dei*, despite religion, race, class, gender expression, or sexual orientation.

Pastoral reflection on social issues must not ignore individual lives and the systems in which people live. All youth and young adult ministry is wiser when it dialogues with and learns from social sciences, social analysis, and reflects upon its contemporary experience with the Christian community.

Catholic pastoral theologians James and Evelyn Whitehead maintain that there are three important ways that pastoral reflection on social sciences and analysis impacts Christian ministry:

1. social sciences and the intellectual perspective of the age, that is, theology has found itself in dialogue with the dominant intellectual categories of the time;

2. social sciences and self-purification of the Christian community, which means that certain social disciplines serve as a resource for the church, offer self-understanding to the church, and provide assistance with the self-critical function of the church, which can aid the church with being self-corrective and self-purifying; and

3. social sciences provide tools for ministry through data collection, research methods and statistics, and providing information and interpretation on questions that impact the Christian community.[19]

For example, over the centuries Christianity has stressed the importance of marriage and family life (religiously a positive effect) as the natural and

17. De La Torre, *Liberating Sexuality*, vii.

18. De La Torre, *Doing Christian Ethics*, 50.

19. Whitehead and Whitehead, *Method in Ministry*, 72–76.

normative expression for Christian couples to express their love and fidelity to each other. Such a practice has resulted in a neglect or negative effect of ministry to the marginalized within the Christian community: unmarried, widowed, separated, divorced, and LGBTQ persons (religiously a negative effect).[20] Christian denominations would be wise to reflect more on their processes of liberation and ministry practices to all ostracized individuals, societies, and structures that oppress and malign. Prayer, coupled with open-mindedness, will help to rid some social oppression. Prayer is the essential element in the next movement in the hermeneutical circle.

Step 3: Praying—A Theological and Biblical Analysis

Prayer is a critical step within the hermeneutical cycle because pastoral dilemmas and ministry conundrums are observed and reflected upon by the lived faith of the community and the *sensus fidelium*. According to Catholic liberation theologian Francisco Moreno Rejón, a salient methodology for bridging the gap between dogma, sexuality, faith, and ministry is liberation theology. Rejón states, "Thus, we are dealing with a moral theology that, far from repeating timeless, ahistorical principles, presents itself as a reflection vigorously involved with people's daily experience."[21] A lived reality of personal experience and prayer are the imminent concern of the marginalized.

Sexual minorities need to feel part of a community and have a place to pray, be open about spiritual struggles, and live freely and unburdened with God. Prayer is a community endeavor as well as a personal encounter. Christian churches have a responsibility to pray for the marginalized, disenfranchised, and outcasts of society, it is part of the liberation process. Therefore, praying for sexual minorities, both personally and communally, is ethical and pastoral. Prayer is a process of interconnecting the reality which people on the margins experience with the broader church: it is action-prayer. In the Franciscan tradition, this type of prayer, which is deeply reflective and active in style, is called *contemplative action*.[22] Contemplative action is a deeper and more introspective prayer, which enabled Francis of Assisi (1181–1226) and Clare of Assisi (1194–1253) to embrace the lepers and social outcasts of their day, and to see them through the eyes of Christ.[23] Matthew Sherman

20. Whitehead and Whitehead, *Method in Ministry*, 74.
21. Rejón, "Fundamental Moral Theology," 217.
22. Pitchford, *Following Francis*, 17.
23. Pitchford, *Following Francis*, 17.

and I state, "It is often overlooked that Francis was discriminatory towards lepers at one point in his life, but he overcame his disgust and 'took the bitter for the sweet' (*FAED*, II:249), becoming invigorated and inspired by lepers."[24] Francis overcame his prejudices and personal biases through contemplative action and by viewing the marginalized of society as *imago Dei*. Christians today are called to do the same!

Disliking someone for being different because of their gender identity and/or sexual orientation creates a cycle of cruelty, oppression, and hatred. Only genuine love for our LGBTQ sisters and brothers, coupled with the peaceful attitude of Christ, will allow Christian congregations to recognize their part in provoking a cycle of cultural bigotry. Martin Luther King Jr. (1929-1968) prophesies,

> Returning hate for hate [only] multiplies hate, adding deeper darkness to a night already devoid of stars. Darkness cannot drive darkness; only light can do that. Hate cannot drive out hate; only love can do that. Hate multiples hate; violence, multiplies violence, and toughness multiplies toughness in a descending spiral of destruction.[25]

King is describing a hermeneutic of suspicion and a cycle of ignorance and fear, which sometimes the Evangelical right, the staunch conservative Catholic, and the outspoken moral majority seem to be missing—to demonstrate *agape*—unconditional love toward all people.

Agape was Jesus of Nazareth's moral message, not bigotry, not so-called sexual sin. Jesus concentrated his efforts on love, affirmation, compassion, and empathy. When Christians say, "love the sinner, but hate the sin," they represent a misguided theology that is *not* grounded in Christ. Jesus welcomed and loved everyone, he did not put conditions on his love, and his love was free, unmerited, and unconditional. Christians are called to love everyone with *agape*, whether the person is of a different sexual orientation, race, ethnicity, faith, class, or gender expression.[26] Opening up our hearts and minds to LGBTQ people, that is, interpreting the Bible with an ethic of openness and affirmation, one from the margins and from the disenfranchised perspective, is the only way to create a disposition and attitude which fosters unconditional love for all God's people. Only through prayer and

---

24. Canales and Sherman, "Franciscan Campus Ministries," 46.

25. King, *Strength to Love*, 37.

26. De La Torre, *Liberating Sexuality*, 142.

conversion will a different attitude take shape. The next movement in the hermeneutical circle moves from praying to implement praxis.

Step 4: Acting—Implementing Praxis

Praxis is concerned with reflection on ministry practice. In this book, praxis is the reflection on pastoral care to and ministry with LGBTQ young people. Ministry from the margins is about *doing* rather than theologizing or theorizing.[27] What does authentic solidarity for LGBTQ young people look like? Merely, theologizing about LGBTQ young people, regardless of a person's best intentions, even the most liberal-minded person, does nothing, changes nothing, and still leaves LGBTQ people on the margins of Christianity and society. Ministry with LGBTQ youth and young adults is accompaniment not chastisement.[28] Action is absolutely required!

Action can take on many forms, but it is seldom taken by the dominant culture. Outside my office door hangs a rainbow flag (3 x 6 inches), which reads "Ally" across it, indicating that I am an LGBTQ ally. One day, not too long ago, a priest from the Archdiocese of Indianapolis stopped by to see me and say "hi," and pointed to the rainbow flag and said, "Art, what's this?" I told the priest that I was an LGBTQ ally and friend to the LGBTQ community on campus, and that I supported the rights of each individual young person to maintain their own sexuality and identity. I think he was a little taken back, but was open-minded to my affirmation of the LGBTQ community on my university campus. He smiled at me and said, "I get it." Therefore, some action is very slight, like I just described above, or some action can also be in terms of larger scale advocacy such as social activism.

Social activism advocates for broader LGBTQ rights and moves community, state, and federal legislation and becomes a catalyst to support large-scale social change. For example, transgender and nonbinary people being able to use public bathrooms because transgender and nonbinary people, who do not identify fully as either male or female, using either the women's or the men's room might feel unsafe, because others may verbally harass them or even physically attack them.[29] Transgender and nonbinary teenagers should be able to use the public restroom that *they* feel the safest using, not the restroom that *others* think they need.

27. De La Torre, *Doing Christian Ethics*, 54.

28. Francis, *Christus Vivit*, §202–7.

29. National Center for Transgender Equality, "Transgender People."

Liberation theologian José Míguez Bonino notes, "In carrying out the needed structural changes we encounter an inevitable tension between the human cost of their realization and the human cost of their postponement."[30] Action will be needed to bring about real systemic change within a ministry, organization, or institution—or even the government? Which orthopraxis (correct action) will be implemented to further enhance or to bring about orthodoxy (correct belief)? Action is necessary to bring about change, but it has to be the correct action, in this case, the correct pastoral action.

It is difficult to discern the right course of action, or in this case, the right pastoral plan to be implemented to support and advocate for LGBTQ young people. The final step in the hermeneutical circle will help to reassess the situation based on the action plan taken. It is the final movement in the liberation process (well, the liberation process is never really accomplished).

Step 5: Reassessing—New Pastoral Perspectives

Liberation pastoral ministry, at its core, is more than raising people's consciousness about the marginalized and disenfranchised. Albeit, consciousness raising is important, there need to be discussions, solutions, and actions taken on behalf of the ostracized and subjugated. Once action is taken, then further introspection and reflection (meta-reflection) is needed. The effectiveness of liberation pastoral ministry is the way it uncovers or reveals the truth from those on the margins, in this case, from the perspective of LGBTQ young people. Doing pastoral ministry from the margins, particularly with sexual minorities, calls for Christian denominations and individual congregations to reassess their ministry to, for, and with LGBTQ young people. Is correct ministry for LGBTQ young people working? Do sexual minorities feel welcome and affirmed at my church? Is there any direct ministry programming provided for homosexual and transgender people in my church? Is my church a safe place for someone to "come out" as gay or lesbian? Has my parish staff gone through any LGBTQ sensitivity training? If some of the answers are no, then the pastoral circle starts all over again with observing.

In the final analysis, reassessing will bring us back to further observation (step 1) and deeper reflection (step 2), and the hermeneutical process continues. Our pastoral practice always informs and re-forms the way churches interact with people and the way we care for these people.

30. Bonino, *Toward a Christian Political Ethic*, 107.

LGBTQ young people are created in *imago Dei* and are worthy of correct and sensitive ministry.

A Pastoral Plan for LGBTQ Young People

Developing a sensible and sensitive pastoral plan with LGBTQ young people is a good step in the right direction for churches trying to be more open and affirming of sexual minorities. The ministry must be practical if it is going to truly invite and attract LGBTQ adolescents and young adults.

British Baptist pastoral theologian Gemma Dunning suggests demonstrating love is the foundation of a good pastoral plan. Dunning gives five ways of demonstrating love toward LGBTQ young people in the church:

1. be explicit in welcoming LGBTQ young people because church, worship, and faith is for all God's people;

2. use inclusive language that does not make assumptions about sexual orientation or gender because the words we say can alienate or invite young people;

3. show an interest in all aspects of the young person's life, not just their sexual status and identity struggles because youth and young adults are still on a journey of self-awareness and self-discovery;

4. connect young people with affirming books, movies, and clubs so they can have resources at their disposal because it is important that they know other Christians who are affirming and that they are not alone; and

5. be physically present to LGBTQ young people as an ally and advocate because along their journey they will need adults to support them and stand in solidarity with them.[31]

Evangelical youth pastor Eric Woods maintains that there are several relatively easy tasks that youth and young adult ministers can incorporate into their daily attitude and mindset regarding LGBTQ young people. He believes that even the most conservative, right-wing Christians can get behind these practical suggestions. Woods lists five practical ways to help sexual minority young people: (1) be pastoral, not a moral cop, (2) be willing to learn about the person, (3) be open, regardless of your theology, (4)

---

31. Dunning, "Integrity and *Imago Dei*," 29.

be about Jesus' mercy, and (5) be unshockable.[32] These practical suggestions remind youth and young adult ministers to meet and experience the LGBTQ young person as they are, *not who they are not*, and to sit and listen to them in the midst of their ambiguity and struggles.

Developing a pastoral plan to, for, and with LGBTQ young people and ministering directly to sexual minorities is a good thing. It is important work! Not everyone always agrees on the methodology (addressed later in the book) for ministering directly to LGBTQ youth and young adults, but if there are any LGBTQ young people in your ministry, then it is *your* responsibility to be welcoming and affirming. Radical love and unconditional love are the hallmarks of youth and young adult ministry. Empowering LGBTQ young people and helping them to further develop their relationship with God is good pastoral ministry.

Parting Remarks

This chapter has demonstrated that the hermeneutical circle has credibility and implications for pastoral ministry in general and for reflecting and acting on behalf of LGBTQ young people in particular. Discussing and discerning the most appropriate pastoral care and advocacy for LGBTQ young people is an important moral decision that youth and young adult ministers will have to come to grips with over the next several years if they have not already begun to think this way. All of God's people need to appropriate and apply pastoral care, and hopefully, the hermeneutical circle for pastoral ministry. Such a pastoral plan will enhance ministers' readiness to work with and for LGBTQ young people.

32. Woods, "Belonging and Transformation," 78–85.

Discussion Questions

1. What are three new things you learned from this chapter?

2. What points did you find surprising, interesting, or perplexing from this chapter?

3. Why is the hermeneutical circle for pastoral ministry important?

4. Do you consider your congregation or parish to be LGBTQ open or friendly?

5. Have you personally witnessed any LGBTQ folks being discriminated against in your congregation or parish?

Chapter 2

Scriptural Analysis through Liberation Lenses

Full sexual consciousness and a natural regulation of sexual life mean the end of [spiritual] feelings of any kind, that, in other words, natural sexuality is the deadly enemy of mystical religion. The Church, by making the fight over sexuality the center of its dogmas and of its influence over the masses, confirms this concept.

—WILHELM REICH
(Austrian Psychologist, 1897–1957)

Opening Comments

REASONABLE-MINDED CHRISTIANS ARE OFTEN outspoken when it comes to homosexuality, same-sex marriage, LGBTQ rights, and transgender issues. Most Christian faithful possess a rudimentary comprehension of the Bible on sexual-specific texts. Truth be told, there are only a handful of Scripture pericopes in both the Old Testament and New Testament that ambiguously pertain to contemporary understandings of homosexuality.

I read and interpret scared Scripture through the lenses of the marginalized. For the purposes of this book, I read and interpret biblical passages through the lens of LGBTQ people. Catholic Scripture scholar Mark

Reasoner would insist that I read and interpret the Bible through the meta-narrative of liberation. He is correct.[1] The methodology that I implore, as discussed in the previous chapter, is the hermeneutical circle for pastoral ministry, which is a process that relies on personal, social, and theological reflection. Many theologians, especially from South America, utilize this method because it is a model that is "motivated by a passion to establish justice-based relationships from which love can flow."[2]

The main goal of the hermeneutical circle for pastoral ministry is to formulate a praxis—a system of pastoral ministry that reflects on its practice—which ultimately tries to change the harsh reality of people who face living in disenfranchised and marginalized ways daily. Perhaps one way of seeing LGBTQ people is not as sexually different, but as sexual and spiritual human beings like heterosexuals and cisgender folks.

A person's sexuality, sexual expression, and sexual identity matters. Eighty-eight percent of churchgoing Christians who self-identify as lesbian, gay, bisexual, or transgender indicated that their pastor was clueless to their sexual orientation.[3] Pastors and lay ministers should not be naïve to the sexual expression and gender identity of their parishioners.

Sexuality and sexual intercourse are extremely important in the Christian life. First, God is the creator and author of human sexuality, sexual intercourse, and pleasurable sexual intimacy. Second, Christian sexuality is a constitutive dimension of the human person and is comprehensive in scope beyond simple genital sex.[4] Third, Christian sexuality is neither incidental to nor detrimental to fruitful spirituality.[5] In fact, to be fully integrated spiritually is to be fully integrated sexually; therefore, sexuality and spirituality are compatible and closely associated.

Moral theologian Marvin M. Ellison and African American theologian Kelly Brown Douglas state, "*Sexuality* is the physiological and emotional grounding of our capacities to love, is intimately connected with *spirituality*, [which is] the response of the whole being [body, mind, spirit] to what we perceive as the sacred in our midst."[6] Sexuality is concerned with complete potential for human relationships and companionships,

---

1. Reasoner, *Five Models of Scripture*, 219–221.
2. De La Torre, *Doing Christian Ethics*, 47.
3. Ellison, "Practicing Safer Spirituality," 4.
4. Ellison and Brown-Douglas, *Sexuality and the Sacred*, xix.
5. Ellison and Brown-Douglas, *Sexuality and the Sacred*, xix.
6. Ellison and Brown-Douglas, *Sexuality and the Sacred*, xix.

while spirituality is about the human person's capacity to connect with God in ways that help to foster the human/divine connection. Therefore, without human sexuality, it would be impossible for a Christian person to have a fully integrated spirituality, because sexuality is the adapter or connector for spirituality.

There are a couple of suggestions to better help heterosexual Christians appreciate the Bible and its impact upon LGBTQ Christians. First, try to read the Bible through the lenses of the oppressed and marginalized and *not* from the dominant culture's perspective: white, male, middle-class, and heterosexual. Second, try to understand the delicate balance and symbiotic association between spirituality and sexuality; that is, a person's sexuality, gender identity, and spirituality are intimately connected. Hopefully both of these suggestions will help heterosexual and cisgender Christians appreciate and affirm LGBTQ Christians living in our midst and worshiping in our pews.

Biblical Passages That Sort of Address Homosexuality

This chapter will highlight several passages from the Bible and will shed light on this darkened corner of Christianity. The six passages that are examined are commonly known as the *clobber passages* or *texts of terror* to LGBTQ folks. They are called *clobber passages* because conservative Christians—Catholic and Protestant alike—use these biblical texts to justify mistreating and bullying homosexual and transgender Christians. Pastor and LGBTQ activist John Shore puts it this way:

> **Heterosexual Christians are being *unbiblical* by using the clobber passages as justification for applying absolute standards of morality to homosexual "sins" that they themselves [heterosexual] are not tempted to commit, while at the same time accepting for themselves a standard of relative morality for those sins listed in the clobber passages that they *do* routinely commit.** (bold text is original)[7]

Figuratively speaking, conservative Christians "beat" homosexual Christians "over the head" with these texts.

LGBTQ author and advocate Susan Cottrell comments further on the clobber passages. She remarks that less is written about same-sex

---

7. Shore, *Unfair*, 3.

relationships, only in seven verses in total out of approximately thirty-two thousand verses in the Bible, which do not hold up to any real scrutiny of biblical exegesis.[8] Moreover, Cottrell points out, "by comparison to 110 verses about slavery, including direct support of slavery and instructions on [the ways] to deal with slaves."[9] Yet, certain denominations within Christianity managed to let go of slavery as inhumane and inexcusable, but still these same churches denounce and condemn homosexuality based on a few *misunderstood* biblical pericopes—the clobber passages.[10]

Which biblical texts are the clobber passages? Well, first, the Bible is not a Christian rule book or moral manual. Second, the Bible is rather a collection of books, a small library, which represent various literary genres—poetry, wisdom writings and prose, songs, prophetic utterances, historical writings, and apocalyptic literature—that allow humans to see God working throughout salvation history. One of the "burning" questions that college students and young adults have on their minds with respect to the Bible and homosexuality is simply: What does the Bible state about homosexuality?

Before I answer the above question, let me start out by making a couple of rudimentary observations as a college theology professor for the past twenty-plus years. First, my experience tells me that the overwhelming majority of Christians do *not* really read the Bible regularly and only have cursory knowledge of various parts of the Bible at best. Second, the term *homosexuality* is really a misnomer in the Bible. The Bible does not mention the words "homosexual" or "homosexuality."[11] The term "homosexuality" is a late nineteenth-century invention and first coined by Karl Maria Kertbeny, who was arguing against Prussian anti-sodomy laws.[12] Third, if the term "homosexual" is in a particular version of a Bible, then it was inserted in the biblical text sometime after the year 1900. The term "homosexual" did not exist in antiquity in the Hebrew or Greek language. Fourth, and this is essential for Christians, Jesus *never*, ever, mentions or addresses anything remotely close to today's understanding of homosexuality. It is baffling that any Christian who has undertaken a thorough reading of the Bible could come away with an understanding that homosexuality is one of the central

8. Cottrell, *"Mom, I'm Gay,"* 119, 127.

9. Cottrell, *"Mom, I'm Gay,"* 127.

10. Cottrell, *"Mom, I'm Gay,"* 127.

11. Himbaza et al., *The Bible on the Question of Homosexuality*, ix.

12. Feray, "Homosexual Studies," 25.

and most pressing moral issues of contemporary North American society.[13] In fact, sex and sexuality is something that Jesus says next to nothing about.

Catholic systematic theologians Kathleen Fischer and Thomas Hart note, "Sex is a subject on which Jesus says very little. There is nothing in the gospels on masturbation, homosexuality, premarital sex, or birth control . . . The gospels hardly constitute a basis for the [Catholic] church's preoccupation with sexual issues."[14] This is not to say that sexual ethics is not important, because it is, but it does not constitute Christianity's negative preoccupation with premarital and homosexual sex. Nevertheless, the debate among Christians regarding homosexuality and same-sex marriages is a lightning rod for many people and their respective denominations. The biblical analysis here is *not* likely to change that debate. My hope is that a cursory survey of the clobber passages will empower some Christians to be a little more open-minded and a little less judgmental about the topic. Furthermore, it is time to stop looking at these clobber passages as a means to mistreat and bully LGBTQ folks.

The Supposed Old Testament Pericopes regarding Homosexuality

There are three biblical pericopes or passages which deal with the question of homosexuality in the Old Testament that merit examination and explanation. The three texts are: Gen 19:1–29; Lev 18:22 and 20:13; and Deut 22:5.

Genesis 19:1–29: The Sin of Sodom (NASB)

> *Now the two angels came to Sodom in the evening as Lot was sitting in the gate* of Sodom. *When Lot saw them, he rose to meet them and bowed down with his face to the ground. And he said, "Now behold, my lords, please turn aside into your servant's house, and spend the night, and wash your feet; then you may rise early and go on your way." They said however, "No, but we shall spend the night in the square." Yet he urged them strongly, so they turned aside to him and entered his house; and he prepared a feast for them, and baked unleavened bread, and they ate. Before they lay down, the men of the*

13. Placher, *Jesus the Savior*, 96.
14. Fischer and Hart, *Christian Foundations*, 84.

city, **the men of Sodom, surrounded the house,** *both young and old, all the people from every quarter; and they called to Lot and said to him,* **"Where are the men who came to you tonight? Bring them out to us that we may have relations [sex] with them."** *But Lot went out to them at the doorway, and shut the door behind him, and said, "Please, my brothers, do not act wickedly.* **Now behold [look], I have two daughters who have not had relations with man; please let me bring them out to you, and do to them whatever you like; only do nothing to these men, inasmuch as they have come under the shelter of my roof."** *But they said, "Stand aside." Furthermore, they said, "This one came in as an alien, and already he is acting like a judge; now we will treat you worse than them." So they pressed hard against Lot and came near to break the door. But the men reached out their hands and brought Lot into the house with them, and shut the door. They struck the men who were at the doorway of the house with blindness, both small and great, so that they wearied themselves trying* to find the doorway. **Then the two** men said to Lot, "Whom else have you here? A son-in-law, and your sons, and your daughters, and whomever you have in the city, bring **them** out of the place; **for we are about to destroy this place, because their outcry has become so great before the Lord** that the **Lord** has sent us to destroy it." *Lot went out and spoke to his sons-in-law, who were to marry his daughters, and said, "Up, get out of this place, for the Lord* will destroy the city." But *he appeared to his sons-in-law to be jesting.* **When morning dawned, the angels urged Lot, saying, "Up, take your wife and your two daughters who are here, or you will be swept away in the punishment of the city."** *But he hesitated. So the men seized his hand and the hand of his wife and the hands of his two daughters, for the compassion of the Lord was* upon him; and they brought him out, and put him outside the city. *When they had brought them outside, one said, "Escape for your life! Do not look behind you, and do not stay anywhere in the valley; escape to the mountains, or you will be swept away." But Lot said to them, "Oh no, my lords! Now behold, your servant has found favor in your sight, and you have magnified your loving kindness, which you have shown me by saving my life; but I cannot escape to the mountains, for the disaster will overtake me and I will die; now behold, this town is near enough* to flee to, and it is small. Please, let me escape there (is it *not small?) that my life may be saved." He said to him, "Behold, I grant you this request also, not to overthrow the town of which you have spoken. Hurry, escape there, for I cannot do anything until you arrive there." Therefore the name of the town was called Zoar. The sun had risen over the earth when Lot came to Zoar.*

Then the Lord rained on Sodom and Gomorrah brimstone and fire from the **Lord out of heaven, and He overthrew those cities, and all the valley, and all the inhabitants of the cities, and what grew on the ground.** *But his wife, from behind him, looked back, and she became a pillar of salt. Now Abraham arose early in the morning and went to the place where he had stood before the Lord; and he looked down toward Sodom and Gomorrah, and toward all the land of the valley, and he saw, and behold, the smoke of the land ascended like the smoke of a furnace. Thus it came about, when God destroyed the cities of the valley, that God remembered Abraham, and sent Lot out of the midst of the overthrow, when He overthrew the cities in which Lot lived.* (italics and bold added)

This passage of Scripture is without a doubt the most famous text that *supposedly* deals with homosexual behavior in the Old Testament and has been used to justify referring to homosexual people and same-sex relationships as *Sodomites* and other perverse names. Therefore, it is a significant passage to unpack this particular pericope. As a father of three, and one of my children happens to be a daughter, I find this biblical text appalling in the extreme! Nevertheless, the pericope merits examination.

The passage indicates that Lot, the nephew of Hebrew patriarch Abraham, received visitors who he did not know. The men in Sodom heard of Lot's visitors (angels) and soon surrounded his house, banged on the door, and demanded that Lot's visitors be sent outside immediately so they could have their way sexually with the two visitors—to abuse and gang rape them. The part of the story that is usually overlooked or ignored by pastors and preachers regarding this passage is that Lot is all too willing to hand over his two virgin daughters for sexual pleasure as a way to appease the angry mob. In my mind's eye, I picture Atticus Finch in the movie *To Kill a Mockingbird* (1962), and the scene where the angry mob is at the local jail wanting to lynch Tom Robinson, an innocent black man, and Atticus and his twelve-year-old daughter, Scout, talk the mob down and turn them away. Lot's logic makes absolutely no sense to the contemporary mind, but remember, women and children had no rights whatsoever in antiquity. Lot was overplaying his obligation as a dutiful host to his two visitors. As the narrative unfolds, thankfully, Lot does not give in to the mob.

Over the decades, if not centuries, many conservative preachers, teachers, and biblical commentaries have judged the sin of Sodom to be homosexuality. Since the majority of Christian denominations and "born-again" individuals proclaim the Bible to be God's truth, especially

Evangelical Christians, then it is only fitting and worthwhile to examine the Bible itself on this issue.

The Prophet Amos (chronologically considered the first of all prophets) prophesied the destruction of Israel for following the same path of selfishness as did the city of Sodom. Amos proclaims, "You who oppress the weak and abuse the needy" (4:1, 11). It seems that Amos condemns the citizens of Sodom for not taking care of the poor and needy. Amos does not mention anything about so-called sexual sin.

The Prophet Isaiah urges the people of Israel to remember the fate of the people who lived in the cities of Sodom and Gomorrah, and their annihilation (1:10–17). Isaiah states, "Wash yourselves clean! Put away your misdeeds from before my eyes; cease doing evil; learn to do good. Make justice your aim; redress the wronged, hear the orphan's plea, defend the widow" (1:16–17). Isaiah is concerned about the Israelites crushing the spirit of the poor and the marginalized. Isaiah does not mention anything about so-called sexual sin.

The Prophet Jeremiah mentions Sodom's sins: "adultery, living in lies, siding with the wicked, so that no one turns from evil" (23:14). For Jeremiah, the real sin of Sodom was their unwillingness to repent. Jeremiah does not mention anything about so-called sexual sin.

The Prophet Ezekiel claims that the crimes or iniquities of Sodom's people were "pride, gluttony, arrogance [and] complacency" (16:49). In addition, the citizens of Sodom "never helped the poor and needy; they were proud and engaged in filthy practices" (16:50). Therefore, according to Ezekiel, the people of Sodom were unwilling to share their resources and abundance with the poor, marginalized, and oppressed. Ezekiel does not mention anything about so-called sexual sin.

The Book of Wisdom (part of the Catholic Bible and Protestant Apocrypha) refers to the city of Sodom and their punishments for mistreating their guests with folly, insolence, and inhospitality, and such deeds were found as grievous in God's sight (19:13–15). The author of Wisdom does not mention anything about so-called sexual sin.

The Book of Sirach (part of the Catholic canon and Protestant Apocrypha) merely specifies that God "spared not the neighbors of Lot whom [God] detested for their pride" (16:8). The footnote from *The Catholic Bible: Personal Study Edition* specifically states that this pericope is regarding the people of Sodom and Gomorrah. Sirach only refers to Sodom's pride. Sirach does not mention anything about so-called sexual sin.

Jesus of Nazareth makes a passing remark to Sodom and Gomorrah as he is instructing the Twelve to go out two-by-two visiting people and evangelizing them. Jesus' injunction reads virtually the same in both the gospels of Luke and Matthew: "Whoever will not receive you or listen to your words—go outside that house or town and shake the dust from your feet. Amen, I say to you, it will be more tolerable for the land of Sodom and Gomorrah on the Day of Judgment than for that town" (Matt 10:14–15; Luke 10:12). These are strong words from Jesus, but he associates the sins of Sodom and Gomorrah with rudeness and inhospitality. Jesus of Nazareth does not mention anything about so-called sexual sin.

Thus, the most famous biblical text that is used so often to judge and condemn homosexuality and same-sex attraction as a serious sexual sin and breach of morality does *not* even address the subject. De La Torre notes, "The sin of Sodom and Gomorrah, according to the word of God [sacred Scripture], is not providing justice to the 'orphans and widows,' the biblical euphemism for the disenfranchised."[15] LGBTQ people today are the social outcasts of contemporary society.

Presbyterian theologian William C. Placher remarks that "Sodomites" are not homosexuals at all; "these sodomites are violent bullies who carry their excess to the point of attempted rape. Such behavior still occurs in the aftermath of battle, in prisons, or among violent gangs."[16] Gang rape is a violation of a person's dignity and freedom and it is a severe act of violence where pleasure is achieved by subjugating and humiliating the victim. Therefore, Sodomites are physical and sexual abusers exercising their own dominance and power to inflect pain and mental anguish upon their victims.

What is the real sin of Sodom? Catholic Scripture scholar Mary Healy claims that the sin of Sodom is "their sexual misconduct, which was part of a larger pattern of pride, greed, and selfishness—all rooted in arrogant disregard for God and [God's] will."[17] The real sin is the lack of love and respect shown to others, to foreigners. This Genesis passage (19:1–29) demonstrates a lack of human dignity and respect shown to the individual. The text is about gang rape and violence; about a people's unwillingness to extend hospitality to the stranger, to the refugee, and foreigner in their midst, it is about coercion, abuse of power, and rape by *heterosexual* men.[18] The passage has

15. De La Torre, *Liberating Sexuality*, 158.

16. Placher, *Jesus the Savior*, 98.

17. Healy, *Scripture, Mercy, and Homosexuality*, 29.

18. De La Torre, *Liberating Sexuality*, 158.

nothing to do with homosexual or transgender people; it has nothing to do with two people loving each other in a committed and monogamous relationship; it has nothing to do with healthy sexuality and genuine love-making. Therefore, the so-called sin of Sodom is *not* about homosexuality.

Leviticus 18 and 20:13: The Law and Holiness Code (NIV)

> *Do not have sexual relations with a man as one does with a woman; that is **detestable**.* (18:22; italics and bold added)

> If a man has sexual relations with a man as one does with a woman, both of them have done what is ***detestable.*** *They are to be put to death; their blood will be on their own heads.* (20:18; italics and bold added)

These are pericopes that I have often heard Christian people and minis-ters—Catholic and Protestant—use to condemn and oppress sexual mi-norities. In other translations, the text uses the word "abomination" (an act incompatible with God) instead of "detestable." Both words are unsettling for the contemporary reader because they smack of racism, judgmental-ism, and triumphalism (self-righteousness).

On the surface, these two passages condemn male homosexual inter-course, but a closer examination might alter that narrow understanding. Leviticus 18 merely disallows same-sex acts and Leviticus 20 specifies the punishment for the same-sex acts.[19] The book of Leviticus has a section known as the Holiness Code, which encompasses chapters 17–26, and had its origins in the sixth-century BCE, which was approximately 2,600 years ago. The Holiness Code is a piece of legislation within the book of Leviti-cus. The prohibition of males having sexual relations with males, like many other laws in the Holiness Code, sought to identify and condemn practices that had always remained, for the most part, foreign to the people of Israel.[20]

The Hebrew people were called to separate themselves or to be holy (Lev 19:2) from other peoples who previously inhabited the land, such as the Canaanites, Moabites, and Ammonites. Hence, as the Israelites took possession of a foreign land, they had to ensure that they did not adopt the customs of the people who surrounded them in this new land. Some of the Israelites who violated the Holiness Code were punished severely or put

19. Healy, *Scripture, Mercy, and Homosexuality*, 31.
20. Coleman, *Homosexuality*, 61.

to death. If we were to read the Bible from a fundamentalist and literalist perspective: we should then put all gay and lesbian people to death? The law in Leviticus also calls for the death of those: committing adultery (Lev 20:10); brides who on their wedding night were discovered not to be virgins (Deut 22:13–21); disrespectful teenagers (Lev 20: 9); and blasphemers (Lev 24:15).[21] The real meaning of these two texts is against temple homosexual prostitution or engaging in sacred sex with a male, which was associated with the worship of pagan gods, and it is that context that led to the denunciation of same-gender sex in Hebrew law.[22]

Today Christians dismiss the killing of disrespectful teenagers or women who are not virgins; however, a large percentage of Christians cannot overlook the two verses regarding homosexuality, maintaining it is an abominable act. Why? This seems unreasonable today based on human dignity of the individual.

The Holiness Code also includes a number of other acts of abomination:

1. offering a blemished animal (Deut 17:1);

2. eating unclean animals, such as shellfish (Lev 11:10), dead carcasses (Lev 11:11), and animals with cloven hoofs, such as pigs (Deut 14:4–8);

3. men may not shave their heads or trim their beards (Lev 19:27);

4. remarrying a former spouse (Deut 24:4);

5. having sex with a prepubescent boy (Lev 20:13), with an animal (Lev 20:15), or with a woman during her menstrual cycle (Lev 20:18–24);

6. the improper use of incense (Num 16:39–40).

The issues in the Holiness Code are actually aimed at ritual purity rather than moral indictments concerning two committed and monogamous lovers.

These abominations in the Holiness Code are hardly taken seriously today by mainline biblical scholars and Christian theologians, and such condemnations no longer apply. Therefore, it is difficult to comprehend the hold these ancient purity and kosher laws of Israel still have on the contemporary understanding of homosexuality within Christianity.[23] Unlike today, it appears that the Holiness Code's concern is not the desire of individual happiness and sexual delight between two people who are in

21. De La Torre, *Liberating Sexuality*, 160.

22. Placher, *Jesus the Savior*, 97.

23. Placher, *Jesus the Savior*, 98.

an exclusive and permanent relationship who are attracted to each other through love and affection.[24] The Holiness Code's primary concern seems to be about the social needs of the community rather than the individual.[25]

Hence, the condemnation of homosexuality in Leviticus 18 and 20 seems unimportant today.[26] De La Torre maintains, "Lying with a sacred male prostitute would be considered an abomination because it follows the ritual practices of those from whom the Hebrews tried to separate themselves."[27] The Leviticus regulations are noticeably irrelevant in explaining Christian hostility toward LGBTQ people and their sexuality. Consequently, then, the Leviticus passages are not condemning the contemporary understanding of homosexuality in terms of a loving, uncoerced, and exclusive relationship.

Deuteronomy 22:5: Wearing Women's Clothes (NRSV)

*A woman shall not wear a man's apparel, nor shall a man put on a woman's garment; for whoever does such things is **abhorrent** to the Lord your God.* (italics and bold added)

This pericope is the one and only biblical text that broaches the condemnation of cross-dressers and/or transgender people. The word *abhorrent* means "objectionable" and "repugnant," but not "you are going to hell" with all fire-and-brimstone motifs. Therefore, this passage, to be clear, is *not* divine condemnation of twenty-first-century societies or transgender people. The covenantal concern for the primary audience of the book of Deuteronomy was to preserve the Holiness Code of Israel. Wearing clothing of the opposite sex was objectionable to Hebrew culture because it was in vogue among fertility worshipers in the Canaanite culture.[28] Preventing cross-dressing might have been a way for the Israelites not to confuse gender roles by swapping clothing like other ancient cultures might have done.

There are three possibilities for this passage: (1) putting and keeping women in their place as property, (2) preserving Jewish traditions by prohibiting other worship services where priests donned the garments of females, and/or (3) preventing the mixing of one category with another—it

---

24. Himbaza et al., *The Bible on the Question of Homosexuality*, 52.

25. Himbaza et al., *The Bible on the Question of Homosexuality*, 52.

26. Coleman, *Homosexuality*, 62.

27. De La Torre, *Liberating Sexuality*, 161.

28. Kellogg, "Transvestism, Transgenderism, and Deuteronomy 22:5," 1.

was prohibited, for example, to wear a garment made from several differ-ent fabrics.[29] This biblical pericope seems to be about maintaining certain social norms and religious customs and is not concerned in the slightest about contemporary American or European fashion and clothing styles. Therefore, the warning of men wearing women's clothing or vice versa can hardly be seen as a condemnation toward transgender people today.

Examining these three Old Testament passages, based upon con-temporary theology and biblical studies, indicates that they are not anti-homosexual or anti-transgender texts, albeit many Christians have used them that way over the centuries. After some scrutiny, these three biblical passages do not justify marginalizing and dooming LGBTQ people. These three Old Testament clobber passages can be explained by offering reason-able exegetical evidence and logical hermeneutical insights.

The Alleged New Testament Pericopes regarding Homosexuality

There are five New Testament passages that allegedly address homosexual-ity. These five texts of terror have been used to harass, shame, and condemn homosexual people. However, there are *no* texts found in the four gospels of Jesus discussing sexuality, sexual ethics, or homosexuality. Should it be assumed that same-sex lovers did not exist in antiquity? The answer is no, of course not. Same-sex attraction and lovers very much existed in Jesus' day. He just had nothing to say about it or perhaps thought it was not as important as love or ushering in the reign of God.

European Catholic Scripture scholars Innocent Himbaza, Adrian Schenker, and Jean-Baptiste Edart state, "The gospels have nothing explicit to say about homosexuality."[30] This silence connected to Jesus demonstrates his great mercy for people regardless of their sexuality and gender identity. Perhaps Jesus' silence on the matter may also be inter-preted as indicating that Jesus tacitly and implicitly approves of homo-sexuality and transgender rights.[31]

Three texts of terror are attributed to the Apostle Paul and are found only in the Pauline corpus. The two main terms that allegedly deal with homosexuality in the Pauline corpus are *malakos* and *arsenokoitēs* in the

29. De La Torre, *Liberating Sexuality*, 161.

30. Himbaza et al., *The Bible on the Question of Homosexuality*, 73.

31. Himbaza et al., *The Bible on the Question of Homosexuality*, 73.

Greek. Therefore, those two terms will loom large while examining the first three New Testament texts.

There are two other texts that require brief consideration; however, they have to do with sex with angels, which is a "stretch" by contemporary theological imagination. Those texts are found in the books of 2 Peter and Jude. Nevertheless, the Apostle Paul's understanding of same-sex genital acts are addressed first in this section.

Romans 1:26–27: Being True to Our "Nature" (NRSV—Catholic Edition)

> For this reason God gave them up to **degrading passions.** *Their* **women exchanged natural intercourse for unnatural,** *and in the same way also the men, giving up natural intercourse with women, were consumed with passion for one another. Men* **committed shameless acts with men** *and received in their own persons the due penalty for their error.* (italics and bold added)

This is an important biblical passage because most Christians today put more emphasis on the New Testament's instructions as distinct from the Old Testament's rules and regulations. Therefore, it is imperative to look at one of the Apostle Paul's most significant books—Romans. I am simply beginning with Romans because its placement is before the books of Corinthians and it is considered his theological masterpiece.

This seems to be the *only* pericope in the Bible that references same-sex relations between women and the most explicit concerning men. Some of the words in the text seem to be the most cause for alarm. The words *degrading passions* is sometimes translated as "shameful lusts" or "vile affections" in various versions of the Bible. During the New Testament epoch, the Roman Empire controlled the majority of the Western world. Roman conquerors of the region frequently, and perhaps openly, engaged in same-sex genital acts between themselves and prepubescent boys.

Shore notes, regarding same-sex genital acts, "such acts are also common between Roman men and their male slaves."[32] Moreover, some male slaves might have been preadolescent or teenage boys. These same-sex genital acts were nonconsensual acts, coercive acts, unequal acts, and acts

---

32. Shore, *Unfair*, 9.

of power and submission.[33] These nonconsensual same-sex acts were normal occurrences in antiquity and socially acceptable to the Romans and their sexual lifestyle. From the Apostle Paul's perspective, these same-sex genital acts were foreign and ghastly. Today in contemporary American society, these coercive, nonconsensual types of acts are repulsive. American society has a term for *forced sexual acts* by the strong upon the weak—rape. We refer to sexual acts with children (ages 5–12) as pedophilia and sexual acts with teenagers (ages 13–17) is ephebophilia. Both are morally reprehensible by today's standards. It is highly doubtful that the Apostle Paul was referring to monogamous homosexuality as practiced today by committed, loving LGBTQ Christians. Therefore, the term *degrading passions*, which the Apostle Paul references in Rom 1:26–27, does not mesh with contemporary homosexuality.

The two main words that Paul uses, *malakos* (literally meaning "soft," "weak," "delicate," or "effeminate") and *arsenokoitēs* (a bit more difficult to translate because it is a term personally coined by the Apostle Paul), in the Greek have several usages. The term *malakoi* can mean "male prostitutes" and can also be slang for boys who played a passive role in sexual intercourse (at least regarding the person who is penetrated).[34] The term *arsenokoitai* is an unusual term in the New Testament, but it appears to mean "men who have sex with other men," "lying with a male," or "men who bed other men."[35] Consequently, neither term, *malakos* nor *arsenokoitēs*, means "homosexual," or has today's contemporary understanding of same-sex marriages as they exist in the United States.

There are four current, scholarly, and well-researched lines of biblical interpretation on this passage by New Testament exegetes. The first interpretation is from Anglican biblical scholar Robin Scroggs, and his book titled *The New Testament and Homosexuality: Contextual Background for Contemporary Debate*. Scroggs notes that "Paul does not condemn homosexual relations as such, but rather the *exploitation* involved in the relations between master and slave, or between young adults (pederasty, the love or use of young boys), or prostitution."[36] For Scroggs, the Apostle Paul is

---

33. Shore, *Unfair*, 9.
34. Placher, *Jesus the Savior*, 99.
35. Placher, *Jesus the Savior*, 99.
36. Scroggs, *New Testament and Homosexuality*, 99.

against the unnatural relationship that exists with pederasty and male prostitution because such relationships are dehumanizing and scandalous.[37]

The second explanation is from psychologist David G. Myers and Evangelical biblical scholar Letha Dawson Scanzoni and their book titled *What God Has Joined Together: The Christian Case for Gay Marriage.* Myers and Scanzoni comment that "Paul had no sense of the notion of sexual orientation. In this passage he is only considering the case of heterosexuals having coerced same-sex relations. One *cannot* therefore use Romans 1 as an argument to condemn the stable union of two homosexuals."[38] For Meyers and Scanzoni, there is no contemporary equivalent to that which is being discussed by the Apostle Paul.

The third analysis of this text is from feminist biblical scholar Bernadette J. Brooten and her book titled *Love between Women: Early Christian Responses to Female Homoeroticism.* Brooten maintains that

> Paul defends the status of the man. According to the model established in the Greco-Roman culture, the man must dominate his sexual partner. Losing this dominating characteristic in homosexual relation (at least regarding the person who is penetrated), he would lose his dignity. In the same way, female homosexual relations, with one woman dominating the other, challenge this model. This cannot be right. The Apostle therefore opposes these types of relations for this reason.[39]

For Brooten's perspective, it is clear that the Apostle Paul does not want a male person to be weak or soft (*malakos*) while engaging in sexual relations. Hence, same-sex intercourse between men would put one person in a passive sexual position. Therefore, in the Apostle Paul's mind, men should not compromise their masculinity or virility; these traits are not necessarily in keeping with contemporary standards. Today, men are taught to embrace their softer or feminine side.

The fourth interpretation is by Protestant New Testament scholar Robert A. J. Gagnon and his book titled *The Bible and Homosexual Practice: Texts and Hermeneutics.* Gagnon simply states that "Paul, speaking here of sins committed by pagans in an imaginary dialogue with a Jew, condemns homosexual relations."[40] For Gagnon, the entire text could come from

37. Scroggs, *New Testament and Homosexuality*, 128.

38. Myers and Scanzoni, *What God Has Joined*, 93.

39. Brooten, *Love between Women*, 195–215; 359–62.

40. Gagnon, *The Bible and Homosexual Practice*, 247.

the fanciful imagination of the Apostle Paul. The rejection of same-sex intercourse by the apostle is irrelevant in today's contemporary context of a committed, loving homosexual relationships.

The common thread of each of these scholarly interpretations is that the Apostle Paul in no way condemns the twenty-first-century understanding of homosexual relationships and marriages. Paul condemns the coercive, dominating, and manipulating causal, sexual intercourse between a male or female in a power-relationship over another same-sex person.

De La Torre has an alternative explanation for the Romans text. He strongly states that this passage is typically read with a heterosexual lens or bias.

> This is not a text about homosexuality, but about exchanging what is *natural* for *unnatural*. If this passage is read with a heterosexual bias, it is easy to assume that the tern *unnatural* is a reference to homosexuality.[41]

The Apostle Paul's concern in this passage is with heterosexual men and women who are having sexual relations with the same-sex partner and not being faithful to their true nature, and therefore, in his mind, their acts are seen as unnatural. However, what if a person's *true* nature is gay or lesbian? Then these persons are *not* acting out against their nature and their sexual acts are *not* be seen as unnatural. Christians who wish to apply this rigid teaching today, either in the classroom or from the pulpit, would be wise to consider this: the truth is that homosexual persons should also *not* exchange their natural orientation for heterosexual practices.[42]

Himbaza, Schenker, and Edart also maintain that in this pericope, the Apostle Paul is referring to heterosexuals having homosexual intercourse, and that homosexual orientation does not fall into consideration for him as a category. Their analysis of the text also concludes them to state three points regarding the possibility of the Apostle Paul's understanding: (1) the loss of freedom, (2) the lack of respect for the body, and (3) the blindness of the conscience.[43] This is a strong interpretation of the text (Rom 1:26–27). However, it does *not* negate the point that the primary intention in these verses is *not* to condemn homosexuality as understood in the twenty-first-century world.

---

41. De La Torre, *Liberating Sexuality*, 162.
42. De La Torre, *Liberating Sexuality*, 162.
43. Himbaza et al., *The Bible on the Question of Homosexuality*, 99.

1 Corinthians 6:9: Sexual Abuses (NIV)

*Or do you not know that wrongdoers will not inherit the kingdom of God? Do not be deceived: Neither the sexually immoral nor idolaters nor adulterers nor **men who have sex with men**.* (1 Cor 6:9; italics and bold added)

1 Timothy 1:10: Sexual Immorality (NAB)

*. . . for the sexually immoral, for **those practicing homosexuality**, for slave traders and liars and perjurers—and for whatever else is contrary to the sound doctrine.* (1 Tim 1:10; italics and bold added)

These two pericopes will be examined together because they are so similar, and both are attributed to the Apostle Paul. However, the majority of Scripture scholars maintain that 1 Timothy was probably not written by the Apostle Paul, but by one of his close disciples.

In the 1 Corinthians text, the Apostle Paul lists several vices that he categorizes as bad behavior for those who follow Christ. However, it is important to remember the social context in which the Apostle Paul was writing, namely, a Greco-Roman, non-Jewish, non-Christian, pagan social order, and not a twenty-first-century American, multireligious culture.

Some translations use the term *boy prostitutes* and/or *sodomites*[44] instead of the phrase "nor men who have sex with men" in 1 Cor 6:9. The debatable words in this text are *malakoi* and *arsenokoitai*, which are often misunderstood and misrepresented as having intimate relations with same-sex partners.[45] In fact, there are several different meanings for these two words, which can be found in different versions of the Bible. A simple chart below illustrates this purpose.[46]

44. I have already addressed the reason the term "sodomite" is *not* an appropriate word to use or the proper interpretation of the word.

45. Achtemeier, *Bible's Yes*, 98.

46. DeYoung, *What Does the Bible Really Teach*, 61. The idea for the chart that I use was taken from DeYoung's book; however, there is little in DeYoung's narrow-minded, fundamentalist, and literalist approach to the Bible that I agree with.

Table 1: Bible Comparison of *Malakoi* and *Arsenokoitai*

Various Bible Versions	*Malakoi & Arsenokoitai* (1 Corinthians 6:9)	*Arsenokoitai* (1 Timothy 1:10)
English Standard Version	men who practice homosexuality	men who practice homosexuality
Holman Christian Standard Bible	anyone practicing homosexuality	homosexuality
King James Version	effeminate, abusers of themselves with mankind	them that defile themselves with mankind
New American Bible	boy prostitutes, practicing homosexuals	practicing homosexuals
New American Standard Bible	effeminate, homosexuals	homosexuals
New International Version	men who have sex with men	those practicing homosexuality
New King James Version	homosexuals, sodomites	sodomites
New Living Translation	male prostitutes, those who practice homosexuality	those who practice homosexuality
New Revised Standard Version	male prostitutes, sodomites	Sodomites
The Jerusalem Bible	catamites (pubescent boys), sodomites	those who are immoral with women or with boys or with men

Is there any wonder why the average Christian does *not* possess an accurate understanding of the Bible on this issue? The chart clearly demonstrates that the words *malakoi* and *arsenokoitai* have a multiplicity of meanings and obfuscate a Christian's comprehension of the Bible. The various interpretations of the words *malakoi* and *arsenokoitai* help to exacerbate this important issue. Most likely, the Apostle Paul coined the term from the prohibitions of the Holiness Code against unequal, nonconsensual, same-sex behavior. However, his condemnation is in no way applicable to twenty-first-century homosexual relationships or marriages that exist today in the United States or Europe.

Understanding the proper historical and biblical context is critical in this situation.[47] It is quite impossible for the Apostle Paul to know the word *homosexuality* as we do today because the term is a late nineteenth-century invention. For the contemporary Christian to conclude that gay men and lesbian women will never inherit the kinship of God is a distortion of biblical and historical context. The context of the apostle's moral argument, in 1 Cor 5 and 6, is challenging the "anything goes" type of Christianity and the "smorgasbord" approach to moral living. Presbyterian theologian Mark Achtemeier notes,

> Paul's possible reference to same-sex behaviors in the last of these three vice lists makes perfect sense when we view it in historical context; the exploitative, cultic, and pederastic forms of same-sex behavior that were prominent in Paul's world were so obviously at odds with God's purposes that they fit the bill perfectly when Paul was looking for illustrations of patently unrighteous behavior.[48]

We do not have to be a Scripture scholar to understand the Apostle Paul's intent here: 1 Corinthians and 1 Timothy are referring to pedophilia, ephebophilia, and boy/male prostitution, and not the loving, consensual, faithful, relationship between two gay men in a mutual life-giving bond.[49] Furthermore, to block LGBT people from entering into loving marriages, that can actually help them to grow in faithfulness, might be quite *unbiblical* and the *antithesis* of the gospels.

Contemporary Christians can feel confident to read these two texts in their proper historical and biblical context, and know that God's love and Christ's blessing are found on any relationship or marriage, whether gay or straight, as long as it is mutual, faithful, life-giving, and equal. At no place in the Bible is there an example of loving and committed relationships renounced—nowhere![50]

---

47. DeYoung, *What Does the Bible Really Teach*, 63. Although DeYoung mentions the term "context," I am not so sure he understands the full meaning of the contextual approach to the Bible, which employs the historical-critical method of Scripture analysis and hermeneutics.

48. Achtemeier, *Bible's Yes*, 99.

49. De La Torre, *Liberating Sexuality*, 163.

50. De La Torre, *Liberating Sexuality*, 163.

2 Peter 4–8 & Jude 1:6–7: Angels Having Sex (NRSV)

*For if God did not spare **the angels when they sinned, but cast them into hell** and committed them to chains of deepest darkness to be kept until the judgment; and if he did not spare the ancient* world, even though he saved Noah, a herald of righteousness, with seven others, when he brought a flood on a world of the ungodly; *and if by turning the cities of Sodom and Gomorrah to ashes he condemned them to extinction and made them an example of what is coming to the ungodly; and if he rescued Lot, a righteous man greatly distressed by the licentiousness of the lawless (for that righteous man, living among them day after day, was tormented in his righteous soul by their lawless deeds that he saw and heard).* (2 Pet 2:4–8; italics and bold added)

Jude 6–7: Sex with Angels (NAB)

*The **angels too**, who **did not keep to their own domain** but deserted their proper dwelling, he has kept in eternal chains, in gloom, for the judgment of the great day. Likewise, **Sodom, Gomorrah,** and the surrounding towns, which, in the same manner as they, indulged in **sexual promiscuity and practiced unnatural vice,** serve as an example by undergoing a **punishment of eternal fire.*** (Jude 6–7; italics and bold added)

Most Scripture experts conclude that the epistle of Jude is strikingly similar to that of 2 Peter, although they both contain independent instructions and ideas. Both texts are typically read from a heterosexual bias and infer that God punishes the people of Sodom and Gomorrah for their "sexual promiscuity" and "unnatural practices." As previously addressed, God punishes the two cities and neighboring cities for their unjust treatment of the traveler. Why do these two ancient cities come up in this pericope? Perhaps the Apostles Peter and Jude want Christians to always be hospitable and to treat travelers and guests with respect and dignity. Perhaps the Apostles Peter and Jude do not want to forget the way God punished the people of Sodom and Gomorrah for their sins of inhospitality, violence, and attempted gang rape.

Furthermore, the two texts seem to be concerned with angels engaging in sexual intercourse with women, thus making the sexual act metaphysical and strange. Some translations read "shameless ways" and "unnatural fornication," and one scholar translates the terms as "other flesh," so he can bash homosexuality.[51] However, there is no evidence in Genesis 19 that the two angels in the story did have intercourse with Lot's daughters. Both of the Apostles Peter and Jude might be referencing Gen 6:1–4, which describes angels having sex with women.[52] No matter which way someone interprets this text, the natural rhythm of two human beings engaging in consensual sex is violated by celestial beings trying to have sex with mere mortals. I suppose the moral of this story is that Christians would be wise to *not* imitate the people of those ancient cities, and try to live wholesome, hospitable, righteous, and godly lives. These two passages have nothing to do with the contemporary understanding of homosexuality and it would be unjust to try and assume that these two texts condemn homosexuality or same-sex marriage.

Matthew 19:11–12: A Text on Transgender— Jesus the Eunuch (NIV)

> *Jesus replied, "Not everyone can accept this word, but only those to whom it has been given. For there are **eunuchs** who were born that way, and there are eunuchs who have been made eunuchs by others—and there are those who choose to live like **eunuchs** for the sake of the kingdom of heaven. The one who can accept this should accept it."* (italics and bold added)

There is absolutely nothing in the gospels about homosexuality. As previously mentioned, Jesus does not discuss the issue of same-sex attraction or relationships whatsoever. Conversely, it does appear that Jesus does discuss some people in antiquity that are likened to transgender people today.

According to pastoral theologian and transgender advocate Justin E. Tanis, "Eunuchs are the closest biblical analogy that [Christians] have for transgender people. Here we see Jesus directly addressing the issue of eunuchs and including them in *his* understanding of the dominion of heaven."[53] Jesus directly speaks about gender variance in this passage and he indicates that there is a range of human expressions apart from a binary

51. DeYoung, *Bible's Yes*, 38.

52. De La Torre, *Liberating Sexuality*, 164.

53. Tanis, *Transgendered*, 72.

(male-female) understanding. Jesus affirms and accepts the sexual outcast of his day—eunuchs. Today's sexual outcasts are transgender people. For Jesus, eunuchs (today's transgender folks) are either created that way from birth or made that way through castration. Either way, eunuchs in antiquity would be parallel to an intersex or transgender person today. Feminist theologian Virginia R. Mollenkott notes,

> Jesus' words about eunuchs in Matthew 19:12 reveal an accepting, respectful attitude that ought to be the norm for the modern Church: *"For there are eunuchs who have been so from birth"* includes at the very least all intersex people; *"and there are eunuchs who have been made eunuchs by others"* includes post-operative transsexuals; *"and there are eunuchs who have made themselves eunuchs for the sake of the kin[ship] of heaven"* includes not only pre-operative and non-operative transsexuals, but all other transgenderists, celibates, and homosexuals who do not engage in reproductive sex.[54]

Jesus seems to understand there is a small section of the population that is seeking one's outer character to reflect more genuinely one's inner and spiritual disposition.

Jesus of Nazareth stands in total solidarity with eunuchs then and intersex and transgender people today. De La Torre writes, "Eunuchs were considered spiritual outcasts, unable to participate in the cultic practices of the faith community."[55] Hence, eunuchs during Jesus' day, and transgender people today, live on the margins of society and are a disenfranchised sexual and gender minority group.

Protestant lawyer, judge, and transgender advocate Victoria S. Kolakowski maintains that

> it is frequently argued by those who hold that Jesus was celibate, that Jesus himself was [mockingly] called a eunuch, and that it was this charge to which Jesus was responding in this statement, placing himself in the third category [of Matt 19:12]. The notion that Jesus placed himself into the third category [*"and there are eunuchs who have made themselves eunuchs for the sake of the kin[ship] of heaven"*] makes this passage particularly fascinating for purposes of the present discussion, since it would place Jesus in direct solidarity with the eunuch. It is very important that there is no

---

54. Mollenkott, *Omnigender*, 120, italics added.
55. De La Torre, *Liberating Sexuality*, 144.

condemnation of eunuchs implicit in this statement; rather, Jesus is placing himself in an analogous situation with the eunuchs.[56]

It might seem bizarre that Jesus self-identifies as a eunuch; however, he is consistent throughout the gospels, namely that he identifies himself as a person on the margins. Jesus seeing himself as a eunuch would be equivalent to self-identifying as a transgender person today. This is not only a word of solidarity from Jesus, but also a powerful display of acceptance and radical affirmation of eunuchs in antiquity, and therefore, of transgender people today.

Jesus of Nazareth serves as a role model for Christians everywhere. Jesus also is a role model for every denomination on the issue of welcoming the stranger, treating the marginalized person with dignity and respect, and affirming the person with love and their life decisions. For far too long, some Christians have used the gospels as a tool of exclusion, malice, and self-righteousness, even though Jesus' own words confront and counter the dominant, heterosexual, White, conservative worldview. Such a display of moral courage cannot be disregarded as a misnomer or an accident.[57] Jesus' own words lead one to dismiss any reading that expresses any type of slander or bigotry aimed at transgender people.

Parting Remarks

The so-called clobber passages or texts of terror have been addressed in this chapter and seem to have been interpreted over the years from a dominant, white, cultural understanding, and with heterosexual biases. The message of the gospels and New Testament is love—overwhelmingly love, not condemnation. If there is any real abomination within Christianity, it is about the way Christians treat people in the LGBTQ community.

Mercy is one of the hallmarks of Jesus the Christ and one of the constitutive dimensions of the gospels.[58] Mercy, compassion, and God's love is proclaimed by Jesus, and is manifested by his acts of kindness and forgiveness. Jesus' message and actions are evidence, especially in the social context of his day and when the Bible was written, that it seems impossible for contemporary Christians to justify the moral outrage on homosexual

56. Kolakowski, "Towards a Christian Ethical Response," 25.

57. Tanis, *Transgendered*, 75.

58. Healy, *Scripture, Mercy, and Homosexuality*, 76. Although I do not agree with most of her scriptural assessment concerning homosexual people, she is correct in her understanding of mercy and Jesus in the gospels.

activity today.[59] Notwithstanding the Apostle Paul's injunctions against same-sex partners concerning male prostitutes and boy slaves, his message is also about love (1 Cor 13:8–13), and in the end, love should never fail (1 Cor 13:8).

The pattern of ministry in the New Testament is clear, that the contemporary understanding of homosexuality and two committed people in a homosexual relationship is not sinful in and of itself. Placher contends that "even if homosexual behavior were a sin, here is precisely not the place to 'draw the line.' Far better to draw it in the face of a sin like greed [and power], which our culture generally treats with something like admiration, especially when it is masked as 'success.'"[60] From my reading of the gospels, Jesus stood in solidarity with the poor, the lowly, the marginalized, and the outcast of society, and stayed away from the self-righteous, the overly religious, and the self-confident. I am cautiously hopeful that this chapter will be a springboard for further discussion and perhaps offer deeper illumination on this highly volatile subject within some denominations of Christianity.

Discussion Questions

1. What are three new things you learned from this chapter?

2. What points did you find surprising, interesting, or perplexing from this chapter?

3. Has this chapter allowed you to understand Scripture in a different light or from a new perspective?

4. What is your understanding of the Greek terms *malakos* and *arsenokoitēs*?

5. How would you summarize this chapter to a friend?

---

59. Shore, *Unfair*, 12.
60. Placher, *Jesus the Savior*, 102.

Chapter 3

Critiquing Current Teachings

Faithful to her own tradition and at the same time conscious of her uni-
versal mission, she [the Catholic Church] can enter into communion with
various cultural modes, to her own enrichment and to theirs too.

—SECOND VATICAN COUNCIL (1965)
Gaudium et Spes, §58

Opening Comments

THIS CHAPTER WILL REASSESS and reexamine the Catholic Church's position on homosexuality. As aforementioned, my tradition is Roman
Catholic, and that allows me the ability to feel free to critique and challenge my own denomination on its views regarding theology, morality,
and pastoral practice. For instance, I do not feel comfortable analyzing or
criticizing Methodist practices because I am not Methodist. Therefore, as a
Catholic pastoral theologian, I can engage in theological and pastoral discourse concerning topics that are usually not discussed on the parish-level.
I am writing as a theologian in my area of expertise—pastoral theology
and ministry. It is from this unique vantage point that I comment on the
Catholic Church's pastoral practice.

Likewise as stated earlier in the book, I am a Hispanic, pastoral theologian, who engages in liberation theology and I do my theological work

and reflection from the margins. Therefore, this chapter offers criticisms concerning the Catholic Church's position regarding homosexual (lesbian and gay) persons. However, the remarks offered here are in the spirit of theological discourse and for the further exploration of knowledge. Additionally, this chapter is concerned with the theological and moral implications that sexual minorities encounter as a direct result of the official position of Catholic teaching on homosexuality.

There are significant theological, moral, and pastoral challenges that merit attentiveness and sensitivity on behalf of Catholic sexual minorities. These challenges that Catholic theologians and ministers face are real, legitimate, and worthy of examination. All of the remarks and recommendations in this chapter (like all the other chapters) are made with a high regard for Catholic teaching on sexuality, gender, and issues surrounding homosexuality. Conversely, though, there is a real need to reexamine and reassess the Catholic Church's teaching on homosexuality. Moreover, I see a real failure in pastoral practice, as a direct result of the theology that governs the Catholic Church's teaching on homosexuality. Therefore, I want to offer new ideas and fresh perspectives in a spirit of open dialog with respect to the traditional views concerning homosexuality.

The Official Catholic Teaching on Homosexuality

There are two official Vatican documents[1] that discuss homosexuality in the Catholic Church: *Homosexualitatis problema* (1986) and the *Catechism of the Catholic Church* (1994). Both documents are part of the Catholic Church's arsenal against homosexual persons and lifestyles.[2] It is advantageous to address both of these documents.

1. There are also two US Catholic documents written by the US Conference of Catholic Bishops on homosexuality: (1) *Ministry to Persons with a Homosexual Inclination: Guidelines for Pastoral Care*; and (2) *Always Our Children: A Pastoral Message to Parents of Homosexual Children and Suggestions for Pastoral Ministers*. Both have the word "pastoral" in the title, but do not provide any real pastoral support, advocacy, or pastoral care to members of the LGBTQ community. In fact, many of the recommendations in the documents are very general and are applicable to all Catholics and Christians.

2. The term *lifestyle* is a "loaded" word because it can have multiple interpretations. Typically, the phrase "homosexual lifestyle" is used in Christian circles to describe a life that Christians feel are contrary to certain Christian ideals. The LGBTQ community finds the term "homosexual lifestyle" offensive. Moreover, the term "homosexual lifestyle" is a false assumption and a prejudice stereotype perpetuated by members of society and mainline, heterosexual, conservative Christianity. Therefore, the term "lifestyle" in

Homosexualitatis Problema

The Catholic Church's position on homosexuality has been officially taught since 1986. This is one of the rare occasions in the Catholic Church's history that an ecclesial document was written in a single theological and moral issue. The definitive teaching first appeared in an ecclesial document promulgated by the Congregation for the Doctrine of Faith (formally called the Holy Inquisition until 1908) titled *Homosexualitatis problema* ("Problem of Homosexuality"), but colloquially titled *Letter to All the Bishops of the Catholic Church on the Pastoral Care of Homosexual Persons*. The document, principally written by then-Cardinal Joseph Ratzinger, who became Pope Benedict XVI. The document clearly acknowledges the distinction between "the homosexual *condition* or *tendency* and the individual homosexual [genital] actions."[3] In other words, the sexual orientation of a person is *not* in question and the homosexual person should be treated with dignity and respect. Only the homosexual genital act is deemed "intrinsically disordered."[4] It is a subtle, but extremely important distinction to be sure within Catholic sexual doctrine.

Another important point that the document makes is this:

> It has been argued that the homosexual orientation in certain cases is *not* the result of deliberate choice; and so the homosexual person would have *no* choice but to behave in a homosexual fashion. Lacking freedom, such a person, even if engaged in homosexual [genital] activity, would *not* be culpable. (italics added)[5]

---

this chapter reflects an openness to affirm homosexual people and their individual rights, and is not seen as a pejorative term. All people live certain and particular lifestyles based on their race, culture, and ethnicity.

3. *Homosexualitais Problema* (English title: *Letter to All Catholic Bishops on the Pastoral Care of Homosexual Persons*), §3. It would be wise to keep in mind that this document is a "letter" and is not to be treated as on par with a Second Vatican Council document or papal encyclical. There is a certain pecking order to Catholic ecclesial documents and certain documents carry more "weight" or heft than others. I will rank them in descending order: (1) the word of God or sacred Scriptures; (2) ecumenical council documents such as the Second Vatican Council documents; (3) papal encyclicals; (4) papal apostolic exhortations; (5) letters from the Congregation for the Doctrine of Faith such as *Homosexualitais Problema*; (6) particular national-church letters, e.g., letters from the US Conference of Catholic Bishops; and (7) individual letters by a particular bishop addressed to his diocese.

4. *Homosexualitais Problema*, §3.

5. *Homosexualitais Problema*, §11.

First, sexual *choice* is highly contested in the lesbian and gay communities. Homosexual people adamantly believe that God created them homosexual. Therefore, choosing to be or not to be homosexual is not an accepted reality for homosexual people. Homosexual people are born homosexual!

Second, the statement is interesting because it indicates that since a homosexual person's sexuality is *not* a matter of choice, then homosexual genital acts are *not* culpable, or deserving blame. Of course, for conservative Catholics, this interpretation might be a difficult to maintain. The main reason for homosexual intercourse is considered morally wrong is because of *sexual complementarity*. Sexual complementarity means that each element finds its proper place within the harmony of the whole. In the Catholic tradition this means that man and woman are naturally ordered, they are complementarity of each other, ordered toward procreation and marriage, and as such, they are the teleological end for woman and man.[6]

Catholic African American and feminist theologian M. Shawn Copeland notes that "this [understanding] admonishes gays and lesbians to repress or sacrifice their sexual orientation, to relinquish genital expression, to deny their bodies, and their selves."[7] However, if the body is a temple of the Holy Spirit (1 Cor 6:19–20 NAB)[8] and if the body is sacrament, according to Catholic principle of sacramentality (everything is a sacrament because it exists from God) and sacramental economy (to express something is to effect something), then homosexual genital expression would not be considered a condemnable offense or unnatural.[9] Copeland asks the question: "Can (artificial) distinction between orientation and act (really) be upheld?"[10] What are homosexual Christians to do with their bodies? What are homosexual Catholics to do with their sexuality, and their selves, especially in a committed, loving, and fruitful relationship? Sexual expression is part of an overall personhood; it is a matter of paramount importance for the overwhelming majority of people.

The response from *Homosexualitatis problema* regarding these questions is less than desirable for lesbian and gay Catholics.

6. Lu, "Eros Divided," 25.

7. Copeland, *Enfleshing Freedom*, 75.

8. 1 Cor 6:19–20 reads: "Do you not know that your body is a temple of the Holy Spirit within you, whom you have from God, and that you are not your own? For you have been purchased at a price. Therefore, glorify God with your body" (NAB).

9. Scanlon, "Postmodernism and Theology," 18.

10. Copeland, *Enfleshing Freedom*, 75.

What, then, are homosexual persons to do who seek to follow the Lord? Fundamentally, they are called to enact the will of God in their life by joining whatever sufferings and difficulties they experience in virtue of their condition to the sacrifice of the Lord's Cross. That Cross, for the believer, is a fruitful sacrifice since from that death come life and redemption. While any call to carry the cross or to understand a Christian's suffering in this way will predictably be met with bitter ridicule by some, it should be remembered that this is the way to eternal life for all who follow Christ.

[The Cross] is easily misunderstood, however, if it is merely seen as a pointless effort at self-denial. The Cross is a denial of self, but in service to the will of God himself who makes life come from death and empowers those who trust in him to practice virtue in place of vice.

To celebrate the Paschal Mystery, it is necessary to let that Mystery become imprinted in the fabric of daily life. To refuse to sacrifice one's own will in obedience to the will of the Lord is effectively to prevent salvation. Just as the Cross was central to the expression of God's redemptive love for us in Jesus, so the conformity of the self-denial of homosexual men and women with the sacrifice of the Lord will constitute for them a source of self-giving which will save them from a way of life which constantly threatens to destroy them.

Christians who are homosexual are called, as all of us are, to a chaste life. As they dedicate their lives to understand the nature of God's personal call to them, they will be able to celebrate the Sacrament of Penance more faithfully and receive the Lord's grace so freely offered there in order to convert their lives more fully to his Way.[11]

The problem with this language and phrasing is multifaceted. First, the document sets up a separation between heterosexuals and homosexuals, referring to lesbian and gay people as "they," "them," "their," which is degrading and not consistent with the respect and dignity of the individual. Second, the document clearly had no input from anyone within the queer community, because it sternly calls homosexual Catholics to live a life of embracing "the Cross" with no regard for sexual intimacy, sexual pleasure, or a person's sensuality. Third, is the document has unrealistic expectations for the typical lay, homosexual Catholic, living a committed relationship. The document mandates that Catholics who are homosexual, through no fault of their own, live a life of forced abstinence, imposed

11. *Homosexualitais Problema*, §12.

self-denial of sexual pleasure, and opt for bodily sexual-asceticism by way of chastity and celibacy.[12] Fourth, the Way of the Cross of Christ is for *all* Christians, whether or not a person is homosexual or heterosexual, cisgender or transgender; the cost of discipleship is a condition for those authentically desiring to follow Christ.[13] Besides, every Christian bears the cross distinctively in their own lives. There are many components and characteristics of Christian discipleship, such as accompaniment, conversion, community, love, morality, faith, spirituality, stewardship, and servant-leadership.[14] Chastity and celibacy are probably toward the bottom of any list of Christian discipleship.

Systematic theologian and Jesuit priest Paul G. Crowley argues that following the Way of the Cross is a spiritual practice for all Christians, but is not necessarily a proper method of sexual self-denial for Catholic LGBT folks, and is a "practice of chaste abstinence, a kind of catharsis from burden of the condition itself."[15] In other words, homosexual Catholics are to purify their lives by remaining celibate from sexual desires with a person whom they love and live a life forced ascetical abstinence as a way to participate in the suffering of Christ. For the homosexual person, this could be a fruitless sacrifice and an unhealthy burden, and one that wreaks havoc on a lesbian and gay spirituality, and perhaps an unrealistic expectation that drives queer folks away from the Catholic Church.

The document *Homosexualitatis problema* tends to treat homosexual activity as if it were some sort of addiction, which homosexual persons need to avoid and need to abstain from: "a disordered sexual inclination which is essentially self-indulgent."[16] The term "disordered" is a lightning rod for LGBTQ folks. I know plenty of homosexual couples. They are in mutual, life-giving relationships or marriages, do not have a self-indulgent addiction, but rather are God-inspired people who live out their sexuality in society, church, and home.

Franciscan theologian Xavier J. Seubert notes that commanding abstinence or to prescribe forced celibacy for lesbian and gay persons simply because that person is homosexual stands in contrast with sacramental

---

12. Crowley, "Homosexuality and the Counsel of the Cross," 508.

13. Copeland, *Enfleshing Freedom*, 76.

14. Canales, *Models & Methods*, 120–54.

15. Crowley, "Homosexuality and the Counsel of the Cross," 508.

16. *Homosexualitais Problema*, §7.

transformation.[17] Sacramental transformation calls all creation: peoples, races, creeds, colors, ethnicities, cultures, sexual orientations, and gender expressions to be in loving communion with Jesus the Christ. Albeit, *Homosexualitatis problema* mentions the Sacrament of Penance for homosexual persons to enrich their lives as chaste and celibate; however, there is absolutely no reference to the sacramental grace and sanctifying grace that accrues during one's baptism or from celebrating Sunday Eucharist, two of the Catholic Church's premier sacraments that unite one more fully with Christ.[18]

English theologian and Catholic priest James Alison maintains that *Homosexualitatis problema* offers a hypocritical and reproachful ecclesiastical message by mandating: love and do not love; be and do not be. Alison states, "The voice of God has been presented as double-blind, which is actually far more dangerous than a simple message of hate, since it destabilizes being into annihilation, and thinks that annihilation to be a good thing."[19] This document might be motivated by moral or pastoral concerns, but it may also introduce Catholics to homophobia because of its lack of affirmation regarding the homosexual person and homosexual dignity.

Finally, the teaching from *Homosexualitatis problema* does not adequately affirm the dignity of the homosexual person. *Homosexualitatis problema* is not collaborative in nature, but coercive in its approach; it is judgmental in tone; it denies a group of people a spiritual-sexual and relational-romantic union; it manipulates the voice of love found in the Gospels; it perpetuates internalized homophobia; and it feeds innuendo and fear.[20] *Homosexualitatis problema* is a difficult document to read from a pastoral-theological disposition that understands that human sexuality cannot be reduced to a sexual or genital act.

The Catechism

The second document the Catholic Church uses regarding its teaching on homosexuality is found in the *Catechism of the Catholic Church* (*CCC* hereafter). The *CCC*'s rendition on homosexuality is traditional and can be found in the following articles:

17. Seubert, "But Do Not Use the 'Rotten Names,'" 74n23.
18. Seubert, "But Do Not Use the 'Rotten Names,'" 74n23.
19. Alison, *Faith beyond Resentment*, 94.
20. Copeland, *Enfleshing Freedom*, 77.

- All human beings are created in the image and likeness of God, known as *imago Dei* (n. 299);

- Love is the fundamental and innate vocation of every human being (n. 2392);

- All human beings deserve to be treated with dignity and respect, which upholds their innate integrity (no. 2284–317);

- Sexuality is a gift that is ordered toward conjugal love (n. 2360);

- Sexuality affects all aspects of the human person in the unity of the body and the soul (n. 2332, 2361);

- All Christians are called to various forms of chastity and to remain chaste outside of matrimony (n. 2348);

- Every person should acknowledge and accept their sexual identity (n. 2333);

- Homosexuality refers to relations between men or women who experience an exclusive or predominant sexual attraction toward persons of the same sex. It has taken a great variety of forms through the centuries and in different cultures. Its psychological genesis remains largely unexplained. Basing itself on sacred Scripture, which presents homosexual acts as acts of *grave depravity*, tradition has always declared that "homosexual acts are intrinsically disordered." [Homosexual genital acts] are *contrary* to the natural law. [Homosexual genital acts] close the sexual act to the gift of life. [Homosexual genital acts] do *not proceed* from a genuine affective and sexual complementarity. Under *no circumstances* can [homosexual genital acts] be approved (n. 2357; italic added);

- The number of men and women who have deep-seated homosexual tendencies is not negligible. This inclination, which is *objectively disordered*, constitutes for most [homosexual persons] a trail. They must be accepted with *respect, compassion,* and *sensitivity.* Every sign of unjust discrimination in their regard should be avoided. [Homosexual] persons are called to fulfill God's will in their lives and, if they are Christians, to unite to the sacrifice of the Lord's Cross the difficulties they may encounter from their condition (n. 2358; italic added); and

- Homosexual persons are called to chastity. By the virtues of self-mastery that teach [homosexual persons] inner freedom, at times by the support of disinterested friendship, by prayer and sacramental grace, they can and should gradually and resolutely approach Christian perfection (n. 2359).[21]

The *CCC* lays out in a concise framework the Catholic Church's teaching on homosexuality. The points represent a concise understanding of the Catholic Church's teaching on homosexuality. The final three articles—2357, 2358, and 2359—are the foundational ecclesial doctrines of the Catholic Church on homosexuality. However, there is nothing new in the presentation of the *CCC* on homosexuality that is different from *Homosexualitatis problema*. Some points may even appear contradictory, and are not so clear-cut, but they will be answered with further exegesis and investigation.

Two Theological Challenges

There are considerable theological challenges to the Catholic Church's position on Homosexuality. This section will examine two challenges: (1) the language of *intrinsically disorder* and (2) explaining the phrase "divergent sexual behavior" for LGBTQ folks.

The Language of Intrinsically Disordered

The first theological challenge concerning the Catholic Church's teaching on homosexuality has to do with language. The philosophical language of natural law can be troubling in this case because it does not take into account a person's life experience. The language of *grave depravity* and *intrinsically disordered* is particularly disturbing. Therefore, the first theological challenge is fleshing out the phrase *intrinsically disordered*.

The terminology *intrinsically disordered* is problematic. The philosophical grounds for this argument reside in the Catholic Church's understanding of marriage and the "permanent union of husband and wife and the procreation of children."[22] The Catholic mindset understands that sexual complementarity means that males and females fall in love, get married in the Catholic Church, have children together, and raise their children as good, faithful, and wholesome Catholics. Thus, a Catholic understanding

21. Pope John Paul II, *Catechism of the Catholic Church*, §§299, 2332, 2333, 2392, 2284–317, 2360, 2361, 2357, 2348 (italics added).

22. Harvey, *Homosexuality and the Catholic Church*, 11.

of sexuality is binary, male and female, and complementary components. Conservative Catholics and Evangelical Christians tend to view homosexuality as a violation of the potential God-given marital bonds between man and woman, which are unitive and procreative. There are other dimensions to marriage, which also stress: sacramental, personal, educative, but they are typically viewed in conjunction with unitive or procreative.

The phrase *intrinsically disordered* is highly contentious in the homosexual community and perhaps rewording may prove to be wise. Wording such as *intrinsically disordered* tends to be divisive instead of binding, and it is offensive and alarming for homosexual persons.[23] Besides being extremely *un*-pastoral, the phrase *intrinsically disordered*, which applies to the homosexual genital acts, can easily be misconstrued by thinking that the message is that all LGBTQ people are intrinsically disordered people, which is a slippery slope.[24] The person with a homosexual orientation, disposition, inclination, tendencies, or condition (as the official documents refer) is not acting wrongly, immorally, or living a life of depravity. In other words, the person with a lesbian or gay orientation is not considered *intrinsically disordered*, only the same-sex genital act carries this negative and stigmatizing distinction. To put it another way, homosexual inclinations are not immoral or "sinful" unless they are acted upon. The slogan of the Catholic Church regarding homosexuality is: "We do not condemn homosexual *people*, only homosexual *acts*." This simple statement gives absolutely no reprieve to the homosexual person.

Systematic theologian Linn Marie Tonstad claims, "Rather than trying to free themselves from cultural opprobrium by using nicer language about gay people, homophobic denominations ought to have the courage of their convictions and admit that they do think homosexuality, the inclination, is sinful."[25] For Tonstad, the Catholic Church, and other churches, should just admit that they really "do *not* love the sinner and hate the sin." For Tonstad, such wording is mere semantics.

The person with a homosexual disposition is a child of God and created in the image and likeness of God. The LGBTQ person deserves love, respect, dignity, empathy, and compassion. Theologians who view lesbian and gay people as *disordered*, view sexual complementarity as the key difference between the sexes and the fundamental characteristic of sexuality:

23. Canales, "Ministry to Catholic LGBTQ Youth," 64.

24. Pope, "Magisterium's Arguments," 549.

25. Tonstad, *Queer Theology*, 44.

meaning that the homosexual relationship simply cannot be reciprocal in the same way as a heterosexual relationship, because it fails to be open to procreation.[26] Catholic theologian Livio Melina suggests that procreation is the completed form of sexual union between a married couple, and children are the crown jewel of marital love, which is inconceivable apart from ready openness to fruitfulness of birth.[27] For Melina, all relationships are imperfect, even the male/female relationship in marriage, but they enjoy procreation, and the homosexual relationship simply cannot enjoy the fruit of procreation, which makes the homosexual relationship less than complementarity.

Traditional Catholic natural law and moral theology acknowledges only two genders or sexes (both are equivalent in natural law) for complementarity: the male and female binary system. Melina provides the Catholic traditional position on complementarity: "The elimination of openness to procreation uproots sexuality from its insertion in time and history through the succession of generations."[28] Traditional Catholic and conservative Christian thinking is that the homosexual relationship subverts the natural order of sexuality and feminine receptivity.

Still, all this philosophical language revolving around the words *intrinsically disordered* does not rule out that a human person is not meant to exist alone (Gen 2:18), and therefore is called to be in intimate relation with another human person. Hence, homosexuals must find another person to live out their lives with and this is usually beyond the binary[29] roles and expressions. The phrase *intrinsically disordered* leaves a loving, monogamous, respectful, and committed homosexual couple in a theological, moral, and practical predicament.

Committed and monogamous, even civilly married, homosexual couples may feel polarized and defamed by the Catholic Church's wording as it stands in tension with the Magisterium's own teaching on the affirmation

---

26. Melina, "Homosexual Inclination," 135.

27. Melina, "Homosexual Inclination," 133–34.

28. Melina, "Homosexual Inclination," 136.

29. Binaries are categories of organization for social existence. Binaries separate reality into neat categories, such as Black/White, light/dark, slave/master, true/false, nature/culture, rich/poor, male/female, and transgender/cisgender. There are many cultural theorists and theologians (Jacques Derrida, Judith Bulter, Patrick Cheng, Linn M. Tonstad, Marcella Althaus-Reid) who maintain that binaries are at the core of many of the social and institutional hierarchies that organize and stratify cultural and social order.

that each LGBTQ person is created in the *imago Dei*.[30] Although many conservative theologians[31] who settle on the *disorder* language insist that such language can be reconciled with an affirmation that we are all made in *imago Dei*, is still an ongoing debate. The *intrinsically disordered* wording disrespects a homosexual person's sexual orientation, identity, and expression, which are qualities comparable to discrimination against race, color, creed, ethnicity, and culture. Nevertheless, regarding homosexuality, the Catholic Church's teaching is firmly entrenched and remains so for the unforeseeable future. Perhaps it is time for new language to be developed to advance the theology of homosexuality.

Divergent Sexual Behavior

The second challenge is to find words that are not as theologically demeaning as *intrinsically disordered*. The term *intrinsically* means "fundamentally" or "inherently," implying that a same-sex genital act is naturally wrong. The word *disordered* means "chaotic" or "messy," inferring that same-sex genital acts are not properly ordered. In my mind, the Catholic Church's message should be more affirming,[32] compassionate, and empathetic to LGBTQ issues, needs, and concerns not stigmatizing and dehumanizing.[33] Moreover, the words *intrinsically disordered* are a philosophical distinction *not* a theological distinction and are based on the natural law or natural order construct.

A natural law approach is rooted in the belief that the will of God can be discerned by human beings within the basic patterns and rhythms of life.[34] The natural law approach has two problems associated with it: (1) it is narrow and exclusivist in its scope and (2) it is "based upon a one-size-fits-all assumption that does not take into account the statistical reality of the significant number of Catholics who experience same-sex attraction."[35]

30. Pope, "Magisterium's Arguments," 550.

31. See these theologians and their respective chapters in the *Living the Truth in Love*: Rachel Lu, Bob Schts, Deborah Savage, Jay Budziszewski, and Livio Melina.

32. The term *affirming* in this context means that Catholic, and hopefully all Christian, youth and young adult ministers would be exercising mercy and grace by acknowledging and welcoming LGBTQ young people as homosexual persons created in *imago Dei*. Affirming does not necessarily mean agreeing with very LGBTQ person's decisions or actions.

33. Pope, "Magisterium's Arguments," 550.

34. Doyle, *What Is Christianity?*, 217.

35. Doyle, *What Is Christianity?*, 217.

There is little to no room for personal experience in the natural law model. Hence, for something to be labeled as *disordered* means that it goes against the natural law or order, and is thus *unnatural* or *disordered*, because it disrupts the natural order and balance of life. For example, a parent should never have to bury their own child; if a child dies before a parent, it disrupts the natural order of life and is hence disordered. In reality, and contrary to natural law, there are many reptiles, animals, bird species, and fish in the natural world that engage in same-sex acts or gender-variant behaviors, such as baboons, orcas, emu, vultures, bearded-dragon lizards, desert tortoise, salmon, and Arctic graying (fish).[36]

Therefore, the ecclesial terminology and wording of *intrinsically disordered* is powerfully negative, alarming, stigmatizing, and dehumanizing and merits changing. The words *intrinsically disordered* belong to the scholastic tradition of Christianity. The period 1100–1700 in Western Europe defended the doctrines of Christianity against rising secular pluralism. Apart from trained moral theologians and philosophers, no one really comprehends or "grasps" its meaning. Perhaps a better phrase for the Catholic Church to implement would be *divergent sexual behavior*,[37] which is better than "intrinsically disordered." A new and improved theology of the body, theology of sexuality, and theology of homosexuality needs to be created within Christianity.

What does *divergent sexual behavior* mean for homosexual persons? It would be theologically prudent to discuss a re-visioning of homosexuality in terms of sexual acts. Alternative phrases such as the two introduced here might be a step in the right direction. The phrase *divergent sexual behavior*, although cumbersome, allows for an acknowledgment that not all sexual attraction and behavior falls under typical or normative sexual behavior of sexes.

The role of sexuality is a fundamental component of personal identity and spirituality. British Catholic moral theologian Kevin Kelly states, "Our sexuality is an essential dimension of our being as human persons and so

36. Moore, *Question of Truth*, 27–37.

37. In 1955, Derrick Sherwin Bailey wrote *Homosexuality and the Western Christian Tradition*, 168–73. Bailey, an Anglican priest, argued for alternative language of "disorder" or "condition." Bailey suggested "inversion" because it is a morally neutral term. I, too, like the term "inversion," because it means "to turn something upside down." I seriously think Catholic moral theologians would be wise be looking for alternative wording to "intrinsically disordered."

it affects our whole approach to life and all our relationships."[38] Sexuality is a powerful and loving force within the human person. Sexuality and spirituality are innately connected. This same sentiment is echoed in the *CCC*: "Sexuality affects all aspects of the human person in the unity of body and soul."[39] Therefore, if a homosexual person suffers a fundamental disorder in sexual orientation, an orientation that is paramount to identity, and through no fault of her/his own, then it is difficult to conclude that such a disorder precludes such persons from engaging in mutual, fruitful, and loving interpersonal and sexual relations. It is because sexuality pervades everyone's spiritual and social identity that allowing a *divergent sexual behavior* for homosexual persons is ethically just and nondiscriminatory.

The table below attempts to make sense of the phrase *divergent sexual behavior* as distinct from typical sexual behavior.

Table 2: Comparing Typical Sexual Behavior and Divergent Sexual Behavior

Sexual Behavior	Sexual Orientation	Healthy Relationship Traits	Position Held
Typical Sexual Behavior	Heterosexual	1. Complementarity of Sexes 2. Consensual 3. Monogamous 4. Loving 5. Faithful 6. Respectful 7. Equality 8. Mutuality 9. Justice Oriented	*Exclusivist* = My position on sexuality is the best, and *all* other positions regarding sexuality are false and misleading.
Divergent Sexual Behavior	Homosexual	1. Non-complementarity of Sexes 2. Consensual 3. Monogamous 4. Loving 5. Faithful 6. Respectful 7. Equality 8. Mutuality 9. Justice Oriented	*Dialogue* = A position on sexuality that is balanced; it is open to dialogue; open-minded; equality oriented.

38. Kelly, *New Directions*, 137.

39. *Catechism of the Catholic Church*, §2332.

The two positions held by each sexual orientation are the exclusivist position and the dialogue position. The exclusivist position maintains that "my" position is the best position. It is the traditional Catholic understanding of a binary system; it is the correct and orthodox position regarding homosexuality, and all other positions are false, misguided, and misleading. There is no room for discussion and this position is the highest position because it reflects divine truth.[40] The dialogue position believes that this is a well-balanced position. This position is more open-minded and progressive; it is concerned with open conversations, exchange of ideas, and is justice and equality oriented. There is a real desire to make sure all God's people are treated with love, affirmation, and hospitality.[41]

Although the phrase *divergent sexual behavior* might not appeal to the homosexual community at large, the phrase is a much better starting point for discussion, dialogue, and discernment than the phrase *intrinsically disordered*. Theology is dynamic, it changes over time, it develops, it breaks new ground, and hopefully, a new and robust theology of homosexuality will emerge, one that is progressive on the subject; if not, the Catholic Church may be accused of being anti-homosexual or homophobic.

The Perception That Catholics and Other Christians Are *Anti*-LGBTQ

There is a perception that Christianity in general dislikes homosexuals and some of the information regarding this premise is alarming.[42] Recent research indicates that *anti*-homosexual feelings run high. There is a strong perception that Christians are prejudiced against homosexuals, and this has reached a critical tipping point. Christian authors and researchers David Kinnaman and Gabe Lyons note, "Outsiders say [Christian] hostility toward gays—not just opposition to homosexual politics and behaviors, but real disdain for [homosexual] individuals—has become virtually *synonymous* with the Christian faith."[43] Using spiteful words such as "hostility" and "disdain" toward the people of God is distressing for all of Christianity. The perception that Christians are *anti*-homosexual is heightened by further realities:

40. Doyle, *Church Emerging from Vatican II*, 271.
41. Doyle, *Church Emerging from Vatican II*, 272.
42. Francis et al., "Sexual Attitudes," 12.
43. Kinnaman and Lyons, *Un-Christian*, 90, italics added.

- Some Evangelical Christians believe that HIV/AIDS are God's wrath on homosexuals;

- Public comments from pastors and church leaders are often perceived as unjustly berating homosexuals;

- Christians use coarse jokes and offensive language to describe homosexuals, such as "faggots," "queers," and "sodomists";

- Some Christian church websites read "God hates fags";

- So-called "born-again" Christians are more likely to disapprove of homosexuality than divorce, despite Jesus never mentioning anything about same-sex relationships;

- A majority of Evangelical Christians, four out of five, maintain the belief that homosexual relations between two consenting adults should be illegal.[44]

Criticism of homosexual people by many Catholics and Protestant Christians runs deep, and this is the backdrop which many lesbian and gay Catholics face. Disdain and hatred are simply forms of oppression.

Many denominations have bloggers whose rhetoric is alarming toward LGBTQ folks, and there are a few Catholic groups as well. There is no shortage of anti-homosexual hate groups, which have websites and blogs and post harmful and damaging homophobia propaganda aimed at both individuals and institutions. One of my colleagues has labeled these groups as the "Catholic Taliban," because disdain and homophobia for homosexual people runs at an all-time high. It must be noted, however, that these anti-homosexual hate groups represent only about one hundred thousand to three hundred thousand Catholics out of an estimated seventy-one million Catholics in the United States. These anti-homosexual groups and their message runs counter to the words and actions of Jesus of Nazareth in the gospels, and continually promotes institutional oppression.

Institutional Oppression

Another way that Christians and Catholics are perceived as anti-homosexual is via institutional oppression. Oppression is the exercise of domination and control by a ruling group or party, and it creates injustice in life circumstances. However, in free societies, democratic countries, and independent

44. Kinnaman and Lyons, *Un-Christian*, 91–93.

institutions, oppression can be a result of a few people's choices, lifestyles, or policies that cause embedded and unquestioned norms, habits, and symbols to arise.[45] In other words, a person or people's rights can be restricted, enforcing barriers that immobilize and reduce a group or category of people.[46] Contemporary thinkers of today understand oppression to be denying people's basic rights: speech, language, education, voting, and other opportunities that might make them feel less than fully human in mind, body, and spirit.

Political philosopher and social justice advocate Iris Marion Young (1949–2006) addresses systematic and institutional oppression in her ground-breaking book *Justice and the Politics of Difference*. Young articulate five "faces" or types of oppression: (1) exploitation, (2) marginalization, (3) powerlessness, (4) cultural imperialism, and (5) violence. Any group, organization, institution, or government that violates just *one* of these types of oppression is guilty of institutional oppression.[47] A brief analysis of these types of oppression in relationship to homosexuality and Christian institutions seems appropriate.

1. Exploitation: Exploitation is normative in class distinctions and is a central part of Karl Marx's (1818–1883) theory of exploitation. Exploitation happens through a fixed process that transfers the results of one social group's work or circumstances to benefit another; it is concerned with other people for one's own gain or feeling of superiority.[48] Exploitation of homosexual people happens in Christian churches when lesbian and gay people:

- are overlooked by church leadership and employers for ministry positions;
- are seen only through the eyes of their sexuality, not as fully functional persons;
- are used as examples by religious leaders as models of inappropriateness.

Exploitation raises basic issues of human dignity. Exploitation takes place when the majority (the "haves") end up manipulating or overlooking the minorities (the "have-nots") within a system.

---

45. Young, *Justice and the Politics of Difference*, 41.
46. Young, *Justice and the Politics of Difference*, 41.
47. Young, *Justice and the Politics of Difference*, 45.
48. Young, *Justice and the Politics of Difference*, 49.

2. *Marginalization:* Marginalization is perhaps the most dangerous form of oppression, because a large spectrum of people can be expelled from useful participation and/or engagement with the community.[49] Marginalization is a process of exclusion. Severe marginalization has the potential to cause injustice, material deprivation, and extermination[50] Christian denominations practice marginalization against homosexuals when:

- they do not allow homosexuals to participate in holy Communion or the Eucharist on Sundays;

- the only preaching gay and lesbian people hear about homosexuality is negative or demeaning;

- LGBTQ folks are perceived as "outsiders" of the norm and are seen as different.

Marginalization raises basic structural issues of justice. Dismantling marginalization is concerned with raising the participation and status of *all* people, not an arbitrary few associated with ecclesial policies and bureaucratic control.

3. *Powerlessness:* Powerlessness is based on the idea that one group has power and other groups do not have power, and thus, the powerful group benefits from the others.[51] The powerless are dominated by the ruling class and are situated to take orders and rarely have the right to give orders. The powerless group lacks decision-making power to make change. The group with power in most hierarchical denominations are ordained bishops and priests. Unfortunately, the powerless group in most organizations are not always seen as respectable or worthy of positive attention. Powerlessness toward homosexual people happens in Christian churches when lesbian and gay people:

- are seen as having a psychological condition or medical condition needing to be "fixed";

- are not included in conversations when decisions are being made about their future;

- are not allowed full participation in *all* the sacraments of the body of Christ.

49. Young, *Justice and the Politics of Difference*, 53.

50. Young, *Justice and the Politics of Difference*, 53.

51. Young, *Justice and the Politics of Difference*, 56.

Powerlessness raises serious issues regarding certain groups of people being stripped of their status to socialize as a group and to exercise their own decision-making power in the dominant group.

4. *Cultural Imperialism:* Cultural imperialism is a term used by sociologists and historians. Cultural imperialism involves the universalization of a dominant group's experience and culture, and establishes it as the norm for all groups.[52] Cultural imperialism is the paradox of encountering oneself as invisible, while at the same time that one is labeled as "different" or an "outcast." The Christian community is built upon a Judeo-Christian belief system, along with a Euro-centric and patriarchal culture, which has persisted over time. Sexuality in general, and heterosexuality and gender expression in particular, has become a common example of cultural imperialism, because the dominant group in church-life is male and heterosexual.[53] Christian denominations practices cultural imperialism against homosexuals when they:

- use the Bible as a weapon to mistreat and violate homosexual dignity;
- imply that "God does not love you" because of a person's sexual orientation;
- do not allow openly lesbian women and gay men to be ordained into or to serve in ministry.

Cultural imperialism raises serious concerns about the invisibility and lack of respect of other groups. The dominant group, male and ordained, holds the majority of power and keeps the lesser groups subordinate and ostracized.

5. *Violence:* Violence includes severe assault, injury, and death, but it also includes incidents of harassment, intimidation, and/or ridicule simply for the purpose of degrading, humiliating, and/or stigmatizing people or groups.[54] Violence is created and supported by organizations in power to maintain unequal and unjust established order and practices.[55] Violence is systemic and coercive because it is a social practice. Violence is directed at members of a group simply because they are different: they look different, they think differently, they act differently, and they react differently than the

---

52. Young, *Justice and the Politics of Difference*, 59.
53. Young, *Justice and the Politics of Difference*, 60.
54. Young, *Justice and the Politics of Difference*, 61.
55. De La Torre, *Doing Ethics from the Margins*, 60.

supposed standard.[56] Organized violence occurs when a group of people are repressed. Repressive or brutal violence is an evil! Violence is a method that uses fear and intimidation to reach desired outcomes or to maintain power.[57] Finally, utilitarian or effective violence approaches legitimacy once it seems to be tolerated by the majority in power, but it is still a form of severe injustice.[58] Christian homosexuals suffer violence when they:

- are fired from Christian organizations or institutions because they are civilly married to a person of the same-sex;
- are asked to go through behavioral counseling or conversion therapy to "get right with God";
- become the objects of pranks, assaults, rapes, and murders because of sexuality.

Violence raises serious concerns about the way certain groups of people are treated within the society and church. All forms of verbal and physical sexism, heterosexism, and genderism are violence. Organized violence blocks the progress of tolerance against its members, and any unjust practices toward any group should be reformed.

The five faces of institutional oppression—exploitation, marginalization, powerlessness, cultural imperialism, and violence—help to perpetuate the superiority-mindset of heterosexuality. Any one of these oppressions creates abuse upon an individual or group of people. As it has been described above, each one of these oppressions is probably manifested in the lives of most homosexual Christians. Homosexual Christians ought to be free to pursue their own life plans, in their own way, based on their own conscience without interference from homophobic Christian denominations.

The Sin of Heterosexuality

Protestant theologians, Marvin M. Ellison and Miguel A. De La Torre, note that anti-homosexual intolerance and prejudice has led some theologians to refer to this behavior as the *sin of heterosexuality*.[59] The sin of

---

56. Young, *Justice and the Politics of Difference*, 62.

57. Young, *Justice and the Politics of Difference*, 62.

58. Young, *Justice and the Politics of Difference*, 63.

59. Ellison, "Practicing Safer Spirituality," 10, 15; De La Torre, "Confessions of a Latino Macho," 62.

heterosexuality makes the dominant culture's sexual experience compulsory on everyone else and views heterosexuality and cisgender as superior to homosexuality and transgender.[60] Of course, such a statement, the "sin of heterosexuality," is electric and the phrase is meant to reflect Jesus' teaching on judging others: "You hypocrite; first take the plank out of your own eye, and then you will see clearly to remove the speck from someone else's eye" (Matthew 7:5). In other words, there is no sin of homosexuality unless there is a sin of heterosexuality.[61] This seems to be a legitimate stance to hold and it has substantial merit. Sin is sin in God's eyes, and no human being has the right to judge another human being for their life circumstances. Judging human beings is left up to God (Matt 7:1; John 8:15).

As these subsections has pointed out, the sin of heterosexuality, the five faces of institutional oppression, and the anti-homosexual agenda that some Christians maintain, is enough to warrant serious theological inquiry, discussion, and speculation regarding a new, more developed, and less abrasive theology concerning homosexual Christians.

Parting Remarks

I conclude this chapter with two incidents that brought national attention. In July 2018, it was reported that a Catholic priest in the Catholic Diocese of Charlotte, North Carolina, denied a fifteen-year-old transgender girl—Max Arbelo—from receiving Communion at a Spanish-speaking Mass.[62] Moreover, in August 2018, Shelly Fitzgerald, a guidance counselor at Roncalli High School in Indianapolis, Indiana, was fired for her sexual orientation and for being civilly married to her partner of twenty-two years.[63] Both Fitzgerald and her wife are Catholics. The story made national news and appeared on the Ellen DeGeneres Show.[64]

Stories such as these are taking place all over the United States in Catholic parishes and Catholic high schools; they are a total disaster for the Catholic Church's pastoral image. Pastorally, incidents such as this "disturb Catholic families and relationships; it rewards [human] disingenuousness

60. De La Torre, "Confessions of a Latino Macho," 62.

61. De La Torre, "Confessions of a Latino Macho," 62–63.

62. Funk, "Was She Denied Communion," 1.

63. https://www.indystar.com/story/news/2018/08/20/roncalli-meeting-postponed-amid-fitzgerald-same-sex-marriage-controversy/1048667002/.

64. https://www.ellentube.com/search.html#search=shelly%20fitzgerald.

as [praiseworthy], then mock[s] women and men whose talents enrich our daily lives and weekly worship."[65] Christians and Catholics should not suffer because of their sexual orientation, sexual expression, or gender identity. Homosexuality is a gift from God, not a form of punishment.

God loves homosexual people. Homosexuality is part of God's grace. The theology of Christianity and Catholicism can change; things do not have to remain the same as they are currently; matters on this issue could be otherwise. Standing in solidarity with the LGBTQ community is a social justice issue, it is an ethical issue, it is a civil rights issue, and it is a humanitarian issue. The Prophet Jeremiah reminds us of God's mandate upon our lives: "Do justice and practice righteousness; deliver the one wronged from the hands of the oppressor; do not oppress the alien, the orphan, or the widow; do no violence; and do not shed innocent blood in this place" (Jer 22:1–3). In this pericope, God reveals to us that it is our duty to help the marginalized and oppressed. Perhaps it is time to deliver Christian homosexual persons from an oppressive theology and moral code that subordinates them to second-class citizens within the Christian community.

Discussion Questions

1. What are three new things you learned from this chapter?

2. What points did you find surprising, interesting, or perplexing from this chapter?

3. Why is the phrase *intrinsically disordered* so polarizing for LGBTQ folks?

4. What are your thoughts on the phrase *divergent sexual behavior?*

5. Have you personally witnessed institutional oppression at work in your congregation or community where you worship?

---

65. Copeland, *Enfleshing Freedom*, 77.

Chapter 4

New Perspectives and Moving Forward

In every age, the church carries the responsibility of reading the signs of the times and of interpreting them in light of the Gospel, if it is to carry out its task.

—SECOND VATICAN COUNCIL (1965)
Gaudium et Spes, §4

Opening Comments

THIS CHAPTER WILL OFFER new perspectives on the principle of *imago Dei,* an important aspect of understanding human dignity in the Christian tradition. Moreover, it is paramount that Christianity is moving forward on the principle of the dignity of the homosexual and transgender person, which is very much part of Christian social justice teachings. Part of moving forward is recognizing the signs of the times and engaging in important issues theologically. Finally, there are indications that Christians in the United States are more open to homosexual couples getting married than in previous decades. Developing new perspectives and moving forward beyond traditional teaching are important in creating a robust theology of sexuality, which includes homosexual and transgender persons.

The Principal of *Imago Dei*

The doctrine of *imago Dei* is a central principal in Christianity and Catholicism. *Imago Dei* is a term that frequently pops up in LGBTQ literature, but it is not always well defined. The aim of this section is to create a robust theology of *imago Dei*, which will influence Catholic theology, morality, and pastoral care. Part of the process involves shifting a person's theological convictions and value system to some extent. I define *imago Dei* as *the image and likeness of God*; hence *all* human beings are created in the image and likeness of the Divine (Gen 1:26–27; 2:21–22; 5:1; 9:6). Ultimately, *imago Dei* finds its fullest expression in the personhood of Jesus of Nazareth as he turned many of the societal rules and religious customs of his day upside down, such as inviting woman to follow him, hanging around questionable people, and healing on the Sabbath. Acknowledging the interior sacredness of all human beings is the cornerstone of *imago Dei*.

Sometimes the doctrine of *imago Dei* can be a slippery slope, because no matter which way someone, some group, or some denomination interprets the principle of *imago Dei*, the other person, group, or denomination can profess the opposite interpretation.[1] In other words, someone might state quite emphatically, "God made me this way," as the immensely popular, internationally renowned 2011 smash hit song by Lady Gaga proclaims, "Born This Way."[2] Meanwhile, the opposite side will argue, "No, God made girls to wear dresses and ribbons in their hair" and "boys to wear slacks and be rough and tough." Both position lacks inclusion and equality.

I have come to believe in some new perspectives in the principal of *imago Dei*. One new perspective is rooted in relational-justice, which is an ethical norm and a central value to pastoral care.[3] The reality is that the doctrine of *imago Dei* is about liberation, justice, and liberative ethics. The doctrine of *imago Dei* encourages doing theology outside the dominant culture and apart from the hegemonic mainstream of Christianity and/or Catholicism. A robust theology of *imago Dei* is concerned with doing theology relationally, justly, and on the margins.[4]

Pastoral theologian Larry Kent Graham maintains that there are five key points that undergird a theology of *imago Dei*:

1. Canales, "Ministry to Transgender Teenagers (Part One)," 200.
2. Canales, "Ministry to Transgender Teenagers (Part One)," 200.
3. Graham, "Role of Straight Allies," 111.
4. Canales, "Ministry to Transgender Teenagers (Part One)," 200.

1. To be created in *imago Dei* means to recognize the sacred worth and dignity of every individual who is created in God's image with unconditional love, value, and goodness.

2. To reflect the image and likeness of God is to be co-creators of novel configurations of life-enhancing relational possibilities; that is, God creates the world for relational possibilities and names it truthfully.

3. To be created in the *imago Dei* is to have enjoyment and delight in the pleasures of intimate relationships and erotically embodied existence and the extension of care, gratitude, and responsibility to those with whom we share these intimate pleasures.

4. To reflect the image and likeness of God is to participate in relational justice; that is, overcoming internalized heterosexism and homophobia, which neither reflects the love of God nor the love of neighbor and is totally inconsistent with God's love.

5. To be created in *imago Dei* is to have respect for diversity, cultural awareness, and multiplicity within the context of a dynamic wholeness, because love is not possible without difference and diversity.[5]

As a liberation and pastoral theologian, as well as a heterosexual and cisgender person, the points that Graham makes above mean that fulfilling a theology of *imago Dei* involves relational-justice, delight and happiness in physical intimacy, the deconstruction of old patterns of thinking, and overthrowing systems of oppression.[6]

A second perspective of *imago Dei* comes from the late Argentinian feminist liberation theologian Marcella Althaus-Reid (1952–2009), who calls for "doing theology with one's panties off" in order to subvert or disturb the status quo of the dominant, white, Euro-centric and America-centric theology.[7] For Althaus-Reid, "doing theology with one's panties off" is a metaphor that helps her (and other theologians) break away from traditional Western theological paradigms based on sexual categories and heterosexual binary systems. There is incredible cultural and Catholic opposition to recognizing LGBTQ people as sexual minorities and as equals. Therefore, Althaus-Reid is advocating a new understanding of sex, gender, and the issues surrounding homosexual, transgender, and

5. Graham, "Role of Straight Allies," 114–15.
6. Graham, "Role of Straight Allies," 116.
7. Althaus-Reid, *Indecent Theology*, 3.

non-gender-conforming folks, because *all* human beings are created in the *imago Dei*.

It would be wise for Catholic theologians to *try* to develop a new understanding and robust theology of *imago Dei*. I have stated in an earlier article,

> *Imago Dei* refers to all people being created in the image and likeness of God, no matter if they are: Black or White, female or male, poor or rich, born below the equator or above the equator, homosexual or heterosexual, or transgender or cisgender.[8]

A theology of *imago Dei* has to involve love, justice, and equality as its binding virtues. There are multiple ways in which people experience God and connect with God. Love, justice, and equality are hallmarks that empower people to see the goodness and godliness in others.[9] Loving the queer person is connecting with the *imago Dei* of the other; demonstrating justice to the vulnerable is part of *imago Dei* because it establishes awareness of conscience; and expressing equality is part of *imago Dei* because it stands with God's solidarity for the marginalized and oppressed.

In the Catholic document *Communion and Stewardship: Human Persons Created in the Image of God*, the principle of *imago Dei* is positively affirmed. The ecclesial statement notes:

> The triune God has revealed [God's] plan to share the communion of Trinitarian life with persons created in [God's] image . . . Created in the image of God, human beings are by nature bodily and spiritual, men and women made for one another, persons oriented towards communion with God and with one another, wounded by sin and in need of salvation, and destined to be conformed to Christ, the perfect image of the Father, in the power of the Holy Spirit.[10]

The document clearly stresses the significance of *imago Dei* in the bodily and spiritual life of individuals, and this bodily and spiritual life would include a person's sexuality. LGBTQ theology places sexuality and spirituality, and all its variables and varieties, as central to the understanding of *imago Dei*. Sexuality and spirituality have a symbiotic association that cannot be dissolved. Again, the document affirms,

---

8. Canales, "Ministry to Transgender Teenagers (Part Two)," 251.

9. Kim-Kort, *Outside the Lines*, 74–75.

10. International Theological Commission, *Communion and Stewardship*, §25.

> Human beings are created in *imago Dei* precisely as persons ca-
> pable of a knowledge and love that are personal and interpersonal.
> It is the essence of *imago Dei* dwelling in them that these personal
> beings are relational and social beings.[11]

God has created human beings to be in relationship and in love with ourselves, each other, and God.

Embracing a more robust theology of *imago Dei* helps to situate its
relevance for Christian formation. Catholic systematic theologian Catherine Mowry LaCugna (1952–1997) understands the principal of *imago
Dei* in relation to the Russian Orthodox concept of *theósis*. LaCugna states,
"*Theósis* means being confronted in our personal existence to God's personal existence, achieving right relationship and genuine communion in
every aspect, at every level."[12] This idea of *theósis* is about recognizing the
intrinsic value of each person's uniqueness: being free to be oneself, free to
be in a just and loving relationship, and free to be odd, queer, or divergent
in one's sexual identity. For LaCugna, then, queer folks are absolutely created in the image and likeness of God based on the concept of rationality.[13]

For LaCugna, lesbian and gay persons are absolutely created in the
image and likeness of God based on the concept of rationality. The theology
of *imago Dei* requires that "everyone is accepted as an ineffable, unique,
and unrepeatable image of God, irrespective of [the ways] the dignity of a
person might otherwise be determined: [sexual orientation], level of intel-
ligence, political correctness, physical beauty, monetary value."[14] A person's
sexuality, gender, and overall personhood is in relationship with and connected to God and their own *imago Dei*.

Consequently, there is a social and sexual undercurrent in the principle of *imago Dei*. This social-sexual undercurrent includes sexual desire
and sexual acts within mutual, committed, monogamous relationships. The
principle of *imago Dei* includes the total person: mind, body, and spirit.
Therefore, it is appropriate to see the connection between social, spiritual,

11. International Theological Commission, *Communion and Stewardship*, §40.

12. LaCugna, *God for Us*, 284. LaCugna borrows from Russian Orthodox metropoli-
tan and historical theologian John Zizioulas, who understands the principal of *imago Dei*
in relation to the orthodox concept of *theósis*.

13. LaCugna did not write specifically about LGBTQ youth and young adults directly;
however, I am reinterpreting and reimagining her position based on her understanding
of *theósis*.

14. LaCugna, *God for Us*, 299.

and sexual activities since God is the creator of these three activities. There is a real danger to spirituality if Christians begin to deny their sexuality.

Theologian Robert E. Goss states, "The denial of human sexuality within spirituality is damaging to the human spirit because it alienates Christians from their own sexual selves and from their own bodies."[15] Human sexual desires and sexual actions are *imago Dei*. If my brother's mark of sexual desire must be hidden, if my sister's mark of queerness must be disguised, if my aunt's mark of civically married lesbianism must be repressed, then we are not *imago Dei*.[16] This is perfectly logical and acceptable, since humans cannot separate their sexuality and sexual identity from their spirituality.[17] The social understanding of *imago Dei* by contemporary theologians has been the means by which they are recovering the value of human community, and the worth of sex, gender, and sexuality.[18] The meta-reflection and rediscovery of *imago Dei* for homosexual persons and transgender people is enormous because it is one way that moves beyond static notions of theology and moves us toward a new and robust theology of queer people.

The challenge for Catholic theologians is that our human understanding regarding sexuality and identity seems to be changing daily, and things that were known through certain theological lenses a few decades ago are seen vastly differently today. It seems apparent that the Catholic Church needs to catch up with the scientific community on certain areas of knowledge regarding sexuality, gender, identity, and intersex.

Imago Dei calls all Christians to participate more fully into the image and life of Jesus the Christ—*imago Christi*. Jesus Christ is "the image of the invisible God" (Col 1:15 NAB), and all peoples, queer or straight, transgender or cisgender, are "being transformed into [Jesus'] likeness with ever-increasing glory, which comes from the Lord, who is the Spirit" (2 Cor 3:18 NIV). The Scriptures remind us that the Christian call is to allow ourselves to be transformed into *imago Christi*. Thus, Jesus of Nazareth

> stands before us not in male perfection, but as the true human into whose image we are transformed as we grow in love, in virtue in

---

15. Goss, "Christian Homo-devotion to Jesus," 113.

16. Copeland, *Enfleshing Freedom*, 82.

17. *Catechism of the Catholic Church*, §2332.

18. DeFranza, *Sex Difference in Christian Theology*, 5.

> faith, in holiness, in hope, by the Spirit who fills us, convicts us,
> breathes life into us, and empowers us for the journey.[19]

Christians would be wise to move beyond older paradigms of myopic interpretations regarding sexuality and gender and allow the principal of *imago
Dei* to move them into newer ways of thinking and treating others.

Presbyterian feminist theologian Mary McClintock Fulkerson regards
the principle of *imago Dei* as a substantial doctrine within Christianity. She
poignantly remarks, "The image [of God] is a symbolic condensation of
what in the Christian tradition it means to be fully human . . . In important
respects the *imago Dei* can serve as an index of *whom* the tradition has seen
as fully human."[20] From Fulkerson, it is logical through analysis, we can see
if the Christian tradition in general and the Catholic tradition in particular,
have viewed and treated all people with the dignity and respect which *imago
Dei* mandates. Have women been historically treated as *imago Dei*? Have
Black people been historically treated as *imago Dei*? Have ethnic minorities been viewed as *imago Dei*? Are sexual minorities today treated as *imago
Dei*? If LGBTQ persons are truly created in the image and likeness of God,
then their sexual identity cannot be fundamentally wrong, it can only be
naturally ordered accordingly to their sexual orientation assigned at birth.

Subsequently, there is an inherent reverence and dignity within each
homosexual person created in *imago Dei*. Finally, in regards to *imago Dei*,
Pope Francis writes in *Evangelii Gaudium* that God

> summons us to the revolution of *tenderness* . . . It is a fraternal love
> capable of seeing sacred grandeur of our neighbor, of finding God
> in every human being, of tolerating the nuisances of life in com-
> mon by clinging to the love of God, of opening the heart to divine
> love and seeking the happiness of others just as [God] does.[21]

Pope Francis's words are at the very heart of seeing and treating every person, regardless of sexuality or gender identity, as *imago Dei* and treating
and respecting that other person with dignity.

---

19. DeFranza, *Sex Difference in Christian Theology*, 288–89.
20. Fulkerson, "Imago Dei," 95.
21. Francis, *Evangelii Gaudium*, §§88 & 92.

The Dignity of LGBTQ Persons

Developing a new theology of homosexuality and a fresh understanding of the dignity of LGBTQ persons is important because of Christian social justice teaching on the life and dignity of the human person. Human dignity is the bedrock of all Christian social justice teachings.

> The Catholic Church proclaims that human life is sacred and that the dignity of the human person is the foundation of a moral vision for society. Our belief in the sanctity of human life and the inherent dignity of the human person is foundation of all the principles of our social teaching.[22]

Consequently, there is no more basic principle than of the dignity of the individual, which is firmly rooted in Scripture and tradition. Christianity firmly maintains the principle of human dignity, and professes that *all* life is sacred because the human person—homosexual or heterosexual, transgender or cisgender—is the most central and clearest reflection of God.

According to social justice advocate Katherine Feely, "human beings have transcendent worth and value that comes from God."[23] Human dignity is "the sign and the safeguard of the transcendental dimension of the human person."[24] This God-given inspiration of human dignity is not based on any human qualities, legal mandates, or individual accomplishments, but is freely given by a generously loving God. God freely gives dignity to the LGBTQ person, and marks the person as holy and sacred, which is a fundamental act of God's being.

According to the US Catholic Bishops,

> When we deal with each other, we should do so with the sense of awe that arises in the presence of something holy and sacred. For that is [the essence of] human beings: we are created in the image of God (Gen 1:27).[25]

The bishops highlight the importance of treating *every* individual with dignity and respect because each human person is created in the image and likeness of God.

---

22. US Conference of Catholic Bishops, *Sharing Catholic Social Teaching*, §4.
23. Feely, "Principle of Human Dignity," 1.
24. *Gaudium et Spes*, §76.
25. US Conference of Catholic Bishops, *Economic Justice for All*, §28.

There are several theological points that envision the dignity of the LGBTQ person and are worthy of consideration:

- The LGBTQ person is *always* capable of knowing and loving God;

- The dignity of the LGBTQ person rests on the foundation of faith that affirms that God is the source and creator of *all* life;

- The dignity of the LGBTQ person is based on divine revelation and finds her/his fullest expression in life with God;

- The dignity of the LGBTQ person is understood as flowing from one's personal relationship with God and is not earned or merited;

- The dignity of the LGBTQ person is grounded in human freedom and the homosexual person is free to accept or reject the ongoing self-communication of God;

- The LGBTQ person is free and only a free person can be morally responsible;

- The LGBTQ person is called to live a morally upright life and to do good and avoid evil, just like every other person;

- The dignity of the LGBTQ person is realized and protected in the community of others;

- The dignity of the LGBTQ person is sacred regardless of age, race, ethnicity, sex, gender, religion, economic status, and political affiliation.[26]

Theologically, it seems evident that there ought to be respect and dignity demonstrated to every LGBTQ person, and that dignity and respect is *not* a suggestion or consideration, but is fundamental for the homosexual person. Ethically, it seems apparent that the respect and dignity of the homosexual and transgender person should be freely given with no constraints and unconditionally.

Homosexual people have a moral right to equality, freedom, and justice. Saint Thomas Aquinas (1224–1274) addresses the virtues of rights and justice in his immense work *Summa Theologica*. For Aquinas, "right is the object of justice," and "people have a right to something."[27] Aquinas is concerned about justice, which has to do with a person's natural rights or

---

26. Krietemeyer, *Leaven for the Modern World*, 21–22; Feely, "Principle of Human Dignity," 2.

27. Aquinas, IIa–IIae, Q57, articles 1–4, and Q58, articles 1–5.

ius in Latin. The term *ius* translates as "right," but it also can mean "the just thing," or "what is due."[28]

Catholic Dominican philosopher Dominic Legge maintains that Aquinas uses the term *ius* most often in an objective dimension;[29] in other words, a person has objective rights. Aquinas maintains that

> *ius* [is] the object of justice, as something that expresses what is fair or equal in a given human relationship or set of relationships, but this has led some to argue that Aquinas presents an understanding of *ius*, and thus of "right" (or "rights"), as exclusively objective, or at least in a predominantly objective sense.[30]

It is clear that Aquinas is discussing rights of all people; therefore, such rights also belong to and include homosexual people and couples. Aquinas's understanding of *ius* or rights is something that is due properly to everyone. Therefore, it is plausible that Aquinas *might* approve of homosexual couples today because their relationship is rooted in justice and equality. Although Aquinas was a community-oriented person (his understanding of rights and justice evolved around society and that which is best for a community), and did not have a twenty-first-century understanding of individual rights; he is clear that people have a right to certain things or aspects of their life. Hence, it is possible to infer from Aquinas that since a homosexual person and/or homosexual couple is created in the image and likeness of God, she/he has a kind of personal right to be respected, acknowledged, and recognized as true and good.[31]

The medieval Franciscan scholar John Duns Scotus (1265–1308) has this distinctive concept known as *haecceitas* (hey-ché-e-tas) or "thisness." For Scotus, *all* human beings are unique in all time and for all eternity because God creates each person freely and individually.[32] Scotus makes the connection that all human beings are individual, unique, and have human qualities and attributes that make each person distinctively different from the next person. Scotus uses the Latin word *haec*, which translates

---

28. Legge, "Do Thomists Have Rights?," 131.

29. Conversely, though, in some instances Aquinas also understands the contemporary notion of subjective rights "as belonging to a person, a kind of moral faculty that characterizes individual subjects" (Legge, "Do Thomists Have Rights?," 131). However, most of Aquinas's accounts of *ius* refer to objective rights and justice.

30. Legge, "Do Thomists Have Rights?," 131.

31. Mizzoni, *Catholic and Franciscan Ethics*, 50.

32. Nothwehr, *Franciscan View*, 48.

as *this*, and uses it to describe the individual and particular uniqueness of each person.

Franciscan moral theologian Dawn M. Nothwehr notes, "The special thing that makes a singular thing what it is and differentiates it from all other things can be called *haecceitas*, which literally means *thisness*."[33] Another way to look at this is that the homosexual person's *haecceitas* makes her/him unique and created by God in such a way that each homosexual person is incapable of duplication.[34] For Scotus, the dignity of the homosexual person is paramount: she/he is a unique and irreplaceable contribution to creation and God's entire plan of reality and salvation.[35] God chose each homosexual person freely, not a different human or person; this invests significance and worth in each homosexual person who is created in the image and likeness of God.[36]

The dignity of the homosexual person is paramount and is rooted in Christian social justice teachings and the US Catholic Bishops affirm this point. Moreover, it is quite possible that both Aquinas and Scotus would understand that accepting and affirming the homosexual person is part and parcel of theological understanding today. This means that homosexual persons are created, loved, and called and gifted by God to live a life with purpose, with an informed conscience, and with an understanding of the signs of the times.

Theology of the Signs of the Times

Understanding of the signs of the times is important to Catholic theology and perhaps even more important to Catholic ministry. The Second Vatican Council (1962–1955) document *Gaudium et Spes* challenges Christians to understand the signs of the times. The actual phrase, as the epigraph at the beginning of this chapter reads, "In every age, the church carries the responsibility of reading the signs of the times and of interpreting them in light of the Gospel, if it is to carry out its task."[37] The Second Vatican Council leaders call on the laity to reflect deeply on matters of faith and life and

---

33. Nothwehr, *Franciscan View*, 48.

34. Wolter and O'Neill, *John Duns Scotus*, 28.

35. Ingham and Shannon, *Ethical Method*, 63.

36. Mizzoni, *Catholic and Franciscan Ethics*, 77.

37. *Gaudium et Spes*, §4.

not merely be a spectator in Catholicism, but to open their eyes and heart to the unfolding issues that societies and cultures encounter.

Catholic Scripture scholar Dianne Bergant notes that with the advent of the Second Vatican Council, changes took place for Catholics: the church changed and people began to change. Bergant states,

> Over the years we have grown into social sensitivity. We take faith-based political stands. At times we even turn a critical eye to the teachings and traditions of the church. Our faith has matured and our devotions have been enriched by reading the signs of the times.[38]

How does this *reading the signs of the times* work today in the twenty-first century? How does it work with regard to homosexuality or transgender folks? Homosexuality is a divisive topic within Catholicism or conservative Christianity. Nevertheless, if theology is going to be authentic, then theology must begin with the living engagement with people in a community. LGBTQ Christians are worthy of theological engagement and thoughtfulness.

Catholic systematic theologian Kevin F. Burke argues that cultural diversity is a gift to theology.[39] Although Burke does not mention sexual minorities per se, homosexual and transgender Catholics are a subculture of Catholic culture and are a diverse and unique population. Regarding a theology of the signs of the times, Burke stresses two points.

Burke's first point is that "theology does *not* directly reflect on God, but on the self-communication of God in history."[40] In this way, homosexuality today is communicated and mediated by historical trends and actualities and it is up to the *sensus fidelium* (sense of the faithful) to help drive these cultural realities which benefit the entire people of God. Therefore, the signs of the times *cannot* be reduced to theological concepts *alone*. Homosexuality and transgender emerges as a *sign* on the level of *steadfast faith* in the struggle and mess of nitty-gritty, everyday, real-world life and *action*.[41] Ethical introspection and theological reflection on homosexuality ought to reflect upon the betterment of all the members within a faith tradition, especially those on the margins, and sharpen its praxis (reflection on ministry practice) with an eye toward interacting with and befriending LGBTQ people within the faith community. A theology of the signs of the

38. Bergant, "Reading the Signs of the Times," 38–39.
39. Burke, "Thinking about the Church," 40.
40. Burke, "Thinking about the Church," 42.
41. Burke, "Thinking about the Church," 42.

times is *not* just a thinking exercise about doctrines. Rather a theology that commits itself to seeing God in different ways and from various perspectives, and to act in ways that Jesus would act, and tries its best to integrate difficult conceptualizations such as the equality, dignity, respect, and justice due to every homosexual and transgender person.

Burke's second point is that "theology not only reflects on cultural diversity, but opts to remain open to further authentic encounters with diverse cultures."[42] Liberation theologians have taught for decades and Catholic/Christian social justice teachings embraced the need for a preferential option for the poor. Similarly, a *preferential option for homosexual people* puts ethicists and theologians (who are usually researching and writing in the comfort of their offices and in their ivory towers) in a place where they might not normally locate themselves: thinking and reflecting about LGBTQ people. What does it mean to have a preferential option for homosexual people? It entails a preferential (favored) affirmation, and acceptance of all sexual minorities and nonbinary people.[43] Catholic theologians, and all Catholics for that matter, cannot forget that preferential openness is for all who are considered outcasts, marginalized, poor, minorities, and all who are victims of racism, classism, sexism, genderism, and for all who have been exposed, excluded, and exploited as subversive, dangerous, weird, and/or queer.[44]

Hugh William Montefiore (1920–2005), an Anglican bishop and theologian, suggested that Jesus' celibacy *might* have been due to him being homosexual and it is something that Christianity cannot ignore.[45] Montefiore's point seems plausible to LGBTQ people because Jesus was always concerned with befriending the friendless.[46] Regarding Jesus' sexuality, M. Shawn Copeland states, "I *neither* propose *nor* insinuate that Jesus Christ was homosexual."[47] Her theological concern is soteriological: *"If Jesus of Nazareth, the Christ of God, cannot be an option for gay and lesbians, then he cannot*

---

42. Burke, "Thinking about the Church," 42.

43. Canales, "Ministry to Catholic LGBTQ Youth," 60.

44. Burke, "Thinking about the Church," 43.

45. Montefiore, "Jesus, the Revelation of God," 109–10.

46. Montefiore, "Jesus, the Revelation of God," 110.

47. Copeland, *Enfleshing Freedom*, 78. However, Copeland does not deny Jesus was not gay either. The truth of the matter is that no one knows with exact certitude Jesus' sexuality, since the Gospels seem to indicate that he was chaste and celibate.

be an option."[48] Christ's mercy, love, and salvation are free for everyone who believes, including queer Christians. Montefiore and Copeland understand that the signs of the times and are trying to eradicate homophobic and transphobic oppression through Christian anthropology and soteriology.

Understanding the signs of the times can challenge the infrastructures that exacerbate justice and mercy and can help to eradicate prejudice and hatred, and move the church to real transformation, which is healing, openness, and acceptance. The impact for having a theology of the signs of the times is critical for developing a new theology of homosexuality and transgender.

Finally, a dynamic theology of the signs of the times presents a central and life-giving change into the way we conceive the nature of faith.[49] In other words, the problem is not having a consensus on homosexuality or a set of propositions regarding homosexuality that Christian hierarchy believes to be true. No, the fundamental question is not: how do we get everyone to subscribe to and follow old standards and ridged beliefs about homosexuality (which is based on flimsy Scripture evidence and heteronormative, patriarchal, and Euro-centric tradition)? But rather, on the quintessential reality of having to deal with the salvific presence of God in Jesus, who continues becoming flesh throughout history and continues to indwell in diverse people, including LGBTQ folks.[50] Theology is engaging, its moves and flows, it develops over time, it breaks new ground, and hopefully, a new and vibrant theology of homosexuality will emerge, and one that is more progressive, that meets the signs of the times.

In recent years, with the advent of Pope Francis's papacy, there has been reason to believe that the signs of the times are happening in the Catholic Church and attitudes are changing on the subject of homosexuality and transgender rights.

Changing Attitudes

Are attitudes changing about homosexuality in the Catholic Church? There is some evidence that suggests that Catholics are becoming more open and affirming toward their lesbian and gay sisters and brothers.[51] There is a grow-

---

48. Copeland, *Enfleshing Freedom*, 78, italics original.

49. Burke, "Thinking about the Church," 43.

50. Ellacuría, "Los Pobres," 148.

51. Canales, "Ministry to Catholic LGBTQ Youth," 60–62.

ing trend in US Catholicism that supports homosexual relationships and marriage. Pew Research Center (a think tank for religion and public life) states that 67 percent of US Catholics support homosexual marriages, which is a significant rise from 2012, when the percentage was roughly 54 percent.[52]

Therefore, the majority of US Catholics support same-sex relationships. In another poll, Pew Research Center found that Pope Francis still needs to do a little more in regards to helping the Catholic Church be more accepting of homosexual people. Forty-one percent of US Catholics would like Pope Francis to do more about homosexuality: opening up dialogue with lesbian and gay Catholics, affirming the dignity and worth of homosexual Catholics, lessening restrictions on homosexual Catholics so they can work in Catholic institutions, and allowing homosexual Catholics to be married.[53]

Pope Francis's popularity numbers have slipped a little over the past few years among US Catholics because many thought he was going to bring about major change in sexual ethics, but that has not happened under his leadership. In 2014, 71 percent of American Catholics favored Pope Francis's agenda, and in 2019, his numbers have decreased a little to 67 percent. Consequently, Pope Francis is still highly regarded in the United States; however, there are signs of Catholics beginning to become disenchanted by his pontificate.[54] He has still not approved simple same-sex nuptial blessings for civilly married lesbian and gay couples, which would go a long way toward repairing ill feelings LGBTQ folks have with the Catholic Church.

If there were a little more discussion and open dialogue with Catholic LGBTQ folks and Pope Francis, perhaps then the Catholic Church would lower its guard regarding homosexual relations and marriages. Today, such activities still constitute "sexual sin" in the eyes of the church. The Catholic Church's strict teaching regarding homosexuality is a malignant issue for the homosexual community and progressive Catholics. As noted, most US Catholics (67%) want the Catholic Church to step into the twenty-first century regarding homosexuality. Most Catholics in the United States would probably prefer that Pope Francis be more of a policy-maker and produce new doctrines that advocate, support, and affirm monogamous and married homosexual relationships rather than rehashing the same old

52. Pew Research Center, "Pope Francis."

53. Pew Research Center, "Most American Catholics," 13.

54. Pew Research Center, "Pope Francis."

theological party line. Unfortunately, US Catholics will have to wait and see if the future brings favorable relief to the homosexual community.

Parting Remarks

It is clear that many Christians today approve of civilly married homosexual couples, even if it is not likely to take place officially in some Christian denominations for some time into the future, probably decades.

The aim of this chapter is to provide new perspectives and ways of looking at an old issue—the notion that homosexuality is wrong or sinful. The goal here is to offer a method of moving forward based on a robust theology of *imago Dei*, the dignity of the LGBTQ person, and understanding a theology that represents the *sensus fidelium* and the signs of the times. The intention was to help persuade the reader to be open to the theological and pastoral issues surrounding the homosexual person. Things are not so black and white, there is gray matter, nuance, and subtlety when discussing matters of homosexuality and transgender rights, and Christians are more attuned to the gospels if they are open and affirming to their LGBTQ sisters and brothers.

Discussion Questions

1. What are three new things you learned from this chapter?

2. What points did you find surprising, interesting, or perplexing from this chapter?

3. Has this chapter allowed you to think of new perspectives or ways of moving forward with regard to homosexual Christians?

4. How would you summarize the phrase *imago Dei*? Does it make sense to develop a robust theology around *imago Dei* for LGBTQ folks?

5. Why is the *sensus fidelium* so important? Explain.

Chapter 5

It Is Time for Openness and Affirmation

"How can we proclaim Christ to a generation that is changing? We must be careful not to administer a vaccine against faith to them." "If someone is gay and seeks the Lord with good will, who am I to judge?" "I remember the case of a very sad little girl who finally confided to her teacher the reason for her state of mind: 'My mother's girlfriend doesn't like me.'"

—POPE FRANCIS
Conversation on route to World Youth Day
July 29, 2013, Rio de Janeiro, Brazil

Opening Comments

POPE FRANCIS'S REMARKS ABOVE direct attention to some difficult and virtually undiscussed concerns about the way the Christian church ministers to LGBTQ youth and young adults. Concerns regarding LGBTQ young people range from serious theological disagreements about ecclesial teachings to ignorance among youth and young adult ministers about the situations that these young people face. LGBTQ youth and young adults often experience fear, shame, and hostility from their peers and from their parents.[1]

1. Durso and Gates, "Serving Our Youth," 4.

I have presented several times over the past few years at various national and international conferences on this subject. It seems that nothing is more controversial and potentially divisive in Christian denominations as the issues of homosexuality and transgender folks. Ministers from various denominations stated that "this is the most pressing and continuous issue" in their churches. This chapter contends that Christian LGBTQ young people deserve, and should expect, proper and competent pastoral care from their parish youth and young adult ministries. The purpose of this short chapter is twofold: (1) to elaborate on the ministry to Christian and Catholic LGBTQ youth and young adults in the United States and (2) to propose more open and affirming youth and young adult ministries that addresses LGBTQ issues and concerns. The question of ministering to Christian LGBTQ young people is both a practical theological matter as well as a ministry dilemma that merits serious attention.

Situating the Discussion

Research suggests that views on LGBTQ relationships vary by Christian denomination and by religious practice.[2] Currently, mainline Christian ministry and pastoral care relating to LGBTQ youth and young adults is likened to ministering to young people with eyes wide shut. The ministerial current presence to the *young church* (a phrase used in youth and young adult ministry that refers to young people's ages 14–29), particularly to Christian LGBTQ young people, is almost nonexistent.[3] The overwhelming majority of youth and young adult ministries in the United States do not cater to, actively attract, or tolerate openly LGBTQ young people. Christian churches in general, and youth and young adult ministries specifically, could be, and should be, doing more to reach out and minister to LGBTQ young people. Christian LGBTQ youth and young adults need a place in the church to be accepted, their gifts empowered, their faith developed, their spirituality nurtured, and their sexuality supported.

As a Catholic pastoral theologian, it is troubling to see the lack of attention LGBTQ young people receive. Therefore, this is my invitation for Christian bishops, pastors, youth and young adult ministers, and parents: (1) to be more hospitable, gracious, and open-minded with the LGBTQ youth and young adult communities and (2) to have LGBTQ young people

2. Francis et al., "Sexual Attitudes," 11.

3. Sanabria and Suprina, "Addressing Spirituality," 54–55.

present at the table for dialogue and critique about the lack of advocacy and pastoral care in Christian youth and young adult ministry. I hope to encourage youth and young adult ministers and lay volunteer catechists "to minister *to, with, by and for*" LGBTQ young people as so beautifully articulated in the original Catholic youth ministry document *A Vision of Youth Ministry*.[4]

Typically, the topic, discussion, and rhetoric surrounding sexual minorities in Christian churches centers around three camps of theological thought. The first camp is the *traditional or conservative*, who are those practitioners and theologians who adhere to the particular denomination's polity, or in the case of the Catholic Church, the Magisterium's[5] position on LGBTQ genital acts with little or no pastoral concern for the LGBTQ person. A second camp is the *mediating* or *moderate*, who are those pastoral ministers and scholars who do not challenge denominational or ecclesial doctrine on LGBT genital acts; however, they place a greater emphasis on the pastoral ramifications for the LGBTQ person. The third camp is the *revisionist or progressive* position, those pastors and theologians who challenge denominational and magisterial teaching on LGBTQ persons.[6] The time might be ripe for a revisionist perspective to try to handle this delicate issue and to provide an open-minded approach toward LGBTQ young people. All Christian people—LGBTQ youth and young adults included—share in the same Christian dignity and worth as heterosexual and cisgender Christians. Every Christian's dignity and worth is equal and shared by virtue of baptism, sealed at confirmation, and nourished at the Eucharistic table.[7]

The Theological Quandary and Moral Conundrum

The theological quandary regarding LGBTQ youth and young adults is directly enmeshed by the rhetoric surrounding the doctrinal and theoretical aspects of Christian understanding on homosexuality. Part of the quandary

4. Department of [Catholic] Education, *Vision of Youth Ministry*, 6–7.

5. The Magisterium (Latin for "office of the teacher"), in the Catholic Church, refers to the authoritative teaching of the universal church, which belongs to the whole college of bishops (Catholic bishops around the world) who are united with the bishop of Rome—the presiding pope.

6. Maher and Sever, "What Educators in Catholic Schools Might Expect," 82.

7. Coleman, *Homosexuality*, 110.

is the obfuscation and misunderstanding of a pastoral plan with and for LGBTQ youth and young adults. The Catholic Church, like many Christian denominations, has not directly written anything substantial concerning LGBTQ young people in its documents on youth and young adult ministry, which is a particularly peculiar phenomenon in this day and age. The Catholic Church has written a few specific documents (addressed below) on the "pastoral care" of persons of homosexual inclination, and although written with empathy and compassion, they lack "teeth" and conviction, and offer precious little by way of authentic advocacy and quality pastoral care for LGBTQ young people.[8] I have already addressed extensively the Catholic position on homosexuality in chapter 3, so no sense rehashing that here.

The Christian custom regarding sex before marriage or outside of a committed, monogamous marriage is seen as fornication and it is considered morally wrong and sinful (Gal 5:19–21). The parameters here do not permit for a full discussion on sexual ethics and morality. Nevertheless, it is wise to understand that the Christian/Catholic *traditional or conservative* view regarding sexual relations is abstinence and chastity. Abstinence is the avoidance of a particular pleasure (food, drink, sexual intercourse) for a determined length of time, usually on certain days.[9] Chastity is a virtue and Christian lifestyle. Chastity is the successful integration of human sexuality within a person, and thus the person's interior life (spirituality) is in unity with the outer life (sexuality).[10] Hence, all Christians are called to chastity; even married couples and spouses are chaste non-virgins to each other.[11] A Christian/Catholic *moderate or mediating* view of sex before marriage or outside of marriage would indicate that sex between two committed and consenting adults is ideally based on genuine mutual respect, companionship, and love.[12] A Christian/Catholic *revisionist/progressive* view of sex before or outside of marriage would maintain that sexual encounters cause no unjust harm, involve free consent, mutuality of sexual desire, and

---

8. Congregation for the Doctrine of Faith, *Letter to the Bishops*; US Conference of Catholic Bishops, *Always Our Children*; US Conference of Catholic Bishops, *Ministry to Persons with Homosexual Inclination*. None of these documents are written to advocate a particular agenda or to endorse a homosexuality, which probably does not engender a warm reception from the LGBTQ community.

9. *Catechism of the Catholic Church*, §2337.

10. *Catechism of the Catholic Church*, §2337.

11. Genovesi, *In Pursuit of Love*, 136.

12. Genovesi, *In Pursuit of Love*, 171–75.

equality of personhood, power, and status.[13] However, monogamy is still the gold standard. Even a Christian/Catholic revisionist perspective would disapprove of so-called "causal sex," "one night stands," or "hooking up" for the night between uncommitted couples. The rationale for bringing up these three views of sex before or outside of marriage is to demonstrate the theological and moral dilemma that pastoral practitioners such as youth and young adult ministers must face, especially with LGBTQ young people.

Despite charged emotions, personal opinions, troublesome psychological theories, and conservative theologies regarding homosexuality, the larger issue remains: LGBTQ youth and young adults deserve, and should expect, proper and competent pastoral care from their parish youth and young adult ministry. If the churches of Jesus Christ are not careful, they may be criticized as suffering from LGBTQ *ephibephobia* (the fear of young people) toward sexual minority youth and young adults.[14]

Official Ecclesiastical Documents That Address LGBTQ Matters

Although this section pertains specifically to the Catholic Church and its writings, it can be applicable and suitable by Protestants as well. In fact, I have plenty of Protestant colleagues who look to the Catholic sources on various theological, liturgical, and ministerial topics and issues. There are five major Catholic Church documents concerning LGBTQ people:

1. The Congregation for the Doctrine of Faith's document entitled *Letter to the Bishops of the Catholic Church on the Pastoral Care of Homosexual Persons.*[15]

2. The United States Conference of Catholic Bishops' document titled *Always Our Children: A Pastoral Message to Parents of Homosexual Children and Suggestions for Pastoral Ministers.*[16]

---

13. Farley, *Just Love*, 216–23.

14. Root and Creasy Dean, *Theological Turn*, 207. *Ephibephobia* is the fear of teenagers and is very distinct from *ephebphilia* the primary sexual desire and attraction of adolescents by adults. I am using the term in the context of the Church could be criticized as having *ephibephobia* toward its homosexual teenagers.

15. Congregation for the Doctrine of Faith, *Letter to the Bishops.*

16. US Conference of Catholic Bishops, *Always Our Children.*

3. The Congregation for the Doctrine of Faith's document entitled *Considerations regarding Proposals to Give Legal Recognition to Unions between Homosexual Persons.*[17]

4. The United States Conference of Catholic Bishops' document titled *Ministry to Persons with a Homosexual Inclination: Guidelines for Pastoral Care.*[18]

5. The Congregation for Catholic Education's document entitled *Male and Female He Created Them: Towards a Path of Dialogue on the Question of Gender Theory in Education.*[19]

All of these documents call for the Catholic Church—institutions, organizations, and ministries—to have an empathetic ear and compassionate heart and to provide pastoral care to the LGBTQ community. However, the five documents provide little by way of real pastoral care and seem out of touch with real LGBTQ issues and daily realities that sexual/gender minorities face.

These five documents leave most LGBTQ people disappointed by their lack of pastoral concentration. Moreover, the documents smack of institutional control as well as exacerbating cultural barriers.[20] It appears that neither the Catholic Magisterium (see footnote 5 in this chapter) nor the US Catholic Bishops consulted critically or dialogued pastorally with anyone from the LGBTQ community.[21] It appears these documents were written by White, middle-aged or older, heterosexual men.

The 1997 US Catholic Bishops' document, *Always Our Children: A Pastoral Message to Parents of Homosexual Children and Suggestions for Pastoral Ministers* provides some reassurance for Catholic parents and recommends the following:

1. Accept and love yourselves as parents;

2. Do everything possible to continue demonstrating love for your child;

3. Urge your son or daughter to stay joined to the Catholic faith community;

17. Congregation for the Doctrine of Faith, *Considerations regarding Proposals.*

18. US Conference of Catholic Bishops, *Ministry to Persons with Homosexual Inclination.*

19. Congregation for Catholic Education, *Male and Female.*

20. Maher and Sever, "What Educators in Catholic Schools Might Expect," 83.

21. Bayly, *Creating Environments for LGBTQ Students,* 85.

4. Recommend that your son or daughter find a spiritual director/ mentor;

5. Seek help for yourself, perhaps in the form of counseling, as you strive for understanding, acceptance, and inner peace;

6. Reach out in love and service to other parents struggling with a son or daughter's homosexuality;

7. Take advantage of opportunities for education and support;

8. Put your faith completely in God.[22]

These are fine words of wisdom, but are also applicable to practically all Christian parents, not only parents of LGBTQ young people.

The 2003 document *Considerations regarding Proposals to Give Legal Recognition to Unions between Homosexual Persons* promulgated by the Congregation for the Doctrine of Faith slammed the door shut on homosexual marriages. "There are absolutely no grounds for considering homosexual unions to be in any way similar or even remotely analogous to God's plan for marriage and family."[23] Despite civil lesbian and gay marriages being legalized in the United States, Canada, Australia, and Europe, the Catholic Church has not updated it policies, and civilly married homosexual couples find themselves at odds with the teaching of the church.

The 2006 US Catholic Bishops' document does not offer anything directly pertaining to LGBTQ young people per se, except for this passing comment:

> Young people, in particular, need special encouragement and guidance, since the best way of helping young people is to aid them in *not* getting involved in homosexual relations or in the *subculture* in the first place, since these experiences create further obstacles.[24] (italics added)

Such a statement hardly constitutes pastoral care and offers no pastoral plan. The language of the document only creates further alienation and ostracization, which the majority of LGBTQ youth and young adults already experience.

---

22. US Conference of Catholic Bishops, *Always Our Children*, 6.

23. Congregation for the Doctrine of Faith, *Considerations regarding Proposals*, §4.

24. US Conference of Catholic Bishops, *Ministry to Persons with Homosexual Inclination*, 21–22.

The 2019 document *Male and Female He Created Them: Towards a Path of Dialogue on the Question of Gender Theory in Education* put out by the Congregation of Catholic Education, a very small and inconsequential office (a one- or two-person bureau) in the Vatican. It advocates for dialogue, but does not provide dialogue with the scientific or medical community on gender issues. The document also confuses gender identity with gender theory. It is not a stellar document in my opinion and should not be touted as if it were of significance. Sadly, the outcome is that the document further alienates transgender folks in the body of Christ.

Questions loom large: Are Christian/Catholic churches providing the best pastoral care to LGBTQ youth and young adults in our parishes/congregations? Are we—the church—doing enough to support, advocate, and minister "to, with, by, and for" LGBTQ young people? What are the best ways to minister with LGBTQ youth and young adults? The Catholic Church is merely obfuscating a pastoral plan with authentic ministry to the LGBTQ community. Moreover, Christian/Catholic youth and young adult ministry seems to be *avoiding* LGBTQ young people instead of *advocating* on their behalf, which is a critique of Catholic youth and young adult ministry.

Assessing Catholic Youth and Young Adult Ministry Documents

Neither the original 1976 *Vision of Youth Ministry* (out of print and vertically out of use) nor the updated version *Renewing the Vision: A Framework for Catholic Youth Ministry* (here after *RTV*)[25] mentions ministering to LGBTQ youth. The exclusion of addressing LGBTQ adolescents in these two youth ministry documents is a glaring oversight. *RTV* is the current benchmark and definitive standard for Catholic youth ministry in the United States. All Catholic youth ministries are strongly encouraged to adhere to its content and follow *RTV*'s framework. *RTV* establishes the criteria and goals for youth ministry, which are expected to be integrated and implemented in Catholic parish youth ministries and Catholic school campus ministries in the United States. *RTV* is the principle pastoral tool that Catholic youth ministers utilize in their pastoral work with young people; unfortunately, there is absolutely nothing written in the document that addresses LGBTQ youth sexuality, issues, dilemmas, or situations.

RTV provides Catholic youth ministers with eight components, which are to help shape the youth curriculum and are to be integrated within the

25. US Conference of Catholic Bishops, *Renewing the Vision.*

youth ministry. The components consist of the following: advocacy, catechesis, community life, evangelization, justice and service, leadership development, pastoral care, and prayer and worship. There are two possible sections in the *RTV* document where ministering to LGBTQ adolescents could have been integrated: the component of *advocacy* or the component of *pastoral care*.[26] *RTV* has beautifully written pages on advocacy with adolescents and pastoral care with teenagers, but nothing in those sections that specifically address the needs, issues, and dilemmas that LGBTQ youth encounter. *RTV* really misses a marvelous opportunity to address the concerns that LGBTQ youth experience on a daily basis. It will be valuable to examine these two ministry components regarding LGBTQ youth more closely.

The Ministry of Advocacy for Catholic Young People

Advocacy for juveniles is an important part of youth ministry, which aids in the fight against economic and social forces that threaten adolescents and their families.[27] The section on advocacy offers four points regarding the rights of Catholic teenagers:

> (1) affirming and protecting the sanctity of human life as a gift from God and building societal respect for those who most need protection and support—the unborn, the poor, the disadvantaged, the sick, and the elderly;
>
> (2) standing with and speaking on behalf of young people and their families on public issues that affect their lives, such as support for education quality housing, employment opportunities, access to health care, safe neighborhoods, and availability of meaningful community activities and services;
>
> (3) empowering young people by giving them a voice and calling them to responsibility and accountability around the issues that affect them and their future; and
>
> (4) developing partnerships and initiatives with leaders and concerned citizens from all sectors of the community to develop a shared vision and practical strategies for building a healthy community.[28]

---

26. For more detailed information of the Ministry Components of Advocacy and of Pastoral Care, see *RTV*, 26–28, 42–44.

27. *RTV*, 27.

28. *RTV*, 27–28.

This would have been an excellent place for the US Catholic Bishops to provide three additional points. A fifth point about focusing on sexual development to all adolescents. A sixth point on practices and policies that will help young people avoid sexual discrimination. A seventh point that reminds youth ministers that all people—homosexual or heterosexual—are created in God's image and likeness. It would have been pastorally prophetic if *RTV* would have added a few bullet points along these lines in this section of the document:

- *Advocacy includes educating all adolescents on psychological development and sexual development, especially those teenagers who are thinking about engaging in sexual relation and those who are already engaged in sexual intimacy.*

- *Advocacy includes standing up for LGBTQ youth and engaging in policies and practices that eradicate discrimination of sexual minority young people and examine and analyze the practices that alienate LGBTQ youth.*

- *LGBTQ youth are created in* imago Dei *and deserve to be treated with dignity and respect and have a right to find a safe place to learn and thrive in their parish's youth ministry.*

Unfortunately, *RTV* fails to advocate for LGBTQ youth in the component of advocacy.

The Ministry of Pastoral Care to Catholic Young People

Pastoral care with teenagers is *sine qua non* for Catholic youth ministry! Without proper pastoral care, healing and growth would not take place within adolescents, their peer relationships, and their families.[29] The section on pastoral care is more developed than the section on advocacy, but it still lacks direct mention of ministering to LGBTQ youth. According to *RTV*,

> The ministry of pastoral care to adolescents involves promoting positive adolescent and family development through a variety of positive (preventative) strategies; caring for adolescents and families in crisis through support, counseling, and referral to appropriate community agencies; providing guidance as young people face life decisions and make moral choices; and challenging systems that are obstacles to positive development (advocacy). Pastoral

29. *RTV*, 42.

care is most fundamentally a relationship—a ministry of compassionate presence.[30]

Again, these are caring words, but there is nothing that is ministry-specific to the needs of LGBTQ youth. In this section, *RTV* lists nine points regarding pastoral care with youth, but one point in particular could have dealt specifically with LGBTQ youth, yet does not: "Pastoral care fosters the spiritual development of young people, and the healthy integration of their sexuality and spirituality."[31] This would have been a perfect location to address the sexual orientation of teenagers as well as connecting LGBTQ sexuality to their spirituality. It is certainly acceptable and reasonable to connect sexuality to spirituality. This would have been an excellent place to add something along these lines in this section of the document:

1. *Pastoral care is concerned about the total person; about the full expression of young people's spirituality and sexuality.*

2. *Integrating our sexuality—whether heterosexual or homosexual—into genuine loving relationships is a matter of greatest importance for identity formation.*

3. *LGBTQ youth deserve and should expect competent and genuine pastoral care.*

Unfortunately, *RTV* fails to offer quality pastoral care to LGBTQ youth in the component of pastoral care.

Ministry to Young Adults

The young adult ministry document entitled *Sons and Daughters of the Light: A Pastoral Plan for Ministry with Young Adults* (hereafter *Sons and Daughters*) is the principle document that young adult ministers are to implement in their ministry with young adults. Unfortunately, *Sons and Daughters* also misses the mark regarding LGBTQ young people, it offers absolutely nothing within its pages on LGBTQ people or issues.

Chapter 3, "A Plan for Ministry," does not address anything concerning LGBTQ persons. In the section entitled "Pastoral Care" the document reads: "The [Catholic] Church has many opportunities to provide adults with pastoral care. At these times, it is important to be sensitive to their

30. *RTV*, 42.
31. *RTV*, 43.

issues and to respond pastorally."[32] I agree with the words here from the US Catholic Bishops, but there is no mention of providing any authentic pastoral care to LGBTQ people whatsoever. There are only a few generalized bullet points, such as, "Form a peer-counseling or support group."[33] Statements such as this are too generic and really do not provide pastoral care. This section could have been a place to insert something like this: *Young adults need a safe space to discuss openly their sexual desires, gender identity, and concerns in a nonjudgmental and nonthreatening place even if their beliefs question and contradict official church teachings.* A simple bullet point along these lines would have shown a greater depth of empathy and compassion toward LGBTQ young adults.

Of course, hindsight is 20/20. It is definitely time for a revised and updated version of *RTV* and *Sons and Daughters*: a new version with a fresh perspective and ideas that meet the needs of *all* Christian young people today.[34] The reality is that the typical mainstream model of parish youth and young adult ministry does not reach LGBTQ youth and young adults because of social, cultural, religious, and sexual differences.[35] Consequently, then, this becomes another of the many reasons *RTV* and *Sons and Daughters* both need updating desperately; knowing full well, of course, that Catholic hierarchy and ecclesial documents are more likely to follow the pioneering ministry or groundbreaking theology rather than setting ministry policy outright. Nevertheless, a new and improved ecclesial youth and young adult ministry document is in the best interest of Catholic youth and young adult ministry. I strongly support a new version that clearly advocates for LGBTQ youth and young adults, and one that clearly states the pastoral care needs of sexual and gender minorities.

In light of Pope Francis's *Christus Vivit*, a new youth and young adult ministry document will need to be written (in fact one is being crafted now), but a document that is bold and honest. A new document that will handle serious questions about sexuality, sexual identity, gender, the connection between spirituality and sexuality, and a plethora of other topics concerning young people.[36]

32. US Conference of Catholic Bishops, *Sons and Daughters*, 37.

33. US Conference of Catholic Bishops, *Sons and Daughters*, 37.

34. Canales, "Ten-Year Anniversary of *Renewing the Vision*," 58–69.

35. Vines, *God and the Gay Christian*, 22–23.

36. Canales, "Pope Francis' Theology of Young People, 104.

The magisterium's two documents and the US Catholic Bishops' three documents mentioned above fail to provide authentic fundamental options to LGBTQ young people as other vulnerable and marginalized groups have received. Therefore, in a real way, the Catholic Church obfuscates a pastoral plan for LGBTQ young Christians and offers generic platitudes, which are not pastorally fruitful or practically fulfilling. It is important that all Christian young people who are sexual and gender minorities receive proper and competent pastoral care and feel they are valued and have a voice and a place within the church. It is the role and responsibility of Christian youth and young adult ministries to reach out and accept LGBTQ young people, who can contribute to the vitality of the ministry, church, and society.

Becoming More Open and Affirming of LGBTQ Young People

It would seem wise if Catholic youth and young adult ministries would become more deliberate and inclusive toward LGBTQ young people. Since the US Catholic Bishops have called for Catholic youth and young adult ministry to be comprehensive,[37] Catholic youth and young adult ministries across the country are going to have to be a lot more systematic and intentional about ministering directly and becoming more open and affirming with LGBTQ young people.

In an unpublished investigation that I conducted back in April 2014, surveying 150 Catholic youth and young adult ministers, the following data was revealed:

1. It seems that many gifted youth and young adult ministers often feel helpless to truly advocate for LGBTQ young people.

2. Many youth and young adult ministers are in fear of losing their job if they came out and supported LGBTQ young people openly.

3. Some youth and young adult ministers felt there would be repercussions for "not following" the letter of the law in the *Catechism of the Catholic Church.*

4. Other youth and young adult ministers are fearful of being fired by a conservative bishop because they are misperceived as "pushing" a ministry agenda too far by advocating for LGBTQ equality in Catholic youth and young adult ministry.

37. *RTV*, 19–20.

5. A few youth ministers simply did not feel comfortable approaching the issue due to a lack of understanding with regard to all the subtleties and nuances of LGBTQ youth.[38]

The anecdotal information gathered through this survey was not surprising, but it did uncover that most Catholic youth and young adult ministers did want to minister directly to LGBTQ young people, but were afraid to advocate and support them with ministry programs through the parish. The reality of the situation is that LGBTQ youth and young adults need authentic advocacy by Catholic priests, from parish youth and young adult ministers, and parents. Authentic advocacy and genuine pastoral care cannot be in the form of: (1) trying to change a young person's sexual orientation, e.g., conversion therapy (2) pressuring adolescents to conform to societal standards of "normal" sexuality, or (3) thinking that God does not love them or does not listen to them because of their sexual orientation.

Protestant youth and young adult ministry scholar Fernando Arzola astutely points out, "If the church does not provide a safe, nonjudgmental environment to help them [LGBTQ young people] process issues and questions, they will undoubtedly go somewhere else for help. Unfortunately, these persons or places—gangs, nightclubs, and the streets—may not necessarily share the values of the church."[39] It is in the best interest of pastors, youth ministers, and parents to collaborate on the best practices for integrating LGBTQ youth awareness into youth ministry.

Catholic youth and young adult ministries would be wise to focus their efforts on being more open and affirming of LGBTQ young people:

1. Teaching adolescents the ways to cope as a teenage sexual minority in the family, school, and church.

2. Helping young people find positive heterosexual and homosexual role models in the community.

3. Providing LGBTQ youth and young adults with a safe place to meet and grow in their faith as part of the parish community and the subcommunity of youth and young adult ministry.

38. Canales, unpublished findings, entitled "A Qualitative Study of the Attitudes of Catholic Youth Ministers toward LGBTQ Youth." The survey was sent out to 150 Catholic youth and young adult ministers, via electronic mail, on April 1, 2014, and was closed and compiled on May 27, 2014. The survey was titled "Questionnaire on LGBTQ Folks & Catholic Youth & Young Adult Ministry" and it asked fifteen questions.

39. Arzola, *Toward a Prophetic Youth Ministry*, 47.

4. Catechizing young people about sexual minorities and about human sexuality, and theology of the body without stigmatizing and shaming.

5. Loving LGBTQ youth and young adults for who they are, and not for who they are not.

6. Developing ways to embrace an LGBTQ young person's sexuality and their Christian discipleship.

Catholic catechesis plays an enormous role in providing justification for schools and parishes to develop programs that help bolster Catholic identity and spirituality in LGBTQ young people.[40]

Becoming more open and affirming with LGBTQ youth and young adults honestly addresses the fundamental human needs of sexual minority young people. All Christian youth and young adult ministry is a response to, and in light of, God's active presence for the life of the world—a presence that reflects and acts on behalf of all adolescents.[41] LGBTQ young people, like heterosexual young people, deserve a lived theological emphasis on a lived experience of soteriology as the natural extension of God's passionate engagement with the world.[42] In other words, those ministering to the young church may want to be more meta-reflective with the ongoing human and spiritual needs of LGBTQ youth and young adults. Pastoral care in Christian youth and young adult ministries is the hope of praxis (reflection on ministry practice), which can be theology in action done well in the name of God, and to, for, and with young people.[43] Therefore, quality pastoral care aims at catering and ministering to the needs of LGBTQ young people, which is a population that is currently being underserved in mainstream Christian/Catholic youth and young adult ministry. To provide competent and proficient advocacy and pastoral care to LGBTQ youth and young adults, development of appropriate pastoral strategies is paramount for Christian youth and young adult ministers.

Parting Remarks

Comprehensive youth and young adult ministry is not a theoretical exercise. Christian youth and young adult ministry is a commitment and

40. Maher and Sever, "What Educators in Catholic Schools Might Expect," 100.

41. Dykstra and Bass, "Theological Understanding," 18.

42. Root and Creasy Dean, *Theological Turn*, 223.

43. Department of [Catholic] Education, *Vision of Youth Ministry*, 6–7.

participation in young people's joys, hopes, and struggles for a full young life, and discernment of God's salvific action in a young person's particular history.[44] Christian youth and young adult ministry is God's work-in-action, embodied, and integrated pedagogically and holistically with critical thinking and theological reflection, and therefore, cannot overlook ministering to, with, and for LGBTQ young people.

It is time for all Christian churches to offer pastoral wisdom and insights on ministering to LGBTQ young people instead of offering insensitive platitudes such as "we love the sinner, but hate the sin." In retort to that dictum, I have heard the following: "I hate the belief, but love the believer." Nevertheless, simplistic answers and once-for-all explanations will not satisfy or pacify the LGBTQ community, and one-dimensional answers should not gratify any Christian youth and/or young adult minister either. Christian youth and young adult ministry would do well to perform emancipatory pastoral practices—be open and affirming to LGBTQ young people—that promote peace through justice, service, and love.[45]

Discussion Questions

1. What are three new things you learned from this chapter?

2. What points did you find surprising, interesting, or perplexing from this chapter?

3. Has this chapter allowed you to think in new ways about being open and affirming with LGBTQ young people?

4. How would you summarize your parish's or congregation's role in advocating and supporting LGBTQ youth and young adults?

5. What are some ways of providing competent pastoral care to LGBTQ young people in Christian institutions, organizations, or ministries?

---

44. Copper-White, *Shared Wisdom*, 186.
45. Copper-White, *Shared Wisdom*, 191.

Chapter 6

Pastoral Care, Support, and Ministry to Transgender Youth and Young Adults

Why can't you just love me the way I am?

—COUNTLESS TRANSGENDER YOUTH

You are the biggest disappointment of my life, and I never want to see you again!

—COUNTLESS PARENTS OF TRANSGENDER YOUTH

Opening Comments

THE ABOVE QUOTES ARE sad reminders that young people need love and acceptance from adults, and that not all parents understand the intricacies and delicacies of transgender issues. This chapter attempts to pursue awareness about transgender youth and young adults, and the issues they face daily. Transgender young people (or *trans*, as used colloquially and for abbreviation purposes), are considered sexual minorities and unfortunately feel the sting of prejudice from family, society, and church on many levels. It is my hope that this chapter provides a glimmer of hope for this particular sexual and gender minority subgroup to feel more supported and appreciated.

This chapter is concerned specifically with the *T* of the LGBTQ acronym. The *T* represents transgender persons, and the scope of this chapter is to dialogue and address the pastoral issues surrounding transgender young people. I work with transgender young people through my work as a college pastoral theology professor and pastoral counselor. As a pastoral theologian, I must admit that I am saddened and deeply troubled by the lack of attention and disrespect this particular sexual and gender minority group receives.

Transgender

Traditionally, assigning someone's sex was a matter of biology, a person's anatomy and chromosomes, and it typically takes place at the hospital, by the obstetrician stating, "It's a girl" or "It's a boy!" Psychologically and medically, *transgender* "describes a person whose gender identity does not match their natal sex or does not align with traditional notions of masculinity or femininity."[1] There are different considerations of gender identity: cisgender, transgender, and intersex.

Transgender is an umbrella and inclusive word that covers a wide range of expressions and experiences, but it is certainly bound by culture and context. Those who self-identify as transgender may consider themselves homosexual, heterosexual, or bisexual. It is possible that someone will consider themselves pansexual, polysexual (the sexual attraction to some, but *not* all multiple genders), or asexual (non-attraction to any gender).[2] As one male-to-female (MtF is a person who is in the process of transitioning from male to female) student told me regarding dress and attire, "Doc, I just consider myself fluid; I go with the way I feel each morning." There is a great deal of gender flux and fluidity in being transgender; for example, movement between specific genders such as when a person moves from school to home or moves from work to the gym. Living as a transgender young person is different and complicated. Some trans youth and young adults tend to *not* experience their gender as something static, but rather as a dynamic involvement and evolvement within themselves.[3] Some trans

1. Gridley et al., "Youth and Caregiver Perspectives," 255.
2. Roberts, *Transgender*, 15.
3. Brill and Kenny, *Transgender Teen*, 82.

youth and young adults might have an array of diverse sides of their gender, and often their gender appearance swings accordingly.

On the other hand, the term *trans*, is used for anyone who identifies, resonates, or expresses with a gender that differs from their gender assigned at birth. Therefore, a teenager whose self-identification is transgender would include transsexuals, transvestites, drag queens, drag kings, and other variations in the transgender world.[4]

In an earlier publication, a few years back, I stated, "Young people who describe themselves as transgender are those persons who exhibit 'gender-non-conforming' characteristics and actions—that is, those individuals who transcend their typical gender paradigms."[5] That is to say, those youth and young adults who are nonbinary in gender or those who are not exclusively female or male in their gender expression do not always self-identify as transgender. Nonbinary gender expression is often captured by the terms "nonbinary," "gender nonconforming," "genderqueer," and "genderfluid." Again, the label "transgender" is a broad term that covers an array of gender expressions and possibilities: from cross-dressers (an aspect of one's genuine gender identity) to people who are intersex (those people born with ambiguous genitalia). Most importantly, in contrast to many common assumptions, if a young person expresses himself or herself as transgender; it is *not* always a reflection of a young person's gender identity or sexual orientation, because gender identity and sexual/affectional orientation are two aspects of a young person's embodiment.

Transgender Myths Debunked

Before going any further, it may be wise to debunk several myths that have been associated with transgender folks. The table below represents myths that are widely prevalent regarding transgender people in many Christian circles, and thus merit debunking.[6]

4. Leone, *The Transsexual and the Cross*, 13.

5. Canales, "Ministry to Catholic LGBTQ Youth," 62.

6. This table comes directly from "Gender Dysphoria," by Taslim, Alshehab, and Canales. Permission was granted by the authors for this table to be published here.

Table 3: Debunking Transgender Myths

Myth #1.	**Transgender people are mentally ill or psychiatric patients.**
Reality	***Mistaken.*** Transgender people are *not* considered psychiatric patients any more according to the scientific research of the last sixty to eighty years. Medical experts believe that transgender is an inherent condition and not in a person's control.
Myth #2.	**Transgender folks are the same as intersex**
Reality	***Invalid.*** Intersex people (those with ambiguous genitalia, hormones, or chromosomes) have developmental defects in their genital organs, which could manifest as ambiguous or immaturely developed genitalia. While transgender people are males or females, with mismatched gender expression. Consequently, intersex have disorder of sexual development, while transgender folks have disorder of gender identity. However, some intersex can be transgender if they are assigned a wrong sex at birth.
Myth #3.	**Transgender people are the same as homosexual persons.**
Reality	***Incorrect.*** Transgender people and homosexual people are distinct phenomena. Homosexuals are attracted to a person of their own sex. Mostly, homosexuals are cisgenders and have no disorders of sexual development or gender identity. Typically, a transwoman (born a biological male) is sexually attracted to men, but this should not be construed as homosexuality. The majority of transgender folks are heterosexuals because their sexuality is driven by their gender expression and not the natal sex.
Myth #4.	**Transgender people can never be treated.**
Reality	***Wrong.*** Ample scientific data support that transgender folks can be reasonably managed with sexual confirmation surgery that can allow a person to live according to their gender feelings and blend in the society like a regular man or woman.
Myth #5.	**Transgender people can be and should always be treated with counseling and psychiatric medications.**

Reality	**Erroneous.** Psychotherapy has been ineffective to reverse gender dysphoria. Behavioral therapies can deteriorate a trans person's mental well-being and can subject them to depression and anxiety. The World Professional Association for Transgender Health guidelines warns against all kinds of reversion therapies through spiritual or psychological means after receiving reports of suicidal death as a result of such therapies.
Myth #6.	**Transgender treatment is strictly prohibited by Islam and Christianity.**
Reality	**Fabrication.** Christian and Islamic scholars are divided as proponents and opponents of the sexual confirmation surgery for gender dysphoria management based on the varying interpretations of the Bible and Quran. Islamic scholars in Iran and Egypt have sanctioned sexual reassignment therapies as a human right of transgender people for those who long to be congruent.
Myth #7.	**Transgender people are sinners and must be avoided.**
Reality	**Untrue.** Transgender-guilt is an experience or phenomenon that comes over transgender folks because they feel their bodies are different. Does that alone constitute a sin? All human beings are created in *imago Dei*, in the image and likeness of God; therefore, a transgender person cannot be a sinner for merely being trans. Matter of fact, the way societies treat their most vulnerable and marginalized members makes them the victims, not sinners.

I hope this chart helps to dispel some of the myths that are prevalent within some Christian denominations and with some misguided individual Christians as well.

An Arduous Road

Transgender teenagers comprise 0.7 percent (13–17 years old) of the total population of adolescents in the United States.[7] This means that approximately 1.5 million young people in the United States self-identify as transgender, which is a significant population and is likely to grow steadily. The period of adolescence and young adulthood brings struggle for identity and a search for meaning as young people look to define themselves as individuals amid their peers, siblings, and parents.

According to transgender expert and advocate Justin E. Tanis, for transgender teenagers, the period of adolescence is particularly difficult

7. Herman et al., *Age of Individuals*, 2–3.

because "physical changes heighten the sense of being betrayed by a body that is developing the *wrong* way for what the teen feels inside."[8] Such feelings of betrayal may cause low self-image in a trans young person.

The road for a transgender teenager is long and arduous. The experience of being "different" as a trans youth or young adult is real because being trans *does* subvert the theoretical coherence between traditional gender expression and sex. Trans disturbs! Being a transgender young person disrupts the conventional imagination of young people; it unhinges traditional expectations, and it sometimes prompts hatred and violence from self and others.[9]

Psychologist Christian Burgess notes that, "because of the internalization of negative attitudes toward gender non-conformity, transgender youth are at an increased risk for low self-esteem, which may manifest itself through depression, substance abuse, self-mutilation, and/or suicide."[10] Transgender young people are on a journey of self-discovery, but trans youth and young adults experience even more gender identity struggles than their assumed gender peers.

From a pastoral care and ministry perspective, the feelings that transgender teenagers experience regarding their own gender dysphoria—the experience of having a psychological and emotional identity as either male or female—looms large.[11] For a trans youth or young adult, gender dysphoria is at the forefront of their life. As one colleague told me, "I do not think a person chooses to experience gender dysphoria." There are a number of feelings that trans youth and young adults might experience: anger, fear, guilt, loss, shame, and worry, as a direct result of their gender identity search and struggles.

Renowned Evangelical psychologist Mark A. Yarhouse recommends strategies that may be beneficial for adolescents and young adults struggling with gender dysphoria. Yarhouse's four approaches are: (1) teaching healthy coping and self-care tactics, (2) treating anxiety, depression, and self-esteem, (3) family therapy to improve the relationships that are strained or severed, and (4) helping navigate gender identity questions (Who am I? Who loves me? Why do I feel this way?) in life.[12]

8. Tanis, *Transgendered*, 34.

9. Brill and Kenny, *Transgender Teen*, 92.

10. Burgess, "Internal and External Stress Factors," 41.

11. Yarhouse, *Understanding Gender Dysphoria*, 19.

12. Yarhouse, *Understanding Gender Dysphoria*, 110–11.

There are a number of issues that threaten the health and well-being transgender young people as a result of their gender nonconformity: homelessness, harassment, bullying, higher rates of alcohol and drug abuse, violence, victimization, and suicide.[13] There are several wonderful Hollywood movies that crystallize the tragedies that transgender young people face: *Boys Don't Cry* (1999), *Transamerica* (2005), *Lawrence Anyways* (2012), *The Danish Girl* (2015), and *Girl* (2018). I would highly recommend youth and young adult ministers watch these movies for their own pastoral understanding. Therefore, in the midst of turbulent adolescence and challenging young adulthood, transgender young people must encounter difficulties that "typical" young people do not face.

Maligned, Marginalized, and Misunderstood

Transgender young people are the most maligned, misunderstood, and marginalized group of youth and young adults within LGBTQ subcultures.[14] While there has been some research on transgender youth and young adults in recent years, it is still an emerging body of work. There is still research needed pertaining to young people who identify as transgender. Unfortunately, many parents, school officials, and especially Christian ministers do *not* know the proper way to respond to lesbian, gay, and bisexual young people once confronted with their coming out, much less to teenagers who move through the complexities of gender identity.

One question some may ask is: What is it that makes transgender youth and young adults misunderstood, marginalized, and maligned in the eyes of others? Or, even sometimes themselves? The reality is that transgender young people are misunderstood because transitioning from MtF or FtM *is* subversive of normative assumptions.[15] The pressure is so great to avoid feelings of unease and unwanted-ness from people in society and any affiliated danger with being trans, leads transgender young people to expedite their transitioning phase to complete womanhood or manhood.

Transgender advocates and biblical scholars Teresa J. Hornsby and Deryn Guest note, "The problem is *not* with [transgender folks]; the problem is with the limitations of cultural norms, employers, and personal relations,

---

13. Tanis, *Transgendered*, 35.

14. Greytak et al., "Putting the 'T' in 'Resource,'" 52–53.

15. Hornsby and Guest, *Transgender, Intersex*, 56.

which compel [transgender young people] to comply with *their* needs."[16] Therefore, it is *not* uncommon for a transgender high school or college students to experience feelings of unwelcome-ness or hostility from school administrators, church figures, coaches, and an array of other authority figures.

Psychologist Gabrielle Owen maintains that

> adolescence is constructed as the moment that gendered *becoming* occurs . . . Transgender phenomena suggest a much more varied and complex range of possibilities for bodily experience and gendered subjectivity, drawing our attention to the contingency of any subjective arrival whether it be normative or trans-identified.[17]

Today, a young person in American society has the potential to develop as a trans person who might reject the typical developmental sequence of adolescent to young adult to adult maturation. Owen also notes, "Trans embodiment disrupts and denaturalizes the development narrative of adolescence, revealing it for what it is—sometimes a story we have been told and sometimes a story of our own making."[18] For transgender youth and young adults, today's gender identity and sexuality is not the gender identity of the 1950s and the "golly gee" world of June and Ward Cleaver in the sitcom *Leave It to Beaver*.

Another problematic and dangerous arena for transgender teenager is *coming out* as trans. Coming out may be the first dose of reality with feeling maligned and the sting of discrimination. Sometimes when a transgender teenager comes out it is not the warm, fuzzy reception she/he anticipated. If this process works positively, it is akin to a "coming-home" party, but for most young people it is not. The term *coming home* refers to an experience of the transgender young person fully embracing their identity.

Some trans youth are told that "you are just confused right now" or "you are too young to know for sure," or "it is a phase, you will grow out of it."[19] Some trans youth and young adults are naively (or rudely) told "gender is a choice." Arguing that transgender people have a choice in their sexual identity and gender is extremely contentious and foolish within the transgender community as well as, the psychological and medical communities. Still, even more distressing are the horror stories that some confront in telling their parents they are transgender. One male trans student told me:

16. Hornsby and Guest, *Transgender, Intersex*, 58.

17. Owen, "Adolescence," 23.

18. Owen, "Adolescence," 23.

19. Huegel, *GLBTQ*, 168.

"When I told my parents I was trans and no longer wanted to be called Tracey, but Travis, my parents said, 'you will never be a male. God created you female! We do not accept you right now!! (yelling at me).'" This is often the sad reality for many youth and young adults who self-identify as transgender, a truth that smacks of abjection and transphobia.

Transphobia and Abjection

The word *transphobia* means the dislike of, or fear of, and prejudice against transgender people. French linguist and psychoanalyst Julia Kristeva coins the term *abjection* in her book *Powers of Horror: An Essay on Abjection*. Kristeva describes *abjection* as "[that which] disturbs identity, system, and order. What does not respect boundaries, positions, and rules. The in-between, the ambiguous, the composite, push transgender people into the domain of the abject."[20] Transgender people seem to throw off the traditional understanding of the two-sex, binary gender system. Abjection refers to the unclear sense of repulsion that permeates the periphery between the self and other.

Psychologist Robert Phillips states that the term *abjection* literally means "to cast out."[21] Abjection refers to the instability of gendered ambiguous bodies—especially those occupied by transgender individuals—which historically and currently has received negative connotations and harsh statements, all of which contribute to transphobia.[22]

Transphobia and abjection link together because they both offer methodological exclusion, repression, and silence of transgender people. Christians exhibit transphobia when they are spiteful, use intimidation, or violence, both interpersonal and systemic, toward transgender people because they seem different. Likewise, Christians express genderism when they postulate that being heterosexual and cisgender are superior and more desirable than being transgender. Conservative Christians engage in abjection when they maintain the argument that "to live transsexually cannot live compatibly with 'orthodox' Christianity."[23] The traditional Christian argument is that female and male humans are the final products of God's imposition of cosmic order on the primordial elements of creation.[24] Trans-

---

20. Kristeva, *Powers of Horror*, 4.
21. Phillips, "Abjection," 20.
22. Phillips, "Abjection," 20–21.
23. Hornsby and Guest, *Transgender, Intersex*, 36.
24. Hornsby and Guest, *Transgender, Intersex*, 36.

gender folks simply see this as another form of transphobia and abjection that continually keeps trans people living on the margins of the dominant culture and their societal rules. Today, Christianity would be wise to seek a new basis for discussion and a new theology for trans people that moves away from narrow-mindedness; otherwise, trans people will continue to suffer rejection from the religious right.[25]

There is incredible cultural and Christian opposition to recognize people with nonbinary genders. Therefore, a new understanding of sex, gender, and the issues surrounding binary—female/male and transgender/cisgender—will help to enhance a new theology of transgender that truly believes and maintains the principle of *imago Dei*. Again, as stated in a previous chapter, I use the principle of *imago Dei* to state that all persons are created in the image and likeness of God no matter if they are black or white, female or male, poor or rich, born below the equator or above the equator, homosexual or heterosexual, or transgender or cisgender. All transgender young people within any Christian community are to be welcomed, affirmed, valued, and cared for as people created in God's image. Moreover, anything that is defaming, dehumanizing, or de-individualizing with regards to a person's sexual orientation and gender expression stands in tension with its affirmation that each transgender person is created in *imago Dei*.[26] To not treat trans youth and young adults with equality, dignity, and respect is an act of discrimination—plain and simple.

Transgender youth and young adults may feel abject for various reasons. Transgender young people feel abjection when they experience gender-based rejection. Moreover, trans youth and young adults experience both internal and external stressors for their gender and sexual minority status. According to gender diversity experts Stephanie Brill and Lisa Kenny, there are four external stressors that cause great misery for trans young people: (1) victimization, (2) rejection, (3) discrimination, and (4) non-affirmation.[27] As a result of the external stressors, Brill and Kenny also maintain there are three internal stressors: (1) negative expectations for future events, (2) internalized transphobia and personal stigma, and (3) concealment or nondisclosure of one's true gender identity.[28] These external and internal stressors produce a sense of abjection within trans youth and young adults.

25. Hornsby and Guest, *Transgender, Intersex*, 38.

26. Pope, "Magisterium's Arguments," 549–50.

27. Brill and Kenny, *Transgender Teen*, 192–94.

28. Brill and Kenny, *Transgender Teen*, 195–99.

Marginalized Transgender Youth and Young Adults

Transphobia contributes to the marginalization of transgender young people. Since gender expression is so visible and obvious, transgender folks are often the brunt of cruel jokes and discrimination. Some trans young people face sexual harassment and gender discrimination on a daily basis.[29] Due to cultural, medical, familial, social, and religious misunderstandings about transgender issues in general, transgender youth and young adults are particularly marginalized. "Transgender [young people] are at higher risk for depression, low self-image, substance abuse, homelessness, HIV/AIDS, and suicide attempts than their non-transgender identified peers."[30] These risk factors are partly the result of trans and nonbinary youth and young adults being "invisible" to the mainline public.[31]

Transgender young people receive more stigmatization, prejudice, harassment, and violence by mainstream culture than any other sexual minority group. "Almost nine in ten [90%] transgender youth have been victimized at school, including more than one-quarter [25%] that had been physically assaulted because of the [way] they express their genders."[32] Such statistics are truly startling! It is important that Christian parents, pastors, teachers, and youth and young adult ministers understand that transgender youth and young adults feel invisible and vulnerable. Transgender young people also feel inaudible when they try to express their inner feelings and thoughts to cisgender people who have no cognitive comprehension or emotional insights of their internal turmoil and struggles.[33] Two main types of struggles that keep transgender young people in the margins of youth and young adult culture are victimization and suicide.

Victimization

Victimization looms large for transgender youth and young adults. Victimization typically correlates with three severity levels: (1) verbal harassment, (2) physical harassment, and (3) physical assault. Victimization toward transgender young people takes place most often in high school

29. Huegel, *GLBTQ*, 187.
30. Reicherzer et al., "Counseling in the Periphery," 184.
31. Bill and Kenny, *Transgender Teen*, 78.
32. Greytak et al., "Putting the 'T' in 'Resource,'" 46.
33. Higa et al., "Negative and Positive Factors," 10–11.

for trans adolescents, on campus for trans college students, and in the workplace for trans young adults.[34] Safety from any type of bullying or harassment is of paramount concern for transgender young people in high school or college. Many places of work have online harassment training that includes LGBTQ harassment, which would benefit young adults who are working full time.

The most common form of victimization for transgender teenagers is verbal harassment. It is estimated that approximately 70 percent of all transgender young people experience some type of physical assault, which is astronomically high.[35] Verbal harassment includes people making fun of their difference in appearance, but there are more extreme examples. One FtM college student reported, "Men keep saying to me, 'I can turn you straight, honey.'"[36] It is common for transgender youth and young adults to experience this type of verbal harassment at their schools or social environments. Unfortunately, even if policies for lesbian, gay, and bisexual students exist in a high school and/or college, those policies do not always protect transgender young people because of their physical demeanor or dress.[37] High schools and colleges/universities with no support strategies or professional resources for sexual and gender minorities usually result in higher rates of absenteeism from trans young people.[38]

Finally, another type of victimization that transgender youth and young adults experience is rejection and isolation. The isolation that transgender young people experience can be deep and painful as a direct result of keeping the secret of their nonconforming gender identity from those they love.[39] The negative effects of isolation put trans youth and young adults at high risk for abuse from others and from themselves, which has the propensity to drain their inner resources from developmental tasks and forces many young people to retreat inward.[40] Experiencing isolation and rejection, as well as incompetent and/or inconsistent caring from most of their parents, pastors, teachers, youth ministers, and schoolmates, has led transgender young people to have a high degree of feelings of unworthiness,

34. McGuine et al., "School Climate for Transgender Youth," 1176.

35. Greytak et al., "Putting the 'T' in 'Resource,'" 52.

36. Grossman and D'Augelli, "Transgender Youth," 124.

37. McGuine, "School Climate for Transgender Youth," 1176.

38. Greytak et al., "Putting the 'T' in 'Resource,'" 52.

39. Tanis, *Transgendered*, 27.

40. Tanis, *Transgendered*, 33.

shame, and embarrassment.[41] Transgender youth and young adults experiencing rejection often leads to social isolation: distancing themselves from their parents and/or friends, doing poorly in school, bouts of drinking, tampering with substance abuse, dropping out of school, being disowned from their parents, and unfortunately sometimes suicide.[42]

Suicide

The ultimate form of victimization, rejection, and isolation transgender young people experience is suicide. Suicide is the third-highest cause of death among American youth and young adults between the ages of fifteen and twenty-five.[43] Since transgender young people are so ostracized and misunderstood by the general public they are at greater risk for suicidal ideation, suicide attempts, and committing suicide.[44] Suicide among transgender young people is usually a direct result of family and society abjection and rejection, not because trans youth are "lost."

A joint study in 2014 by the American Foundation for Suicide Prevention and the Williams Institute, the nation's preeminent LGBTQ think tank, out of UCLA, found that "suicide attempts among trans males (46%) and trans females (42%) were slightly higher than the full sample (41%). Cross-dressers assigned male at birth have the lowest reported prevalence of suicide attempts among gender identity groups (21%)."[45] Suicide attempts are higher (50%) for those who disclose to everyone that they are transgender or gender nonconforming.[46] Suicide is a real and present danger for transgender youth and young adults.

One survey of over nine hundred youth and young adults in Alberta, Canada, reported that approximately 65 percent of trans young people between the ages of fourteen and twenty-five have had suicidal ideation. That is a tragic statistic! Such shocking statistics reveal the need for competent advocacy, pastoral care, and legitimate concern from church leaders and ministers.[47]

41. Grossman and D'Augelli, "Transgender Youth," 124.
42. Grossman and D'Augelli, "Transgender Youth," 125.
43. Grossman and D'Augelli, "Transgender Youth," 527.
44. Grossman and D'Augelli, "Transgender Youth," 530.
45. Haas et al., *Suicide Attempts*, 2.
46. Haas et al., *Suicide Attempts*, 3.
47. Wells et al., *Being Safe, Being Me*, 7–38.

Another study, for Cincinnati Children's Hospital Medical Center, reports that 30 percent of transgender young people report a history of at least one suicide attempt, and nearly 42 percent report a history of self-injury, such as cutting or burning. The same study also discovered a higher frequency of suicide attempts among trans young people who are dissatisfied with their weight.[48] Alarmingly, one-quarter (25%) of *all* transgender youth and young adults report suicidal ideation and have attempted suicide, and one-third (33%) have engaged in self-injurious behaviors; males are more likely to burn themselves and females more likely to cut themselves, both of which point to the specific vulnerabilities that trans young people encounter.[49]

Familial rejection, low body esteem, and childhood abuse all play a part in a transgender youth and young adult's feelings of estrangement, and such feelings of hostility to oneself can lead from suicidal ideation to suicide.[50] Resiliency and self-determination play a crucial role in transgender young people's worldview fighting against discrimination and low self-image.[51] Therefore, all of these areas—transphobia, abjection, marginalization, victimization, and suicide—are harmful to transgender youth and young adults. Public discourse and exposure might be the only way to increase sensitivity and empathy to transgender young people.

This first part of the chapter has opened the discussion regarding transgender youth and young adults in Christian congregations by pursuing awareness and understanding about issues facing transgender youth and young adults. The next part of this chapter will address the importance of pastoral care, support, and advocacy. The focus will be on the ways in which Christian communities can help transgender young people.

Providing Pastoral Care, Support, and Advocacy

In one of his many public addresses, Archbishop Desmond Tutu stated, "The ultimate evil is not suffering . . . which is meted out to those who are God's children. The ultimate evil of oppression . . . is when it succeeds in making a child of God begin to doubt that he or she is a child of God."[52] As Tutu warns, if Christianity is not careful, it might be responsible for

48. Peterson et al., "Suicidality, Self-Harm," 476–77.

49. Dickey et al., "Non-Suicidal Self-Injury," 3–4.

50. Grossman and D'Augelli, "Transgender Youth," 532.

51. Reicherzer et al., "Counseling in the Periphery," 184.

52. Tutu, "South Africa's Blacks," 131.

perpetuating the misperception that transgender youth and young adults are not children of God just because of their gender identity. Such a misperception is a mistake and would be a travesty. This section hopes to share some insights regarding pastoral methods for those who work with young people and who specifically want to provide pastoral care to and ministry with transgender teenagers, college students, and young adults.

As discussed in the previous chapter, the proper stance for Christian communities to all God's people is one of openness and affirmation, because of the theological reality of *imago Dei*.[53] Christian communities would be wise to begin to think about appropriate ways to minister to trans youth and young adults and begin to provide proper pastoral care, support, and advocacy to this particular sexual and gender minority group. For the parameters of this chapter, I have scaffolded or ordered these three categories from easiest to most difficult; that is, pastoral care should be the easiest for Christian communities to integrate into ministry practice, while advocacy would be more difficult for congregations to implement; of course, it may also depend on the personality and demeanor of the church community.

A. Pastoral Care

Competent pastoral care and counseling is steeped in kindness, compassion, and empathy of the trans person—adolescent or adult. There are two areas of pastoral care that merit consideration for those working with and ministering to transgender young people: (1) welcoming the trans young person and (2) utilizing a pastoral care checklist with trans youth and young adults.

Welcoming the Trans Young People into Our Communities

The first step for any Christian church, organization, or ministry would be to acknowledge that transgender youth and young adults exist, and that it is an acceptable gender expression and a satisfactory way of living.[54] Second, welcoming churches, youth and young adult ministries, and

53. DeFranza does a great job of addressing the principle of *imago Dei* from various Christian perspectives in her book *Sex Difference in Christian Theology*. For DeFranza, *imago Dei* needs to be liberated from a "normal," two-sex, binary model of gender identity (23), as well from a white, middle-class, evangelical and Roman Catholic, heterosexual, virgin-until-married, cisgender, female and male identity for doing theology (xv).

54. Grossman and D'Augelli, "Transgender Youth," 125.

para-youth and young adult ministry organizations would be pastorally sensible to adopt a posture of acceptance, openness, and affirming the human dignity of each and every person who walks through the doors, promoting an ethic of empathy and compassion for all.[55] Third, catechize the entire congregation, but especially the youth and young adult ministry, about the transgender issues and their struggles as sexual minorities in society. Fourth, and this is a bit risky for a traditional, heterosexual, and cisgender congregation, preach on transgender topics at Sunday worship—again, from a loving and genuine pastoral position, embracing the person created in *imago Dei*, and preaching from a place of openness not judgment. Fifth, offer accompaniment and discipleship programs for sexual and gender minorities in church to help enhance their faith life and increase their spirituality—all Christians can benefit from further growing in Christ. Sixth, it might be wise if adult members of Christian congregations were catechized and informed about society's gender constructs and the way those concepts contribute to trans youth and young adult vulnerability and devalue the spiritual, emotional, physical, and social well-being of transgender teenagers.[56] Seventh, and this relates to a larger systemic problem, address the negative attitudes and theological convictions that Christian adults have toward trans young people. Negative attitudes and theological convictions play a role in harming transgender teenagers and young adults.

Episcopal and intersex scholar Megan K. DeFranza notes that communities of faith would be wise to reflect *imago Christi* in their attitudes, which replicates love, goodness, and kindness.[57] DeFranza states, "*Imago Christi* requires not only just dealings and the recordings of societal oppressions, but also the cultivation of personal holiness, a life of worship, prayer, humility, kindness, generosity, and other virtues."[58] In other words, to help eradicate larger systemic issues that exist toward trans young people, Christian communities would be wise to focus on gospel values and become *imago Christi*—created in the image and likeness of Christ.

Pastoral theologian and transgender advocate Justin E. Tanis recommends a good list for those communities which genuinely want to welcome transgender people into their congregation. He lists eight:

55. Canales and Sherman, "Franciscan Campus Ministries," 46.

56. Grossman and D'Augelli, "Transgender Youth," 126.

57. DeFranza, *Sex Difference in Christian Theology*, 282.

58. DeFranza, *Sex Difference in Christian Theology*, 282.

(1) offer genuine hospitality,

(2) provide nondiscrimination policies and attitudes,

(3) demonstrate appropriate and inclusive language,

(4) create a visible and audible presence of transgender people and programs,

(5) establish provisions of meaningful rituals to mark changes in people's lives,

(6) propose outreach to transgender groups and individuals,

(7) generate opportunities for the congregation to learn accurately about transgender issues, and

(8) build restrooms that the gender-variant can access.[59]

This list is a good guide for communities to get started and to maintain a welcoming and affirming disposition for all trans people.

Presbyterian minister James R. Oraker and small group process leader Janis Hahn suggest that designing a program of dialogue might be the path of least resistance for helping Christian communities and ministries discuss sexual minorities. They offer this brief template as a welcoming model for sexual and gender minorities, which can be used for pastoral care to and ministry with transgender young people. Here are five recommendations:

(1) direct dialogue, an initial and open discussion about trans youth and young adults, which includes inviting trans young people to the table of discussion;

(2) process, which moves beyond dialogue and examines the strengths and limitations of the issue—in this case—engaging trans youth within the church and inviting and calling (as distinct from texting or e-mailing) trans young people to the ministry;

(3) small groups, which allows for voices to be heard, stories to be shared, and mutual understanding and discovery about the one person's life and journey;

(4) establish an event, such as a days of reflection, retreat, or conference, and work with the larger community toward that end; and

59. Tanis, *Transgendered*, 122.

(5) an action plan, which is planning, organizing, and implementing the desired ministry event and bring it to completion.[60]

These are just a few ways that Catholic parishes and Christian congregations, organizations, and ministries can welcome transgender young people.

A Pastoral Care Checklist for Trans Youth

Pastoral care is a relationship and it is primarily concerned with human benevolence, empathy, and compassion. Technically, there are no "official" set standards for pastoral care, but some basic competencies for pastoral care are: accompaniment, empowering, liberating, listening, healing, sustaining, guiding, reconciling, and nurturing a person toward God, self, or the other.

Queer author and advocate David J. Kundtz and sexual minority scholar Bernard S. Schlager (2007) give a checklist for pastoral caregivers who serve sexual and gender minorities. I use their checklist, with minor alterations, in hopes that it might serve as a rudimentary rubric for pastoral ministers who work with transgender youth and young adults.

1. Examine your own assumptions—assume that:

    a. being trans may *not* be the issue that brings the youth or young adults to seek pastoral care;

    b. young persons may *not* wish to explore their sexual identity;

    c. because of social pressure and fear, sometimes trans youth and young adults avoid identifying themselves as transgender; and

    d. nothing is surprising about transgender behavior.[61]

2. Be informed about:

    a. advocacy programs, help lines, books, web pages, films, and teaching videos;

    b. of pastoral counselors, spiritual directors, and psychologists who work with trans people;

    c. the doctrines and practices of various Christian denominations regarding transgender issues; and

    d. the words and terms you use describing and referring to transgenderism, transsexuality, and gender identity.[62]

60. Oraker and Hahn, "Church in Action," 122–23.

61. Kundtz and Schlager, *Ministry among God's Queer Folk*, 81.

62. Kundtz and Schlager, *Ministry among God's Queer Folk*, 82.

3. Be self-aware of:

   a. your own attitudes, biases, and responses, regardless of your own sexual orientation;
   b. your own limitations concerning your scope of pastoral care;
   c. your own feelings toward the person receiving your pastoral care; and
   d. all the boundary issues in your pastoral care relationship.[63]

4. Respect your transgender care-receiver's:

   a. orientation, identity, personal integrity, cultural assumptions, and lifestyle;
   b. privacy by not asking inappropriate medical questions pertaining to surgery;
   c. personal pain, suffering, and continual struggle with their internal conflicts; and
   d. individual capabilities to find their own pastoral solutions.[64]

Providing pastoral care to trans youth and young adults may not come easy for most people who work with young people. The natural inclination is to give advice, but try *not* to give advice, because it could backfire, just listen and be supportive. The above checklist is a helpful rubric for those who truly want to empower trans youth and young adults through pastoral care.

B. Support

What does *support* look like? Support, like advocacy, comes in a myriad of ways. First and foremost, the cultivating of new conversations must take place within our churches and ministries. Baptist pastoral theologian Cody J. Sanders invites his readers to contribute to the "lagging literature" in our pastoral and practical fields concerning transgender people and issues. Sanders states, "We have failed to give equally serious and sustained attention to the concerns of trans people."[65] Cultivating a culture for transgender young people to flourish would be ideal, but creating a climate that does not breed fear, intimidation, harassment and one that fosters a spirit of wellness, openness, affirmation, and integrity would also be wonderful.

63. Kundtz and Schlager, *Ministry among God's Queer Folk*, 82.
64. Kundtz and Schlager, *Ministry among God's Queer Folk*, 83.
65. Sanders, "LGBTQ Pastoral Counseling," 1.

Parents, pastors, and youth and young adult ministers will all have to be unified in this front of cultivate a culture of trans awareness and openness.

Second and simultaneously, as pastoral ministers, support for transgender youth and young adults often comes by way of helping parents who struggle with their teens' or young adults' gender and sexuality. Supportive parents are on this transitioning and transgender journey with their youth and young adult sons and daughters.[66] In addition, young people require reassurance from parents and pastoral ministers because there is a large gender spectrum, and adolescents and young adults are often not aware of the existence of nonbinary and nonconforming identities.[67] According to Brill and Kenny, "Some teens struggle with claiming their gender identity because they think that all transgender and nonbinary people are gay or lesbian, and they do not feel that they are gay or lesbian."[68] Explaining to adolescents and young adults that gender and sexuality are two distinct facets of their self is helpful for transgender young people as they embark on their journey of self-discovery. Furthermore, it may be worthwhile to help the trans young people to understand that being transgender or nonbinary is about a person's individual gender identity; while sexual orientation is about whom the young person is sexually attracted. Therefore, it is perfectly reasonable for different transgender teenagers and young adults to claim any gender because they are still evolving in their nonbinary gender.[69] Do not expect young people to have all the answers or to have everything figured out regarding the nonbinary gender identity.

Third, transgender youth and young adults often experience various forms of discomfort. Understanding discomfort will be a great asset to their overall emotional health and spiritual wellbeing. Every trans adolescent and young adult figures out differently and *comes out* in their own way and in their own time. Coming out is a transition period; the time that a young person decides to disclose her/his sexual orientation and/or gender identity.[70] Coming out is part of the transgender maturation process

66. There are several resources parents can use in the process of adjusting to their transgender youth and young adult's gender identity. Moreover, these sources can also help to alleviate some of the common instinctive reactions that parents might experience. Here are a few of my favorites: Brill and Kenny, *Transgender Teen*; Riggle and Rostosky, *Positive View of LGBTQ*; Huegel, *GLBTQ*; Sanders, *Brief Guide*.

67. Brill and Kenny, *Transgender Teen*, 70.

68. Brill and Kenny, *Transgender Teen*, 171.

69. Brill and Kenny, *Transgender Teen*, 171.

70. Huegel, *GLBTQ*, 201.

and a positive step in cultivating personal grown, gaining self-esteem, and becoming self-actualized. When trans young people finally do come out, sometimes there are specific areas of discomfort or a more global sense of unrest. Hence, coming out is not always a pleasant process; in fact, for the majority of young people, coming out to parents, friends, and coworkers is stressful and uncomfortable. Transgender teenagers and young adults may experience a variety of discomforts:

a. *gender role discomfort:* feeling like their assumed gender is not a good fit for their gender identity and their gender presentation,

b. *gender expression discomfort:* feeling awkward or strange in traditional gender-conforming clothes;

c. *body/self-image discomfort:* feeling of discomfort with their body beyond the usual adolescent;

d. *gender identity discomfort:* uncomfortable with the terms *cisgender* and *transgender;*

e. *pronoun discomfort:* feeling that pronouns make a difference; some youth are more comfortable using one pronoun over another to describe themselves; and

f. *name discomfort:* feelings of dissatisfaction with their baptismal/given name.[71]

One teen explains her gender role discomfort: "I am suffocating by the expectations everyone has for me. It seems like every sentence begins with 'Girls aren't supposed to' . . . But I'll never be a girl in the way they want me to be."[72] This young person's statement calls for parents and pastoral workers to be attuned and sensitive to the young person's issues, but also to recognize that not every trans person's issues are the same. Prudent parents and pastoral workers will be ready to provide practical guidance for their transgender teenagers. Practical guidance may come in the form of listening, asking probing questions in a kind and sensitive manner, and offering compassion and empathy.

Fourth, support is comprised of inviting parents and families of trans youth and young adults into the church. This process is more akin to "inviting-in" as distinct from a "coming-out" event. Pastorally, trans youth

71. Brill and Kenny, *Transgender Teen,* 175–84.
72. Brill and Kenny, *Transgender Teen,* 179.

and young adults need help with the inviting-in process; it requires young people to muster up a great deal of honesty and courage, which may need facilitation from a trusted adult. During the inviting-in process, transgender teenagers and young adults should experience God's engagement and love through a nonjudgmental Christian community. Sanders states,

> The most vital thing to remember in the process of working with the families of [trans] youth is this: in the process of "inviting family in," the [trans] youth are always the hosts—deciding *who* to invite in, and *when, how quickly,* and with what *levels of access* to the sacred spaces of their hearts and souls.[73]

This process allows for questions to arise, listening to misconceptions, and feelings to be shared in a safe environment.

The "inviting-in" method also allows for six supportive scenarios for churches to help transgender young people and their families:

a. coping with initial family rejection,

b. addressing conflict between parents and among families,

c. helping shift family narratives from negative to positive,

d. providing hurting youth with family support,

e. creating supportive communities for parents and families, and

f. inviting *new* family members into the process.[74]

The "inviting-in" process is one of dialogue and support that allows for family narratives to find meaning and to work through any disappointment, bitterness, and shame, but it also creates a safe space for the trans young person to be heard and feel invited. Sometimes this coming-out/inviting-in process is affectionately called *coming home.* Coming home refers to an experience of the transgender teenager fully embracing her/his identity: it is a coming home to themselves; a coming home to their family, perhaps for the very first time; a coming home to God too. When done successfully, most transgender young people state that coming out is more akin to a coming-home party—a fiesta of choice food and drinks and friends and family gathered around enjoying themselves. One young person noted,

73. Sanders, *Brief Guide,* 67.

74. Sanders, *Brief Guide,* 69–79.

"My coming out was more a coming home to God: You made me this way, you love me this way. I am lovable. And I will find love in my life."[75]

Support for transgender young people comes in different forms and it is important for parents and pastoral ministers to be ready and willing to help and support these young people with their unique life and identity situations. Beyond offering practical guidance, parents and pastoral workers can "move the needle" even farther by advocating for transgender young people; this, for most congregations, is the hardest hurdle to overcome.

C. Advocacy

There are many forms of advocacy. Christian parents, youth and young adult ministers, and pastors can employ a myriad of advocacy options. A few rudimentary forms of advocacy that will be easy to implement for Christian parents and congregations are providing role models, mentoring, and social activism. All three of these forms of advocacy are part of a larger matrix of Christian social justice.

Adult role models. The importance of adult role models for transgender youth and young adults cannot be overstated. Baptist practical theologian Amy Jacober notes that adult role models help teenagers shape their worldview and remove the social disconnect between adults and adolescents.[76] Finding a role model for trans youth and young adults should not be a problem. Role models come in all shapes and sizes, from all walks of life, and from various Christian denominations. Adult role models can be a powerful ally for young people. Ideally, trans youth and young adults would be with trans adult role models, but this might not always be possible in some communities.

Being a role model is a relatively easy venture because it may be a private activity that occurs within own's own families and/or in a person's local community.[77] Many transgender young people would be wise to seek role models from their own extended families: aunts, uncles, and cousins who can be a little more impartial than their own parents.[78] Trans youth and young adults can also find adult role models in the larger community, as well, such as coaches, teachers, and other working professionals they

75. Graham, "Role of Straight Allies," 115.

76. Jacober, *Adolescent Journey*, 88–89.

77. Riggle and Rostosky, *Positive View of LGBTQ*, 113.

78. Riggle and Rostosky, *Positive View of LGBTQ*, 113.

might know. There is nothing incorrect or wrong with a trans young person working with cisgender role models, but there might be more in common with and more to learn from a trans role model. The ultimate purpose of finding a good role model for transgender teenagers is so they can begin to adopt some of their insights, habits, and life practices.

Mentoring. Distinct from role models is mentoring. Mentoring is typically a more formal process between two people. Mentoring is an active process of cultivation and supervision of the personal growth and development of someone else.

Mentoring is a ministry of the church because its nature is to act in ways that Jesus Christ acts towards his people: by exercising the ministry of presence and loving without conditions.[79]

According to gender diversity scholar Ellen D. B. Riggle and psychologist Sharon S. Rotosky, "Perhaps one of the biggest needs in the community is mentoring for [transgender] adolescents and young adults as they come out and transition into their adult lives."[80] Transgender young people, like all youth and young adults, would benefit greatly from adult mentors, those inside and outside the trans community. Some of the common elements for being a good mentor for transgender teenagers are: (1) be open to becoming a trans ally, (2) be available to meet regularly, (3) be a good listener, (4) be able to engage in meaningful conversations, and (5) be empathetic and compassionate.[81]

Mentoring transgender youth and young adults also involves affectionate orientation toward young people. Presbyterian pastoral theologian Carrie Doehring maintains that hearing young people's personal narratives is an essential part of mentoring and pastoral care.

> Stories allow [youth] to lament with each other—express anger and question all they know about life—without imposing meanings prematurely . . . When pastoral care is experienced as narrative it becomes more relational and communal.[82]

Part of mentoring is listening intently to stories, which helps trans youth and young adults to ask about making-meaning of their lives, introspection

---

79. Campbell and Carani, *The Art of Accompaniment*, 22.

80. Riggle and Rostosky, *Positive View of LGBTQ*, 111.

81. Brill and Kenny, *Transgender Teen*, 162–65.

82. Doehring, *Practice of Pastoral Care*, xv.

about their gender identity, and understanding preferences and hopes for their future.

Sanders states that there are several essential areas that heterosexual and cisgender ministers and pastoral care givers may want to provide transgender young people in mentoring relationships. There are five to consider:

a. asking personal questions to young people, even if you might be uncomfortable with the answers;

b. inviting personal stories from young people so they can share their journey, hopes, and fears;

c. talking openly about sex and sexuality with a non-judgmental attitude;

d. helping young people reflect theologically on their experiences of being trans; and

e. assisting youth and young adults in exploring their spirituality as a trans person.[83]

These five suggestions will help both the mentor and the mentee in their working relationship.

As a transgender ally and mentor, I have four-prong foci with my mentees, which is part of the accompaniment process and the ministry of presence: (1) pastoral counseling, (2) spiritual direction, (3) vocational discernment, and (4) moral guidance. This four-prong approach allows me to work through their personal and familiar issues, discuss their faith life or spiritual life, help them to discern the direction of their career and vocation, and provide moral guidance should they ask me for moral advice. All of the above mentoring techniques will help an adult mentor to become a better and more affective mentor with the transgender teenage mentee.

Social activism. The third level of advocacy is social activism. This can be a scary term for some Christians, but it need not be, and activism has lots of leeway. Catholic moral theologians Jozef D. Zalot and Benedict Guevin note that social activism is part of social justice work, which seeks fair and equal treatment of all human beings in important social, economic, political, and sexual issues.[84] Social justice is the cherished principle that finds its footing in the bedrock of sacred Scripture and Christian doctrines.[85] Social activism toward transgender young people begins with

83. Sanders, *Brief Guide*, 86–91.

84. Zalot and Guevin, *Catholic Ethics in Today's World*, 47.

85. Zalot and Guevin, *Catholic Ethics in Today's World*, 48–51.

treating trans youth and young adults with dignity, respect, empathy, and compassion, from both adolescents and adults alike, because transgender young people are created as *imago Dei*.

In the transgender community, social activism may be simply attending a transgender-awareness meeting or being part of a local conversation that sparks local grassroots efforts. On the other hand, social activism could be something larger that advocates for transgender rights and moves community, state, and federal legislation and becomes a catalyst to support large-scale social change. For example transgender and nonbinary teenagers not being able to use public bathrooms in their schools or businesses. Transgender and nonbinary young people, who do not identify fully as either male or female, do not feel comfortable using either the women's or the men's restrooms, and might feel unsafe, because others may verbally harass them or even physically attack them.[86] Transgender and nonbinary young people should be able to use public restrooms that *they* feel the safest and most comfortable using.

Whether it is being a role model, mentor, or social activist, transgender youth and young adults will probably need all three forms of support. Whichever form of advocacy one chooses to be a part of, doing *something* is the most important part of advocacy. As one transgender male from Tennessee notes, "I have learned to fight for my rights instead of just being a victim."[87] Christian congregations are acting hospitable, affirming, and prophetic when they choose advocacy for transgender teenagers.

Providing competent and proficient pastoral care, support, and advocacy to transgender youth and young adults may also require development of appropriate pastoral strategies for Christian youth workers to employ. Unfortunately, too many pastoral care providers, youth and young adult ministers, college campus ministers, and pastors remain ignorant about the subject or simply ignore the feelings and experiences of transgender young people.[88] The importance of transgender youth and young adults for pastoral care professionals and ministers is enormous.

---

86. National Center for Transgender Equality, "Transgender People," 1.

87. Riggle and Rostosky, *Positive View of LGBTQ*, 123.

88. Huegel, *GLBTQ*, 168.

Parting Remarks

Transgender issues are complex, challenging, and changing. Nevertheless, transgender youth and young adults are in nearly every Christian community, even though it might not be evident. Christian congregations would be wise to work toward inclusiveness. This chapter has given parents, pastors, and youth ministers a few tools to work toward that inclusiveness and to further enhance their ministries with transgender young people by examining three areas: pastoral care, support, and advocacy.

It is time that Christian denominations begin to reflect on ways to help transgender young people. Parents especially, but also pastors, directors of Christian education, youth and young adult ministers, coaches, and all people of good will who work with young people have a tremendous responsibility. The obligation is to ensure that this generation of transgender young people stops becoming targets of oppression and condemnation, and starts to be understood and seen as authentic individuals whose nonconforming gender can be respected and admired. I hope and pray that our Christian churches can begin to minister more openly and effectively to all transgender people, but especially trans youth and young adults.

Discussion Questions

1. What are three new things you learned from this chapter?

2. What points did you find surprising, interesting, or perplexing from this chapter?

3. Has this chapter allowed you to think in new ways of being an advocate, a support, and an activist for transgender young people?

4. How can you help your parish's or congregation's role in advocating and supporting transgender youth and young adults?

5. What are some ways of providing competent pastoral care to transgender young people in Christian institutions, organizations, or ministries?

Chapter 7

Queer Theology & Ministry

We know through painful experience that freedom is never voluntarily given by the oppressor; it must be demanded by the oppressed![1]

— MARTIN LUTHER KING JR.
Why We Can't Wait, 1964

Opening Comments

WHEN I TELL AVERAGE churchgoing folks that I research and study about queer theology, I often get a blank stare or a polite smile and nod of their head. Typically, the average Christian sitting in the pews does not really know about or understand queer theology. Here I will attempt to shed some light on the subject of queer theology as a whole and to examine its placement in Christian youth and young adult ministry.

This chapter is divided into four main parts: (1) What is queer? (2) What is queer theology? (3) Strands of queer theology; and (4) Queer theology and youth and young adult ministry. The hope is that this chapter can help straight—heterosexual and cisgender—folks to better understand queer theology and that ministers might take a radical chance on integrating more aspects of queerness into Christian youth and young adult

1. King, *Why We Can't Wait*, 80.

135

ministry. As a result the findings here are subjective judgment based on individual information collected and the understanding of a particular group of people—queer people—and the ethnographic[2] finding of such theological inquiry.

What Is Queer?

Defining the word *queer* is the first order of business. The *Oxford English Online Dictionary* defines *queer* as "strange," "odd," "peculiar," and/or "eccentric," as well as "relating to homosexuals or homosexuality." The term *queer* is the "inside" and *preferred* word used within the LGBTQ community, and terms such as *homosexual* and *homosexuality* are dated, and are used more from those people, organizations, and institutions that desire to keep queer people and queer theology away from mainstream society, culture, and church. The same holds true for the term "same sex attraction," only folks outside the queer community use this outdated terminology.[3] Therefore, *queer* has had a negative connotation in the past and has been a derogatory term. However, the queer community has turned it into a positive term; an insult reclaimed for power and identity.

Queer is an inclusive or all-encompassing term for all sexual minorities: gay, lesbian, bisexual, and transgender persons. Queer refers to anyone who lives outside of or beyond heterosexual and gender-conforming norms of society and culture, for example, a young adult woman might refer to herself as *pansexual*, which means she is a person who experiences sexual attraction to any and all genders. The word "queer" can also include straight and cisgender "allies" who do not self-identify as lesbian, gay, bisexual, transgender, intersex, or questioning, but stand in unity and solidarity with queer people in hopes of cultivating a more just and equitable church, society, and world with respect to sexuality and gender identity.[4] Queer is also used in academic literature and is understood from a dynamic, inquisitive, and research-based manner in several disciplines, such as anthropology, biology, feminism, women's studies, gender studies,

2. The term *ethnographic* provides insight into human behavior. Ethnography is a branch of anthropology that systematically and intentionally studies individuals, cultures, and groups. Ethnography tries to understand the way certain groups or populations of people live their lives.

3. Greenough, *Queer Theologies*, 127.

4. Cheng, *Radical Love*, 3.

historical criticism, sociology, queer theory, and theology.[5] The term *queer* will be used throughout this chapter to mean anyone who self-identifies as lesbian, gay, bisexual, or transgender.

What Is Queer Theology?

Queer theology means different things for different people. There are many strands of queer theology. In fact, there are queer religious beliefs that are not Christian, nor do they want to be labeled as Christian. For the parameters of this chapter, queer theology refers to and is concerned with Christian theology and ministry. Queer theology, for the most part, entails Christian theologians talking about God and Christ from an LGBT worldview. Moreover, queer theology focuses on issues of nonnormative sexuality that represent LGBTQ people, while simultaneously moving beyond sexual expression and gender identity, or being anti-identity, as a critical approach.[6] In addition, queer theology involves Christian theologians reflecting upon and writing about queer people and their relationship with God and Jesus the Christ. Furthermore, queer theology is talking, reflecting, and writing about the misnomers, challenges, and deconstruction of hegemonic, postcolonial, totalitarian or traditional theology (T-theology)[7] that pigeonholes natural binary classifications of sexual and gender identity.[8] Christian queer theology usually indicates theologies: (1) in which sexuality and gender are addressed, (2) that affirm and represent a queer person's worldview, and (3) that do apologetics for queer folks.[9] In the final analysis, queer theology is Christian theology done by and with queer theologians and queer allies. Many people come to study or read queer theology because of their own self-identification or that of a loved one.

---

5. Sanders, *Brief Guide*, 9.

6. Greenough, *Queer Theologies*, 126.

7. The term "T-theology" refers to traditional, patriarchal, heterosexual, and dominant Northern Hemisphere–centric theology; it does not have the capacity to wrestle with the complexities of people's sexual experiences; it cannot question the approved official script of Christianity on sexuality, gender, and women (Althaus-Reid, *Indecent Theology*, 52; Tonstad, *Queer Theology*, 85). Moreover, T-theology contributes to religious stigmatization and to sexual and social oppression (Tonstad, *Queer Theology*, 85).

8. Althaus-Reid, *Indecent Theology*, 7.

9. Tonstad, *Queer Theology*, 3.

Queer theologian Gerard Loughlin states that "theology is a queer thing. It has always been a queer thing."[10] Loughlin's point is that from an outside or non-Christian perspective, it may seem that theology is odd, strange, peculiar, or bizarre, or that it does not make sense on the surface. Queer theology is about erasing boundaries and binary systems and "it views sexuality as something that is continually undergoing negotiations and dissemination, rather than mere natural (let alone medical) fact."[11] Hence, queer theology questions; queer theology challenges; queer theology analyzes the status quo.

Argentinian queer theologian Marcella Althaus-Reid (1952–2009) claims that queer theology is a personal experience based upon solidarity and empathy for the marginalized, but also disruptive practices that can subvert normative "straightness" in loving relationships. She states:

> This is one of the most important challenges that queer theologies bring to theology in the twenty-first century: the challenge of a theology where sexuality and loving relationships are not only important theological issues, but experiences which un-shape totalitarian theology (T-theology) while re-shaping the theologian. For instance, queer theologies do not disregard church traditions. However, the process of queering may turn them upside down, or submit them to collage-style processes by adding and highlighting from them precisely those elements which did not fit well in the construction of the church tradition and thus were excluded or ignored. To queer theological sources in church traditions could simply mean to gather together all the dispersed fragments of love and sexuality identity struggles in people's live, and add to that the struggle for spaces of freedom and social justice which constitutes the real queer traditions of the church, which are characterized by processes of sexual ideological disruption in Christianity, and not by its continuity.[12]

For Althaus-Reid, the lives of queer people within the queer community influence queer theology. Moreover, at times queer theology can be disruptive because it is based upon real people's sorrows and struggles and seeks personal and communal transformation. Queer theology differs from other theologies, not because of people's lived experiences, but because

10. Loughlin, "Introduction: The End of Sex," 7.
11. Foucault, *Religion and Culture*, 277.
12. Althaus-Reid, *Queer God*, 8–9.

queer people are more marginalized and ostracized more than other people.[13] Althaus-Reid also maintains that queer theology must also be about sexuality and sex. "It is from human sexuality that theology starts to search and understand the Sacred [God], not vice-versa."[14] Accordingly, sexuality, spirituality, and theology are intimately connected.

⟶ The quest for transformation and equality in queer theology has come about over the last few decades by implementing four areas of Christian influence used by Protestants and Catholics: (1) Scripture, (2) tradition, (3) reason, and (4) experience.[15] This fourfold method is the "Wesleyan Quadrilateral Theory." Using these four areas of influence or sources indicates that queer theology is thoroughly Christian. These four sources are meant to be a "checks and balances" to one another.[16] Therefore, it is worthwhile to describe these four sources of influence on queer theology.

Queer Scripture

Queer theology utilizes the Bible and biblical narratives just as other Christian theologies. The difference may be that queer biblical scholars apply the Scriptures in creative ways and interpret the Scriptures in modes that move queer people from the margins to the mainstream. Queering Scripture will always be a project related to rereading the patriarchs and dissecting harmful biblical passages, because texts from antiquity may not always reflect transcendental (God's) presence; in fact, some texts are downright inhospitable.[17] Althaus-Reid notes, "Queering [Scripture] is also the art of deconstructing laws in search of justice, an art which comes from experiences of love at the margins of the lawful or, to use Christian terms, outside the redeemable."[18] Consequently, destruction of laws must take place and queer hermeneutics of liberation will need to be constructed. For example, queer Scripture scholars have taken the traditionally six or seven oppressive,

---

13. Canales, "Ministry to Transgender Teenagers (Part One)," 196–97.

14. Althaus-Reid, *Indecent Theology*, 146.

15. Waltz, *Dictionary for United Methodists*, 91. This fourfold method is sometimes called the "Wesleyan Quadrilateral Theory."

16. Cheng, *Radical Love*, 11.

17. Tolbert, foreword to *Take Back the Word*, vii.

18. Althaus-Reid, *Queer God*, 77–78.

anti-homosexual passages, known as "clobber passages"[19] or "texts of terror"[20] in the queer community, and have interpreted these pericopes with new light and in affirmative and beneficial ways that are alternative to T-theology.

Queer biblical scholars and theologians have gone beyond simply re-envisioning and re-interpreting the seven "clobber passages" to read, interpret, and research all biblical narratives in creative and positive ways that are more meaningful and affirming for queer people and their experience.[21] The Bible is not supposed to be used as a weapon against people; therefore, queer Scripture scholars reinterpret and redefine biblical narratives for the exhortation and edification of the entire People of God. Queer biblical scholars write in "ever-surprising capacities and can be disruptive, unsettling, and unexpectedly, but delightfully *queer*."[22] Consequently, the approaches that queer biblical scholars employ come from a wide spectrum of hermeneutical choices. For instance, queer biblical scholars use the 4-R method or principle for queer hermeneutics: resistance, rupture, reclamation, and re-engagement.[23]

It may be meaningful to briefly look at the 4-R methodology. Reading the texts with resistance and suspicion is a strategy the reader uses to examine the Scriptures more critically from an oppressed perspective.[24] Rupture emphasizes the way Christian institutions and traditions have used certain biblical passages to enforce heterosexuality and cisgenderism.[25] Reading the biblical texts with an eye for reclamation allows the Scriptures to come alive for queer folks, and truly, to explore the Bible with the mindset of coming-home.[26] Reengagement is an approach of reading the Bible that grapples with the texts and forgives or absolves the Scriptures themselves for wrongdoing to the queer community. This means that biblical pericopes

---

19. Shore, *Unfair*, 3. These passages are called this because conservative, heterosexual Christians "clobber" queer Christians "over the head" with these passages.

20. Trible, *Texts of Terror*, 1–5. These texts are referred in this way because white, conservative, heterosexual, homophobic Christians "terrorize" queer Christians with these texts. The clobber texts are: Gen 19:1–29; Lev 18:22; 20:13; Deut 22:5; Rom 1:26–27; 1 Cor 6:9; and 1 Tim 1:10. Please see chap. 2 for a more thorough Scripture analysis.

21. Wilson, *Our Tribe*, 111–64.

22. Guest et al., *Queer Bible Commentary*, xiii, italics original.

23. Guest, *When Deborah Met Jael*, 110.

24. Guest, *When Deborah Met Jael*, 124.

25. Hornsby and Guest, *Transgender, Intersex*, 57. Hornsby and Guest refer to the rupturing process of Scripture as the "transgender gaze."

26. Hornsby and Guest, *Transgender, Intersex*, 73.

that were once toxic, dangerous, and injurious can no longer be because "their capacity to kill by arguing it is the interpretation of the Scriptures, not the Scriptures themselves that have been condemnatory."[27] The 4-R methodology is a powerful tool for queer folks to read, study, and interpret the Bible. Queer Scripture scholars use this 4-R methodology to combat hetero-suspicion to find new ways of retelling biblical truths.

Queer Tradition

Queer theology uses tradition in the same manner as T-theology: examining church history, studying various theological dogmas and doctrines, and trying to discern the *sensus fidelium*. Queer theologians, like queer Scripture scholars, draw upon tradition in unique ways because for the most part, Christianity has been anti-queer in its rhetoric and theological stance. It is important to scrutinize and reconsider Christian doctrines in light of new revelations. "Truth claims that cause harm to ourselves or others must be questioned and questioned again."[28] Attention to the ways that churches and Christian denominations affect other persons, creatures, and the creation around us merits introspection.[29]

However, in the last two decades, queer theologians have had to reexamine and reinterpret T-theology from a queer worldview, and have made great strides and advancements in queer theology. Queer theology does not jettison T-theology, but rather reclaims it and repositions it for a queer audience and from a queer perspective. Some queer theologians have re-examined and re-interpreted Augustine of Hippo (354–430), Peter Damian (1007–1072), Thomas Aquinas (1224–1274), and Martin Luther's (1483–1546) theological discourses.[30]

Queer Reason

Beyond tradition, queer theology also utilizes queer reason. Theology has always maintained that both faith and reason are sources of authority and a person can come to know God with these two criteria alone. However,

---

27. Guest, *When Deborah Met Jael*, 247.

28. Schneider and Ray, *Awake to the Moment*, 54.

29. Schneider and Ray, *Awake to the Moment*, 54.

30. Burns, *Sex Lives of Saints*; Moore, *Question of Truth*.

reason integrates and uses more philosophy than it does theology.[31] In the Catholic heritage, philosophy has always played a role in theological education, especially reason and natural law. In Catholic philosophy, great Christian thinkers have always recognized reason and abstract knowledge.[32] Thomas Aquinas was a brilliant philosopher as well as theologian and came up with his famous five proofs for the existence of God, and they are an example Catholic philosophy and reason influencing theology.[33] Reason is normally understood as the principles for critical thinking and methodological inquiry, whether intellectual, moral, aesthetic, or religious.[34] Reason has not always been an affable source of queer theology in large part because of the Roman Catholic traditional view that same-sex, genital acts are *always* "acts of grave depravity" and "intrinsically disordered" because they supposedly deviate from natural law.[35]

Conversely, queer reason does not view same-sex attraction or homosexual genital acts as unnatural, "intrinsically disordered," or "acts of grave depravity," but as something entirely accepted and good. In reality, and contrary to Catholic natural law understanding, there are many reptiles, animals, bird species, and fish in the natural world that engage in same-sex acts or gender-variant behaviors, such as Baboons, Orca, Emu, Vultures, Bearded-Dragon Lizards, Desert Tortoise, Salmon, and Arctic Graying (fish).[36]

Queer theory and queer reason within queer theology do *not* reject outright the traditional view of sexuality (heterosexual/homosexual) and gender variance (female/male), but want to reshape, challenge, and transform sexuality, loving relationships, and gender for contemporary society and culture.[37] Queer reason simply argues for and acknowledges that sexual and gender categories are socially constructed and conditioned. Catholic moral theologian Margaret Farley indicates that queer reason understands that there is no "fixed" or "natural" continuum when it comes to gender

---

31. Cheng, *Radical Love*, 16–17.

32. Gilson, *Spirit of Mediaeval Philosophy*, 30.

33. Kreeft, *Summa of the Summa*, 65–70. Here are Aquinas's five proofs for the existence of God: (1) from motion, (2) from efficient cause, (3) from possibility and necessity, (4) from the gradation to be found in things, and (5) from the governance of the world.

34. Swindal, "Faith and Reason," 1.

35. Canales, "Ministry to Catholic LGBTQ Youth," 64. *Catechism of the Catholic Church*, §2357.

36. Moore, *Question of Truth*, 27–37; Bagemihl, *Biological Exuberance*. Also see *Wikipedia*, s.v. "List of Animals Displaying Homosexual Behavior."

37. Althaus-Reid, *Queer God*, 8.

and sexuality, the only borders or boundaries with adults are do no unjust harm, free and consensual of partners, mutuality, equality, commitment, fruitfulness, and respect for persons as sexual beings in society.[38] It may be commonsense to note, then, that a person's genitalia does not define the whole person: people prefer different styles of clothing, wear their hair and make-up differently, select different careers, and choose divergent sexual paths.[39] Finally, queer reason disrupts the status quo of T-theology, and pushes the boundaries of sexual fluidity and gender variance, even if it subverts traditional Christianity's notion of sexual ethics.

Queer Experience

Theology encompasses a person's individual and communal experiences and relationships. Queer experience is an important dynamic within queer theology. Christianity maintains that God acts in people's lives within certain settings and parameters—*contexts*. The contexts that queer folks come from is lived experience: a lived-practice that has largely been ignored from mainstream theological discourse. Queer lives and their experiences of anguish, happiness, and love will necessarily enlighten and empower the Body of Christ.

Multicultural theologian Stephen B. Bevans notes there are four important contexts or experiences that people encounter. First, context includes the experiences of a person's (or groups) personal life: successes, failures, spirituality, sexuality, and relationships.[40] Second, personal or communal experience is possible only within the context of culture, which expresses the way people communicate, act, perpetuate, and establish knowledge and attitudes toward life. Third, contexts revolve around a person's community or social location: it matters if a person is female or male, black or white, poor or rich, born below or above the equator, from the margins or from the center. It matters because people's daily encounters are different coming from different contexts. Fourth, the reality of present-experience—the now or immediate—in human contexts involves the reality of social change. No context or culture is static; it is moving and growing.[41]

---

38. Farley, *Framework for Christian Sexual Ethics*, 231.

39. Cheng, *Radical Love*, 18.

40. Bevans, *Models of Contextual Theology*, 5.

41. Bevans, *Models of Contextual Theology*, 5–7.

The point of contextual theology is to demonstrate that beliefs about God and the practices of certain beliefs and customs are not the same everywhere. Throughout history, local customs and cultures differ in their religious beliefs and practices.[42] Therefore, queer theology today takes account of all these aspects of people's experience. For example, if a person's experience is transgender, she/he (they) love God, and want to serve God by opening up a soup kitchen for homeless transgender folks, then such a spirituality needs to be cultivated. Queer experience is a paramount source for doing theology from a queer viewpoint.

These quadrilateral sources of queer theology—Scripture, tradition, reason, and experience—help queer theologians navigate, advocate, and support the *doing* of theology from a queer perspective. Beyond these four sources of theology, which inform and influence queer theology, there are also four strands or categories of queer theology that have emerged and merit brief attention.

Categories of Queer Theology

There are four categories of theology, which influence and affect the development of queer theology: (1) apologetic theology, (2) liberation theology, (3) relational theology, and (4) queer theory and theology.

Apologetic Theology

Apologetic theology is the earliest factor of queer theology and can be summed up with this pithy phrase: *gay is good*.[43] The early theologians who defended homosexuality were primarily concerned with moving Christianity away from the stereotypes and labels that were harmful toward gay and lesbian people. The advocacy from these theologians is that, since homosexuality is an inherent and apparently, an unalterable state, it must be morally neutral then.[44]

These early queer theologians also stressed a message of love and acceptance for all God's people, but especially God's gay and lesbian people. There were several pioneering books in the second half of the twentieth

---

42. Greenough, *Queer Theologies*, 63.

43. Cheng, *Radical Love*, 27.

44. Bailey, *Homosexuality and the Western Tradition*, 168–73.

century that helped promote queer (mainly homosexual) rights, sexuality, and spirituality within Christianity.[45] These early queer apologists have led to other avenues of thought to influence queer theology.

Liberation Theology

The second influence on the development of queer theology is liberation theology. Initially, the main thrust of liberation theology was the concern for the poor and oppressed. Liberation theology looked to Jesus of Nazareth for its example as a liberator. Eventually, liberation theology intersected with queer theology. Liberation theology has helped queer theology to de-emphasize heterosexuality and cisgender as the only possible natures that human beings possess. Moreover, liberation theology allows people to find their authentic self in sexuality and gender. Liberation theology has also helped to unmask the hidden biases and prejudices that lurk within Christianity, such as transphobia and homophobia, and has helped queer folks find freedom.

Liberation theology works toward righting injustices for those on the margins: those who experience oppression, those who are financially poor, and those who are disenfranchised. Hence, liberation theology affirms and accepts same-sex relationships, same-sex marriages, the ordination of women, the ordination of openly gay/lesbian people, homosexuals, and transgender people, and no longer accepts passively the discriminatory practices of injustices by the various denominations within Christianity.[46]

Gay theologian Robert Williams argues that,

> in Liberation Theology 101, only lesbians and gays can determine for themselves what constitutes sin and morality . . . Any straight [pastor or priest] attempt to define sin for gays and lesbians is patriarchal and condescending and ultimately blasphemy.[47]

Williams maintains that straight folks cannot determine that which is sinful for LGBTQ folks. However, 30-years ago, queer theology was just

45. Wood, *Christ and the Homosexual* (1960); Jones, *Toward a Christian Understanding of Homosexuality* (1966); Perry, *The Lord Is My Shepherd and He Knows I'm Gay* (1972); Pittenger, *Time for Consent?* (1976); Boswell, *Christianity, Social Tolerance, and Homosexuality* (1980); McNeil, *The Church and the Homosexual* (1993); Scanzon and Mollenkott, *Is the Homosexual My Neighbor?* (1994).

46. Johnson, "Good News of Gay Liberation," 91–92.

47. Williams, *Just As I Am*, 151–52.

getting started and there was really no notion of queer allies. I do not think Williams is implying that only queer ministers can only minister to queer congregants or parishioners. In liberation theology, the people with lived experiences are the real religious experts, not those who sit comfortably in their offices away from those who live on the margins of society (like theologians and bishops).

Relational Theology

Relational theology is the third strand of queer theology. Relational theology grew out of feminist theology. Relational theology is constructed with feminist principles and women's experience of love, sex, and spirituality.[48] Relational theology concentrates on finding God, love, relationships, and in the middle of appropriate intimate conversations and sexual episodes.

Lesbian theologians such as Barbara B. Gittings, Del Martin, Phyllis Lyon, and Sally Gearhart have pioneered relational theology, distinguishing it from gay theology, and dispelling the myths that lesbians are over-sexed, masculine women, only interested in trying to seduce one another.[49] Relational theology does theology from the margins of lesbianism and from a feminist perspective. Both lesbians and heterosexual woman reconnect with each other through feminism and relationships.[50]

Moreover, relational theology maintains that God is present in the lustful desires and that erotic sexual actions are sacred actions because God is *not* foreign to gender, sexuality, or intercourse.[51] Relational theology differs from traditional Christian thought on the matter of premarital sex and people's bodies (not that I am advocating for this with youth and young adults). Relational theologians embrace queer bodies as spiritual wholeness and expression; the body is sacramental.[52] In fact, God fully participates and engages in human gender and sexuality and the variety of erotic and lustful particularities, that queer people might prefer.[53] Relational theology is not

48. Geenough, *Queer Theologies*, 12.

49. Gittings, "The Homosexual and the Church" (1969); Martin and Lyon, "Lesbian Approach to Theology" (1971); Gearhart, "Miracle of Lesbianism" (1974); Heyward, *Touching Our Strength* (1989).

50. Gearhart, "Miracle of Lesbianism," 128, 133.

51. Cheng, *Radical Love*, 34.

52. Kim-Kort, *Outside the Lines*, 74–76.

53. Cheng, *Radical Love*, 34.

necessarily bound by T-theology's sexual parameters, although monogamy is still preferred by most lesbian, feminist, queer theologians. Concerning friendships and mutual hospitality, relational theology maintains that it is in constructing loving relationships where God is ultimately found.[54]

Fundamentally, relational theology acknowledges God's interaction with all humanity and God's embrace of human beings and their various idiosyncrasies and hidden peccadilloes. God is *not* separate from God's creation. God relates to the creation that God creates and that creation makes a difference to God.[55] God loves all of us at all times. Therefore, it follows that God creates, interacts, and deeply cares and loves queer people.

Queer Theory and Theology

Queer theory and theology, motivated by liberation theology and relational theology, moves contextual theology to new limits and alternative ways of thinking about sexuality, gender, and politics.[56] Queer theory is the intentional and critical theory that works to disrupt normative ways of thinking. Queer theology is not interested in the status quo of patriarchal and colonial visions of traditional or totalitarian theology and/or the normative human sexual expressions and identities.[57] Queer theology is interested in the real sexual experiences of lesbian, gay, bisexual, and transgender folks, and the ways that God interacts with them in their daily lives.

Queer theory challenges compulsory ideas of binary gender and interrogates heterosexuality and cisgender. Queer theory has come to be applied in the following ways: (1) it resists ideas of categorization, (2) it challenges the ideas of essentialism, (3) it contests "normal," (4) it removes narrow binary thinking and presumptions, and (5) it exposes and disrupts power relations or hierarchies.[58]

The task of queer theology is to help God "come out of the closet" and move into a new contextual and experiential theology. Queer theology has to push beyond the static notions of hegemonic T-theology: white privilege, male privilege, wealthy privilege, heterosexual privilege, and cisgender privilege. Queer theology has an ethical imperative to move toward

---

54. Stuart, *Just Good Friends*, 236.

55. Oord, "What Is Relational Theology?," 2.

56. Althaus-Reid, *Queer God*, 2.

57. Tonstad, *Queer Theology*, 72.

58. Thomas, *Straight with a Twist*, 26.

new limits and claim its queerness and "shake off the shackles" of moral assumptions of heterosexuality and the categories of contamination of values associated with so-called Christian straight people.[59]

Queer theology is contextual. Queer theology is sexual. Queer theology has to sexually deconstruct T-theology and make it indecent, as distinct from decent theology, which is heterosexual, cisgender, patriarchal, and white T-theology. There must be space for theological claims such as,

> God, the Faggot; God, the Drag Queen; God, the Lesbian; God, the heterosexual woman who does not accept the constructions of ideal heterosexuality; God, the ambivalent, not easily classified sexuality.[60]

These queer labels may seem severe, but this is the only way LGBTQ Christians can reclaim their sexuality and gender from ridicule, harassment, and marginalization. It is the groundwork for a different epistemology that challenges appropriately and positively spiteful words that have been used to humiliate and hurt queer folks over the decades.[61]

In the final analysis, queer theory and theology exposes privilege, but it can also be a catalyst for change in ministry. Consequently, then, queer theory and theology can influence and impact youth and young adult ministry in positive ways.

Queer Theology and Youth & Young Adult Ministry

What does queer theology have to do with youth and young adult ministry? Everything. The queering of youth and young adult ministry is similar to the queering of other parts of the Christian tradition such as God, theology, Christology, ecclesiology, liturgy and worship, sacraments, and Scripture interpretation. What is the place of queer theology in youth and young adult ministry? What does queering youth and young adult ministry look like? These questions are considered below.

---

59. Althaus-Reid, *Queer God*, 20.

60. Althaus-Reid, *Indecent Theology*, 95.

61. Althaus-Reid, *Indecent Theology*, 95.

The Place for Queer Theology in Youth & Young Adult Ministry

Queer theology within youth and young adult ministry is in confrontation with binary awareness and understanding. Rudimentary cognizance and comprehension about queerness is essential for youth and young adult ministers in today's multicultural and complex world.

The fields of youth and young adult ministry have always been about openness and hospitality with other young people. Therefore, one placement for queer theology is in openness and affirmation of individual queer young people.[62] Another place for youth and/or young adult ministers is to try to do their ministry with a queer lens while remaining faithful to their particular tradition, e.g., Catholic or Presbyterian.[63] The term *queer lens* refers to youth and young adult ministers trying to integrate a worldview that looks at ministry from the margins to include, and perhaps give preferential treatment to the marginalized. Creating ministry from the margins will reshape traditional youth and young adult ministry to give queer theology a more prominent place in work with Christian young people.

Queering Youth & Young Adult Ministry

Can youth and young adult ministry be queer? Absolutely. The starting point for queering ministry is queer lives and queer relationships.[64] Queering youth and young adult ministry requires that feelings, interests, and issues of queer young people are heard, understood, and supported. At a minimum, there should be some ministry alternatives for queer young people in youth and young adult ministries. An integrated ministry is ideal, but a specialized and separate ministry can also work. These alternatives do not have to disrupt the integrity of the ministry or its programming.

Queering youth and young adult ministry means moving away from "vanilla ministry" that cannot question or oppose an approved ministry script or that does not risk change and alternative viewpoints on pastoral care with those who live in the margins like queer young people.[65] The unadventurous vanilla youth and young adult ministry will not help the disenfranchised young people in society or churches. If youth and young

---

62. Canales, "Ministry to Catholic LGBTQ Youth," 69–70.

63. Greenough, *Queer Theologies*, 35.

64. Althaus-Reid, *Queer God*, 146.

65. Althaus-Reid, *Indecent Theology*, 52.

adult ministers are afraid or ashamed of discussing sexual minority issues openly and in a spirit of respect and dignity for the human person, then it only feeds into T-theology and the dominant heteronormative view that produces more alienation, suppression, homophobia, and transphobia.[66]

The merits of queering youth and young adult ministry include a realization that queerness is a gift from God. As Althaus-Reid states, "Queerness is something that belongs to God, and . . . people are divinely queer by grace."[67] Queer lives matter in youth and young adult ministry because queer people have stories to share, lives to be in relationship with, and experiences that can also help shape heterosexuality and cisgenderism.[68]

It is awesome to witness youth and young adult ministries becoming a bit more liberative with issues surrounding queer young people and begin to cater more directly to this unique and odd (queer) population. The more comfortable a youth and young adult ministry becomes (ministers, peer leaders, and young people) with openness and affirmation of queer folks, the more transformation happens in the lives of young people. This has happened to a church in Washington, DC, that I have been consulting with for a few years, and pastoral methods that were integrated in the church's youth ministry have led to the entire congregation being more accepting and affirming of queer people throughout the congregation. Most significantly, the youth ministry in particular has implemented some pastoral methods for advocating, supporting, and promoting queer culture in the youth ministry.

Parting Remarks

This chapter has addressed the nature of queer, the sources of queer theology (Scripture, tradition, reason, experience), categories of queer theology (apologetic, liberation, relational, queer), and the placement of queer theology in youth and young adult ministry. I have also considered the place for queer theology in youth and young adult ministry and queering youth and young adult ministry. My hope is that this chapter will empower academics and practitioners (even those who are reticent to the topic) for openness when it comes to affirming queer young people in Christian youth and young adult ministry, because queer lives matter.

66. Althaus-Reid, *Queer God*, 91.

67. Althaus-Reid, *Queer God*, 34.

68. Greenough, *Queer Theologies*, 132.

I think it is important for queer experiences and narratives to be integrated into mainstream Christian youth and young adult ministry, even if it is only gradual and sporadic. The queering of youth and young adult ministry does not have to be lurid or outrageous. It simply does not need to be so taboo. Queer theology, queer lives, and queer experiences ought to be addressed and discussed openly, even celebrated, because queer folks living and worshiping in churches are *Christians*. Integrating queer theology into youth and young adult ministry takes temerity and requires courage. This is so because it takes place not at the center of mainstream Christianity, but at the margins, with the oppressed.

Discussion Questions

1. What are three new things you learned from this chapter?

2. What points did you find surprising, interesting, or perplexing from this chapter?

3. Has this chapter allowed you to think in new ways about queer theology as distinct from T-theology?

4. Why is having a preferential option for queer young people important for youth and young adult ministry?

5. How can you help your parish's or congregation's role to advocate and support the queering of youth and young adult ministry?

Chapter 8

Pedagogical Approaches and Pastoral Strategies for Implementation and Practice

Methodology [or pedagogical approaches and pastoral strategies] seeks to help the youth and young adult ministers see something practical and pastoral and in ways which the method can be implemented and utilized.

—ARTHUR DAVID CANALES
Models & Methods for Youth & Young Adult Ministry, 24

IT IS MY SINCERE hope that all the good folks reading this book, especially youth and young adult ministers, do *not* jump immediately to this chapter before reading the previous chapters. Such an action is a big mistake and does not properly inform or form the person or minister with the proper theory and theology that undergirds the particular pedagogical approach or pastoral strategy for implementation. This chapter offers suggestions and guidance for those youth and young adult ministers to discern the best possible methodological practice that will suit the young people in ministry contexts.

There are numerous LGBTQ pastoral strategies and pedagogical approaches that a youth or young adult minister can be implement into a youth and young adult ministry. Before offering the pastoral methodologies, a few preliminary remarks are in order.

1. It is important that the youth and/or young adult minister discuss this with the pastor and inform the pastor of the nature and scope of the strategies.

2. It would be wise for the youth minister to address this with parents as well, to gauge the reaction and position of the parents, and to get permission slips for the events, some parents may be reticent to the idea, and that is okay.

3. It is advisable to discuss queer theology and issues with the catechists or volunteer adult leaders in the ministry. Anticipate some tension and hesitation, especially from people who do not have any understanding of queer issues.

4. Discuss queer issues with the young people who are regularly attending and participating in either youth or young adult ministry. Answer basic questions that young people want to know surrounding queer issues.

5. Do some research on the topics, preview movies and music, get an outline from any guest speakers, sit down with core leaders and other volunteers who minister and support the ministry.

6. Follow up each event with journaling, small faith-sharing groups, or theological reflection, to engage young people in introspection and in discussing their feelings and emotions regarding a sensitive topic. It is prudent to remember that some topics might make people cagey and emotionally charged.

In my experience, the overwhelming majority of young people are much more open to thinking and talking about LGBTQ issues and concerns than are adults.

This chapter will provide fifteen methods or pastoral strategies for consideration to help youth and young adult ministries to become more hospitable and affirming of LGBTQ young people, but also to be more aware of LGBTQ issues and culture. These strategies are merely suggestions and afford youth and young adult ministers with pedagogical approaches that may be utilized for purposeful catechesis with young people in youth and young adult ministry settings. These fifteen strategies are designed to assist youth and young adult ministers in areas of empathy, encouragement, and empowerment with young people to whom they serve. This chapter also offers pragmatic and pastoral tactics, which can be readily infused and integrated into either a youth or young adult ministry curriculum.

I humbly offer these fifteen strategies for consideration: two or three are specifically intended to make people aware of transgender young people and the others are to make young people aware of gay, lesbian, or bisexual young people. I hope that youth and young adult ministers find these useful.

Strategy #1: LGBTQ Youth and/or Young Adult Speaker Series

The first pedagogical strategy is rather simple to do, and that is to bring in LGBTQ speakers within the community (congregation or neighborhood) to address and discuss their personal struggles, issues, and concerns of growing up in a Christian church. It might prove to be prudent if a different speaker came in and presented a different sexual minority group. There-fore, the LGBTQ Youth and/or Young Adult Speaker Series is primarily to address the young people of the congregation. For example, the series could be a four-week series.

- The first evening could be with a lesbian speaker who shares from her experience as a lesbian woman living in the world.
- The second session could be a gay presenter who can testify from his familiarity as a gay man participating in the church.
- The third week a bisexual person could express their unique situation as a bisexual person and as a Christian believer in the faith.
- The fourth lecturer could discuss transgender issues and the struggles that a transgender person suffers.

This could be a powerful consciousness-raising series for all young people involved in the youth and young adult ministries. It may be wise for the youth or young adult minister to meet and discuss the format of the evening with the presenter and ask the speaker for an outline of the presen-tation a week before she/he presents. In this way, the speaker's outline will be able to be shared and discussed with the catechists of the youth or young adult ministry ahead of time. It may be a good idea if there were small faith-sharing groups following the speaker to help young people process the topic and to engage in theological reflection. I think this is a relatively easy and simple method to integrate into youth and young adult ministry settings.

Strategy # 2: Lesbian, Gay & Bisexual Awareness Film Series

A second pastoral approach is to develop a lesbian, gay, and bisexual film series—transgender films will be covered in a later strategy—that strives to develop cultural awareness and sensitivity to the issues that queer young people encounter. Young people enjoy watching movies as a group and discussing them; it becomes a social experience for youth and young adults.[1] This is perhaps one of the simplest approaches to organize and implement; however, it can potentially be one of the most graphic for young people. Queer cinema covers an array of LGBTQ topics and issues: first same-sex kiss, sexual discrimination, taboo cultural customs, violence because of sexual identity, and multicultural LGBTQ young people.

Granted that some of these movies will need permission slips from parents (who have teenagers involved in the youth ministry) because they are rated R (Restricted) and will probably also need permission from the pastor to show some of these movies at the church. Here is a list of movies that cover a variety of lesbian, gay, and bisexual themes: *My Beautiful Laundrette* (1985); *My Own Private Idaho* (1991); *Philadelphia* (1993); *Weekend* (2001); *Go Fish* (1994); *The Birdcage* (1996); *Brokeback Mountain* (2005); *Milk* (2008); *Circumstance* (2011); *Pariah* (2011); *Blue Is the Warmest Color* (2012); *Dallas Buyers Club* (2013); *The Normal Heart* (2014); *Boy Erased* (2018); *Uncle Frank* (2020); *Boy Meets Boy* (2021).

It is highly recommended that the youth and young adult minister preview the film with the adult volunteer leaders (catechists or core team members) of the ministry so they can discuss and discern the direction of the evening and prepare small group discussion questions. It may be prudent for the youth and young adult minister to hand out journals for each student to write her/his thoughts out and to reflect on certain aspects of the movie and the way the movie made them feel (affectively, emotionally) as they watched the movie. Then after a period of journaling time, enlarge the small groups into a few semi-large groups to discuss their thoughts and feelings. Both youth and young adult ministers should be aware that each evening may be emotionally charged due to the content of the movies.

---

1. Jacober, *Adolescent Journey*, 90.

Strategy # 3: Parent Series on LGBTQ Young People

A third practical tactic would be to host a parent series on LGBTQ young people, which could be launched once a year to discuss LGBTQ issues and raising LGBTQ students in the Christian churches. The series could be publicized as "Embracing Unity through Diversity," "Embracing All Our Sisters and Brothers," or "Embracing LGBTQ Christians," and could involve a variety of themes or topics. Guest speakers such a theologians, psychologists, pastors, school administrators, and parents could be invited to share their expertise in certain areas. A six-week series might look similar to this:

- *Week One:* Human Sexuality & Spirituality: God's Gift and the Interconnection between the Two

- *Week Two:* The Challenges of Being LGBTQ at Home, School, and Church

- *Week Three:* The Societal Stigmatization and Dangers That LGBTQ Youth Confront Daily: Harassment, Bullying, and Violence

- *Week Four:* Creating a Parish and School That Welcomes and Loves All People

- *Week Five:* Growing in Faith and Love: Loving God, Church, and All God's People

- *Week Six:* Created for Love: What's a Committed, Loving, Gay or Lesbian Couple to Do?

All these topics are suggestions and they can be changed and altered to meet the needs of the youth and young adult ministry or the congregation.

This might be a good time for Catholic parents to discuss the USCCB document *Always Our Children* (1997) that was addressed in chapter 5. Immediately following each presentation, a brief question-and-answer session could be provided, and perhaps after that, some light refreshments and *hors d'oeuvres* could be served to stimulate further causal conversation. A series such as this would potentially illuminate the hearts and minds of all its participants; however, one of the drawbacks would be getting parents to commit to attending six weeks due to hectic family schedules and perhaps lack of openness to the series.

Strategy # 4: Support LGBTQ Month

This fourth pragmatic method involves a few separate activities. These activities are to be implemented throughout the entire year or a particular month such as October, which has been coined "LGBTQ History Month," or June, which is coined "LGBTQ Pride Month" by the LGBTQ community in the United States.[2] Each of these activities can be used interchangeably with any activities mentioned here in this strategy or with the other pedagogical practices listed in this chapter.

One activity that youth or young adult ministers could do to cultivate a spirit of openness and acceptance among LGBTQ youth and young adults is to create LGBTQ peer-led student ministry, which could be a sub-ministry of the youth or young adult ministry. A separate LGBTQ peer-led sub-ministry that caters to the issues, needs, and concerns of LGBTQ young people would be highly desirable for sexual minorities. The LGBTQ ministry could be called Alliance, Affirmation, Blessed, Dignity, or Diversity.

A second activity within LGBTQ month is to sponsor a "Stop the Hate Campaign." The purpose of the Stop Hate Campaign is to help highlight LGBTQ social justice implications. It is a method designed to integrate Christian social teachings[3] and to discuss the discrimination and persecu-

---

2. Lesbian, Gay, Bisexual, and Transgender Pride Month (LGBT Pride Month) is currently celebrated each year in the month of June to honor the 1969 Stonewall riots in Manhattan. The Stonewall riots were a tipping point for the Gay Liberation Movement in the United States. In the United States, the last Sunday in June was initially celebrated as "Gay Pride Day," but the actual day was flexible. In major cities across the nation, the "day" soon grew to encompass a month-long series of events. Today, celebrations include pride parades, picnics, parties, workshops, symposia, and concerts, and LGBT Pride Month events attract millions of participants around the world. Memorials are held during this month for those members of the community who have been lost to hate crimes or HIV/AIDS. The purpose of the commemorative month is to recognize the impact that lesbian, gay, bisexual and transgender individuals have had on history locally, nationally, and internationally. In 1994, a coalition of education-based organizations in the United States designated October as LGBT History Month. In 1995, a resolution passed by the General Assembly of the National Education Association included LGBT History Month within a list of commemorative months. LGBT History Month is also celebrated with annual month-long observances of lesbian, gay, bisexual and transgender history, along with the history of the gay rights and related civil rights movements. National Coming Out Day (October 11), as well as the first "March on Washington" in 1979, are commemorated in the LGBT community during LGBT History Month. This source is from the Library of Congress website: http://www.loc.gov/lgbt/about.html.

3. The Catholic/Christian social teachings are as follows: (1) the dignity of the human person, (2) community and the common good, (3) human rights and responsibilities,

tion that surrounds LGBTQ youth. The Stop the Hate Campaign could be a series of four evening lectures, which are open to the entire community and which highlight various themes. Some lectures may be the following:

- *Presentation # 1:* The Dignity and Equality of the Human Person
- *Presentation # 2:* Putting an End to Homophobic Bullying
- *Presentation # 3:* Debunking Myths and Stereotypes about LGBTQ Persons
- *Presentation # 4:* Why Can't We All Just Get Along?

These lectures will thoroughly ground young people with Christian social teachings and allow them to connect their faith with the larger global realities that other people face daily.[4]

These two activities can really aid Christian congregations during LGBTQ Youth and/or Young Adult Month to become more open-minded and inclusive about same sex issues and in the process learn a tremendous amount.

Strategy # 5: Weekend Retreat

A fifth pedagogical scheme is to offer a weekend retreat, which highlights certain youth and/or young adult LGBTQ themes. Retreats are an excellent way to enhance faith formation and are the spiritual "backbone" of a comprehensive youth and young adult ministry.[5] Retreats have a way of moving teenagers away from an individualistic (self-centered) mentality to a communal mindset (other-centered), which is most appropriate for reaching out to LGBTQ young people.[6] The retreat theme could be "Dispelling Myths," "Affirmation & Acceptance," or "Dignity & Equality." The retreat could offer a variety of presentations on various topics that are beneficial for LGBTQ youth and young adults, such as:

---

(4) compassion for the poor, (5) participation in civil society, (6) work and the rights of workers, (7) stewardship of creation and environmental responsibility, (8) solidarity with citizens of the world, (9) the role of government, and (10) the promotion of peace. For more information on Catholic Social Teachings, see Krietemeyer, *Leaven for the Modern World.*

4. Canales, "Transforming Teenagers," 79–80.

5. Canales, *Noble Quest,* 93.

6. Canales, "Christian Discipleship," 42.

- "Knowing Yourself, Loving Yourself,"
- "Understanding LGBTQ Spirituality,"
- "Being Queer and Being Christian,"
- "Loving God and Loving Neighbor," or
- "Living LGBTQ Christian Discipleship."

The list of topics for retreat talks is limitless and the retreat could be as broad or narrow as the youth and/or young adult minister discerns.

An essential element of a youth and young adult retreat that highlights LGBTQ themes to concentrate the retreat on aspects that will raise the conscious awareness about LGBTQ issues as well as engage all young people on the topics. Retreats are great avenues for bolstering youth and young adult spirituality in young people, and since retreats typically take place on a weekend format they have greater potential to transform teenagers' lives and call them more deeply into a relationship with God.[7]

Strategy # 6: Host a Queer Dance

A sixth pastoral tactic is to host a queer dance at the parish or congregation. This strategy is fun to prepare and host. The youth and/or young adult ministry could get a committee together to plan, organize, and implement a dance, but this particular dance will be for queer folks and queer allies. The dance would be more "queer-friendly" if queer-only bands and/or queer musical artists performed at the dance, or a disc jockey played queer-oriented music. There are numerous queer musical artists to select music from: Elton John, Queen, Village People, Indigo Girls, KD Lang, David Bowie, Melissa Etheridge, The B-52's, Ty Herndon, Culture Club, George Michael, Frankie Goes to Hollywood, Pet Shop Boys, Cyndi Lauper, Gloria Gaynor, Lady Gaga, Christina Aguilera, Chely Wright, Panic! At the Disco, King Princess, Miley Cyrus, and many more.[8]

It may be sensible for youth and young adult ministers to preview the songs in advance for lurid or vulgar lyrics. Nevertheless, this could be a really fun strategy to implement and has potential to build and foster community.

7. Canales, "Biblical-Hermeneutical Model," 246.

8. For more information on queer musical artists, see *Wikipedia*, s.v. "LGBT Music."

Strategy #7: A Coming Home Party

A seventh pastoral approach is to cohost LGBTQ coming home party. The coming home party is described in Larry Kent Graham's chapter titled "The Role of Straight Allies in Pastoral Care of Lesbians and Gay" in Miguel A. De La Torre's book *Out of the Shadows into the Light: Christianity and Homosexuality* (2009). It is also alluded to in Cody J. Sanders's book *A Brief Guide to Ministry with LGBTQIA Youth* (2017).

A coming home party is akin to an individual person's coming out as gay, lesbian, bisexual, or transgender, but with a celebration attached to it in some way. Being true to who they are for the first time with themselves and their family. For example, I think of a soldier who has been overseas for a couple of years and has returned safely home to his mom and dad and to his family. Coming home is fully embracing one's sexual expression and gender identity, perhaps for the very first time, but also celebrating that reality with family members and close friends. It is a coming home to God, too.

When planning a coming home party, it should be a celebration and festival that supports the person's sense of self-worth and identity. A coming home ideally is a coming home to friends, to family and to God.[9] The young person should feel the love of her/his community, family, and friends. It should be a joyful affair! Sanders refers to this coming home process as "inviting the family in" to the celebration.[10] Support and advocacy of the young person and their self-awareness and self-expression of their new sexual expression or gender identity is of paramount importance. Sanders points out that the LGBTQ young person is the real *host* of the coming home party and is the person who invites the proper people to the celebration. I am advocating here that the youth and/or young adult minister be encouraging of this process and be open and willing to cohost the coming home party at the church. Helping to cohost the party demonstrates affirmation and solidarity with the young person who is coming out.

Strategy # 8: Plan and Create an LGBTQ Worship Service

This eighth pedagogical method is to plan and create an LGBTQ worship service. Prayer is an essential component within Christian discipleship, but it is also the bedrock of the Christian/Catholic faith. One scenario could

9. Graham, "Role of Straight Allies," 115.
10. Sanders, *Brief Guide*, 67.

be to bring in a liturgical planning team to plan, create, and implement an LGBTQ worship service for either youth or young adults. However, one crucial element of the planning must be taken seriously, that is, queer youth and young adults must be part of the liturgical planning team.

The spirit of the worship service is to have all people gathered in steadfast faith to feel welcomed, affirmed, comfortable, and safe to express themselves fully, openly, and without judgment or harassment. The worship experience would ideally be open to the entire parish and could be on any night of the week. I would imagine the service looking something like this:

- The worship service could begin with song and with a liturgical procession or liturgical dance.

- A reading from the Lectionary or Bible (Prov 11:14; Matt 5:39; John 15:19; Gal 3:28; Rom 1:16; 13:1–2; 14:5; 1 Cor 9:22; 10:23; Acts 5:39; 2 Tim 2:1–15; 4:3; Rev 7:9);

- A variety of music selections, both contemporary and classical, a variety of musical instruments being played, perhaps a procession with rhythmic dancers;

- PowerPoint slides of pictures representing sexual minorities could be shown while the service is taking place;

- A dynamic and energetic pro-LGBTQ preacher—and this is an absolute must—perhaps delivered by an ordained minister or from another denomination who is an LGBTQ ally;

- The worship service could end with a concluding prayer, song, and a liturgical recession or liturgical dance.

A small reception afterward would be a nice addition to the evening.

The purpose of this strategy is to be multidimensional: (1) to help eradicate prejudice, (2) to welcome LGBTQ young people, (3) to embrace diversity and multiculturalism, (4) to break down social barriers, (5) to provide people with a dynamic and inspirational prayer experience, and (6) to worship God in prayer, song, and dance. This strategy could do wonders for a community that was struggling to be more affirming of LGBTQ people in the community and holding on tightly to the belief that the only valid relationship is between a man and a woman.

Strategy # 9: Transgender Film Series

A ninth pastoral technique is for a youth or young adult minister to develop and host a five- or six-week film series on transgender issues and discuss the pertinent themes that a given movie addresses. Like the lesbian, gay, and bisexual movie series, this strategy also may require permission slips to be handed out in advance, since most films are R rated. Transgender cinema covers an array of gender topics and issues: gender dysphoria, gender discrimination and violence, taboo cultural customs, suicide because of gender, intersex, sexual confirmation surgery, and multicultural transgender teenager topics. Here are some of my favorite transgender movies: *Boys Don't Cry* (1999), *Beautiful Boxer* (2003), *Transamerica* (2005), *Tomboy* (2011), *Laurence Anyways* (2012), *3 Generations* (2015), *The Danish Girl* (2016), *They* (2017), *Strong Island* (2018), *Girl* (2018), *Work in Progress* (2020), *Cowboys* (2021), and *Framing Agnes* (2022).. The youth and/or young adult minister should preview each of these films for substance. Moreover, keep in mind that the evening may be emotional due to the content of the movies.

Strategy # 10: Create an LGBTQ Book Club

A tenth pragmatic approach is to create an LGBTQ book club. Read and discuss a different book each month with a group of interested young people. The benefit of this implementation strategy is that it can take place on the church campus or off the church property. Below is a list of LGBTQ books that one state's department of education has included in their high school reading list.

1. *Orlando: A Biography* (1928), by Virginia Woolf

2. *Giovanni's Room* (1956), by James Baldwin

3. *The Color Purple* (1982), by Alice Walker

4. *Oranges Are Not the Only Fruit* (1985), by Jeanette Winterson

5. *Middlesex* (2002), by Jeffrey Eugenides

6. *Boy Meets Boy* (2003), by David Levithan

7. *Rose of No Man's Land* (2005), by Michelle Tea

8. *Luna* (2006), by Julie Anne Peters

9. *Fun House: A Family Tragicomic* (2006), by Alison Bechdel

10. *Hero* (2007), by Perry Moore

11. *I Am J* (2011), by Chris Beam

12. *Refuse* (2011), by Elliott DeLine

13. *The Difference between You and Me* (2012), by Madeleine George

14. *Being Emily* (2014), by Rachel Gold

15. *Some Assembly Required* (2014), by Arin Andrews

16. *The Art of Being Normal* (2015), by Lisa Williamson

17. *If I Was Your Girl* (2016), by Meredith Russo

18. *Tash Hearts Tolstoy* (2017), by Kathryn Ormsbee

19. *It's Not Like It's a Secret* (2018), by Misa Sugiura

20. *If You Only Knew* (2019), by Jamie Ivey

21. *Felix Ever After* (2020), by Kacen Callender

There are thousands more that are applicable and appropriate for a book discussion club. The purpose of this strategy is to allow LGBT+ young people to understand themselves while also allowing the larger youth and/or young adult community to befriend them and come to know their struggles and stigmatization as a sexual minority.

Strategy # 11: Build or Remodel a Transgender Bathroom

This eleventh strategy is a pragmatic, fun, and a hands-on approach for young people. Transgender youth and young adults are often seen as the "lepers" of today. Transgender young people are the marginalized and are the outcasts, and Christians are called to minister and include. I have seldom seen a transgender specific bathroom in a youth and young adult ministry space or church. A good initiative for youth and young adult ministry is to rebuild or remodel an existing bathroom for transgender young people.

If I were a youth or young adult minister serving a particular congregation, I would paint the bathroom in colors that appeal to the young people of your congregation. Use bright and vibrant colors, not simply white or beige; it would have cool lighting and a colored toilet and sink, and most importantly, the sign on the door would read "Trans Bathroom" or "Gender-Neutral Washroom," or "Unisex."

This may seem like an insignificant strategy, but it is designed to create a safe environment and provide privacy for transgender young people, who are more likely to suffer maltreatment and violence, verbal harassment (54%), physical attack (24%), and sexual assault (13%) than non-transgender young people.[11] Therefore, Christian youth and young adult ministers would be wise to lead by example in this battle taking place in our country that many politicians are calling the "bathroom bill." By building a transgender bathroom, ministries are normalizing transgendered persons, affirming their personhood, and creating a safe place. Remember, transgender rights are human rights issues.

Strategy # 12: Hold an LGBTQ Town Hall Meeting

This twelfth methodology is useful because it can allow all people in the parish or congregation to be heard. The main reason to hold a town hall meeting would be to identify the objectives of the youth and young adult ministry. One scenario could be to discuss the best way to approach being open and affirming to LGBTQ young people. Another scenario could be to discuss the best and most direct way to minister to the LGBTQ young people in the congregation.

The town hall meeting should invite everyone in the parish to attend and participate. However, key members of the parish should be invited: parish staff, adolescents, young adults, lay ministers, and parents of tweens and teens. The event should have widespread promotion, at least two months in advance through written and verbal announcements, but also on social media and the parish website. The aim of the town hall meeting is to promote awareness about the realities that LGBTQ young people face daily, but also to do something as a parish for sexual minorities by way of ministry.

Strategy 13: Plan an LGBTQ Walk/Run

A thirteenth practical approach is to plan and host a walk/run called "Stand Up!" The walk/run could be either a full marathon (26.2 miles), half marathon (13.1 miles), or 10-K (6 miles). The walk/run could be advertised at local schools, churches, and youth, campus, and young adult ministries to raise awareness of about LGBTQ young people. Such an event would

11. James et al., *Report of the 2015 U.S. Transgender Survey*, 4.

begin to create moral and transformational leaders for those young people who helped to plan, organize, and implement the walk/run.[12] The run/walk would need to be planned at least six months in advance to get publicity and the proper exposure out to the public. The purpose of this strategy is to raise awareness about the social stigmas that face LGBTQ young people. However, the event could also be a fund raising activity for the youth and/ or young adult ministries. At the event, there could be locations where pamphlets and literature are provided about LGBTQ young people and the social stereotyping they face and endure on a daily basis. Besides being a physically healthy alternative method for raising public awareness about LGBTQ young people, it is also a great way to collaborate with other nonprofit organizations (YMCA, adoption agencies, social services, United Way, etc.) on this important issue.

Strategy 14: Providing Ongoing Spiritual and Pastoral Care

A fourteenth pragmatic technique is probably the most rudimentary of all the strategies. This approach provides basic spiritual accompaniment, pastoral care, and moral guidance to LGBTQ young people for a variety of reasons: depression, loneliness, frustration (anger), same-sex attraction, feeling rejected, being bullied, gender dysphoria, and suicidal ideation. Not all young people's needs are serious; it may be that a young person simply wants someone to listen to her/his needs.

Pastoral theologian Carrie Doehring insists that young people simply need a place where they feel comfortable and safe, and feel encouraged to tell their stories. "Stories allow people to lament with each other—express anger and question all they know about life—without imposing meanings prematurely."[13] This type of listening and pastoral care is more akin to *mentoring* and having a ministry of *presence*, which invites and encourages dialogue and personal narratives to emerge.

Catholic psychologist Janelle Hallman notes that there are several pastoral care tips for youth and young adult ministers to engage in with LGBTQ young people. Hallman offers ten guidelines for youth, campus, and young adult ministers to utilize while working with LGBTQ young people:

1. Show delight in young people,

---

12. Canales, "Models of Christian Leadership," 41.
13. Doehring, *Practice of Pastoral Care*, xv.

2. Become their student and learn from them,

3. Stop speaking carelessly,

4. Resign from being God's "moral cop,"

5. Develop into a person who can offer empathy and mercy,

6. Refresh your own understanding of love,

7. Challenge your own beliefs,

8. Exchange fear-based relating with heart-focused connection,

9. Be different and open-minded, and

10. Be courageous and preserving in compassion and grace.[14]

These ten guidelines seem very doable for any caring and competent minister.

Certainly, the majority of youth, campus, and young adult ministers can provide a listening ear and basic pastoral care to their flock; however, something more delicate may require more in-depth training and education. Therefore, it would be wise for larger parishes to have a professionally trained and certified spiritual director and/or pastoral counselor on staff. Congregations that offer spiritual direction and pastoral counseling to LGBTQ young people demonstrate their affection and affirmation for them as young people.

Strategy 15: Utilizing the Queer Theology of Miguel A. De La Torre

This fifteenth and final strategy is ambitious and utilizes one particular queer theologian—Miguel A. De La Torre (one of my theological heroes), and applies his queer theology to youth and young adult ministry. This is a strategy that gears itself to a more experienced youth or young adult minister who has read significantly about queer theology. There are plenty of brilliant queer theologians, but I think De La Torre's work is more accessible for most youth and young adult ministers.

For this strategy, I recommend three of De La Torre's books: *Reading the Bible from the Margins* (2002), *Out of the Shadows into the Light: Christianity and Homosexuality* (2009), and *Liberating Sexuality: Justice Between the Sheets* (2016). The books are to be used as the main curriculum that

14. Hallman, "Do No Harm," 219–43.

a youth and/or young adult ministry uses throughout the ministry year. Some parts of his work can be used as a main topic for evangelization and catechesis, while other parts could be used as weekly Bible study topics.

Here is a simple eight-week methodology using De La Torre's books for a Sunday evening large gathering, which is more evangelistic and catechetical in scope.

- **Week One:** Learning to Read the Bible (*Reading the Bible from the Margins*, 1–35).

- **Week Two:** Reading the Bible from the Center (*Reading the Bible from the Margins*, 36–54).

- **Week Three:** Unmasking the Biblical Justification of Racism and Classism (*Reading the Bible from the Margins*, 54–81).

- **Week Four:** Unmasking the Biblical Justification of Sexism *Reading the Bible from the Margins*, 82–103).

- **Week Five:** Sex and Sexism (*Liberating Sexuality: Justice Between the Sheets*, 62–95).

- **Week Six:** Confronting Sexual Abuse (*Liberating Sexuality: Justice Between the Sheets*, 96–117).

- **Week Seven:** Confronting Sexism (*Liberating Sexuality: Justice Between the Sheets*, 118–41).

- **Week Eight:** Confronting Heterosexism (*Liberating Sexuality: Justice Between the Sheets*, 142–65).

These presentations and discussions will move youth and young adults into a much deeper understanding of the subtleties and nuances of biblical interpretation and the danger of taking a literal perspective of the Bible.

Concurrently with the above scheme, but on another night of the week, let's say on Wednesday evenings, an eight-week Bible Study could be done around some of the clobber passages in the Scriptures utilizing De La Torre's book *Liberating Sexuality: Justice Between the Sheets* (ch. 19, 142–46, and ch. 21, 156–64). Here is a suggested sample using De La Torre and the NIV translation of the Bible:

- **Week One:** The So-Called Sin of Sodom (Gen 19:1–29).

- **Week Two:** The Sin of Ham (Gen 9:20–27).

- **Week Three:** The Law and Holiness Code (Lev 18:22; 20:13).

- **Week Four:** Wearing Women's Garments/Cross-Dressing (Deut 22:5).

- **Week Five:** Being True to Our "True Nature" (Rom 1:26–27).

- **Week Six:** Exclusion of Sexual Abusers (1 Cor 6:9; 1 Tim 1:10).

- **Week Seven:** Sex with Angels—Really? (2 Pet 2:4–8; Jude 6–7).

- **Week Eight:** Jesus, Eunuchs, and Transgender Folks (Matt 19:12; Acts 8:26–40).

These eight weekly Bible studies will give young people a great comprehension of the biblical texts that will empower them to use twenty-first-century logic and love in supporting and advocating for queer folks.

Of course, the scheme listed above just scratches the surface of the type of ministry programing that can be accomplished by integrating De La Torre's books. Once a youth or young adult minister decides on and reads De La Torre's books and hopefully studies them with her/his core team of volunteers, then the ministry team can decide the best course of action using this pastoral method.

Parting Remarks

I hope that these pastoral strategies will excite youth and young adult ministers to feel more confident in their abilities to address and discuss LGBTQ issues within their respective ministries. My hope is also that youth and young adult ministry educators and scholars will use these pedagogical methods in their classrooms when addressing the reality of ministering to LGBTQ young people.

Taken together, these fifteen pastoral strategies and approaches offer pedagogical support and pastoral implementation methodologies for Christian youth and young adult ministers. These ideas can benefit the entire youth and young adult ministry and will demonstrate that youth and young adult ministry can stand in solidarity with LGBTQ young people. These pastoral methodologies addressed engage young people on several LGBTQ issues, themes, and principles, but they are *only* suggestions, and youth ministers, campus high school ministers, and young adult ministers will have to discern which pedagogical practices work best for their circumstances and parish constituents.

Reflection and/or Discussion Questions

1. Which of these pastoral strategies do you like the best? Explain.

2. Which one of these pedagogical approaches do you think you could implement the easiest in your youth or young adult ministry?

3. What keeps you from experimenting in utilizing one of these practical strategies in your ministry?

4. What or who is the biggest obstacle for your congregation or parish to begin the planning process to integrate one or two of these suggested methodologies?

5. Can you think of any other pastoral strategies for LGBTQ young people that was not listed in this chapter?

Conclusion

God has created all human beings equal in rights, duties, and dignity, and has called them to live together as brothers and sisters . . . The transcendent dignity of the human person who, as the visible image of the invisible God, is therefore, by [her] very nature the subject of rights that no one may violate.

—POPE FRANCIS
Fratelli Tutti, §§5 & 273

PASTORAL CARE TO AND *Ministry with LGBTQ Youth and Young Adults* has been about advocating for LGBTQ folks in general, and LGBTQ youth and young adults in particular. My sincere hope is that readers have been able to glean several new insights from this book, as well as a few ideas to integrate in their own ministries or in the classroom.

This book is for a wide audience: pastors, parents, youth and young adult ministers, and youth and young adult ministry educators and scholars. The book has offered both sound theology and solid pastoral practice with the anticipation that youth and young adult ministers will utilize its content in both theory and practice.

The theology that has been utilized and discussed throughout this book to help youth and young adult ministers is both pastoral theology and liberation theology. The methodological tool to help situate this pastoral care and ministry model for LGBTQ young people is the hermeneutical circle of observing, reflecting, prayer, acting, and reassessing. It is that theological framework that undergirds this book because it takes into account the oppressed, marginalized, and disenfranchised person—in the case of this book—LGBTQ young people.

Praxis or reflection on pastoral practice is another facet of this book. The book reflects on the way Christians do ministry with LGBTQ young people. It is clear from reading the book that Christian ministry practice can be more open and affirming with LGBTQ young people. It is also evident that advocacy, support, and pastoral care may come in different forms and practices.

Three areas are significant to me that I have tried to communicate throughout this book. I believe they are important for empowering young people and their journey of self-discovery and self-actualization. The points are: (1) accompaniment, (2) ecumenism, and (3) interculturality.

Accompaniment: This book has provided ways for youth and young adult ministers to accompany LGBTQ young people. As these chapters have shown, there are a myriad of ways that youth and/or young adult ministers can accompany LGBTQ people: acknowledging them as human beings, listening to their specific needs, supporting their personal decisions without being judgmental, advocating for their personal autonomy, and helping them on their journey of self-discovery. Accompaniment is about walking with the LGBTQ young person and being in solidarity with them as they discern *their* direction and life path.[1]

Accompaniment brings to mind two Scripture pericopes: (1) the Good Samaritan and (2) the Road to Emmaus. The Good Samaritan parable (Luke 10:25–37) emphasizes the need to help others, to accompany them, not abandon them in times of distress and uncertainty. The accompaniment motif is strong in this passage and indicates that God's reign is radically inclusive and God's love is emphatically hospitable. The Road to Emmaus narrative (Luke 24: 13–35) is about being open to the stranger and listening to her with an open mind and heart with no expectation other than to accompany the other person. Just as Jesus takes, breaks, and blesses the Eucharistic bread in this story, he takes, breaks, and blesses young people's brokenness, pain, insecurity, loneliness, and fear.

---

1. Canales, "Pope Francis' Theology of Young People," 100–101.

Accompaniment with LGBTQ young people is the minimum pastoral care that needs to be happening in our Christian congregations, high schools, and college campuses. Moreover, accompaniment is also something that will generate much trust, respect, and friendship between the youth and/or young adult minister and the LGBTQ young person.

Ecumenism: The second and significant aspect of this book is that it is ecumenical. LGBTQ people, the issues surrounding LGBT folks, and their rights are every Christian denominations' responsibility. In my mind, Christian youth and young adult ministry should always be ecumenical and sensitive to others' beliefs. Those who work in youth and young adult ministry are called to build bridges, to be inclusive, and to collaborate with others toward unity.

Working with an ecumenical spirit is paramount because it demonstrates openness and respect toward all Christian churches and maintains that not any particular denomination holds all the truth of Christianity. However, working together can be challenging at times. Collaboration is part of the ecumenical process and is part of ensuring that LGBTQ young people be seen, heard, and valued.

Interculturality: Any ministry with young people today needs to be multicultural and inclusive. Cultural diversity is part of sexual minorities' realties. Inclusive ministry is the "name of the game" in youth and young adult ministry because young people will simply not tolerate anyone who is not open-minded toward folks who are different than they appear.

Intercultural youth and young adult ministry is necessary for LGBTQ young people to feel welcome. Today's young people live, work, and play in a multicultural and multifaith world, and youth and young adult ministry would be wise to focus of the cues of society to help in their pastoral care to and ministry with LGBTQ young people.

Embracing sexual minorities is part and parcel of being intercultural, culturally diverse, and inclusive. Youth and young adult ministry has a duty to embrace all God's children, LGBTQ folks included, and to do otherwise would be offensive in the extreme. Youth and young adult ministry has a real opportunity to lead Christian churches in tolerance, unity, and diversity.

These three areas—accompaniment, ecumenism, and interculturality—are essential elements to youth and young adult ministry. The future task of youth and young adult ministry is to move forward in these three areas to help enhance ministry with the LGBTQ community.

Christian churches need bold initiatives, fresh ideas, and new thinking when it comes to pastoral care to and ministry with LGBTQ young people. This book is an attempt to help youth and young adult ministers to: (1) *equip* them with knowledge of LGBTQ issues and topics, (2) *increase* their understanding of pastoral care to and ministry with LGBTQ people, and (3) *enhance* their skill set of pastoral strategies and pedagogical methods for working with LGBTQ young people. There is much work that needs to be done with LGBTQ youth and young adults, but I am confident and optimistic that Christian churches will open their minds and hearts to welcome and affirm this marginalized group.

LGBTQ youth and young adults are often alienated and misunderstood, but that does not mean that Christianity should be indifferent to their importance. LGBTQ youth and young adult lives matter! LGBTQ lives matter because queer young people are created in the image and likeness of God. LGBTQ lives matter because queer youth and young adults are fellow sojourners on the earth. LGBTQ lives matter because queer lives are sexual and gender minorities in a world that still needs equality and liberation.

Finally, I sincerely believe that those who support LGBTQ people, and advocate for LGBTQ rights and issues, stand on the factual side of the Gospels, stand on the correct side of justice, stand on the accurate side of humanity, and stand on the right side of history. I have been proud to stand in solidarity with my LGBTQ sisters and brothers over the years!

I have spent almost ten years writing, researching, and speaking (nationally and internationally) on LGBTQ youth and young adult ministry topics. For the most part, my thoughts and ideas have been widely appreciated and respected. However, I do believe that the Good Lord is calling me to reflect and write in other areas. Therefore, this *might* be one of my last publications on this particular topic; but do not worry, I still have much to say and write on other theological and ministry topics.

About the Author

ARTHUR DAVID CANALES, DMIN, is a third-generation Mexican American. Dr. Canales and his wife, Tanya, have three children: Alex, Anna, and Albert. They live in Indianapolis, Indiana, where Dr. Canales is professor of pastoral theology and ministry at Marian University. Dr. Canales is considered one of the foremost Catholic youth and young adult ministry scholars and educators in the United States and abroad. Dr. Canales also teaches ministry courses at Boston College in the summer. Dr. Canales teaches two courses that center on LGBTQ theology and ministry: Christianity and Sexual Minorities at Marian University; and Ministering to the LGBTQ Community at Boston College.

Dr. Canales began his education career at Ohio University (Athens, OH), and transferred and earned a baccalaureate degree from Florida International University (Miami). He holds a master of arts degree from University of Miami (Coral Gables, FL), a master of divinity degree from the Catholic University of America (Washington, DC), and a master of arts in liturgical studies degree from the University of Notre Dame (South Bend, IN). Dr. Canales earned his doctor of ministry degree from the Catholic University of America (Washington, DC) with a major areas of specialty in pastoral theology and liturgical and sacramental theology and areas of concentration in pastoral care and counseling. His doctoral dissertation is titled "Toward a Theological, Liturgical, and Pastoral Understanding of Sunday Parish Worship with Deacon and/or Lay Presiders."

Dr. Canales has previously served as a parish youth minister (Miami; Washington, DC; and Beltsville, MD), a college campus minister (Coral Gables, FL), diocesan director of youth and young adult ministry (Austin, TX), and as an assistant/associate professor of theology and ministry at Silver Lake College of the Holy Family (Manitowoc, WI) and Saint Edward's University (Austin, TX). Dr. Canales is also the creator of and an instructor for the Diocese of Austin's Youth Ministry Certification Program. Dr. Canales has written approximately forty pastoral-theological and catechetical-educational essays for the *Herald Times Reporter* newspaper in Manitowoc, Wisconsin (2000–2006) in their Beliefs section.

Dr. Canales has written for various pastoral and scholarly publications: *Pastoral Music* (1996), *Ministry* (2000), *Living Light* (2002), *Journal of Pentecostal Theology* (2003), *Journal of the Association of Franciscan Colleges and Universities* (2004, 2016), *Catechumenate* (2005, 2005), *Apuntes Reflexiones Teológicas* (2005, 2005), *Religious Education* (2006, 2014), *Journal of the American Academy of Religion* (2006), *New Theology Review* (2007, 2016), *Stewardship Reflections* (2008), *Emmanuel: Eucharistic Spirituality* (2009, 2010), *International Journal of Children's Spirituality* (2009), *Journal of Youth Ministry* (2010, 2021), *Pastoral Liturgy* (2010), *Chicago Studies* (2011), *Verbum Incarnatum* (2011), *International Journal of Religious Education* (2012), *The Bible Today* (2013), *Journal of Youth and Theology* (2015, 2022), *Journal of Pastoral Theology* (2018), *Journal of Pastoral Care & Counseling* (2018, 2018), *Religions* (2020), and *Psychiatria Danubina* (2021).

Dr. Canales has also written chapters in two books: "Early Adolescence: Venturing toward a Different World," in *Human Development and Faith: Life-Cycle Stages of Body, Mind, and Soul*, edited by Felicity B. Kelcourse (Chalice, 2015, pp. 211–30), and "Providing Pastoral Care and Spiritual Care to Transgender People in Chaplaincy Settings," in *Multifaith Perspectives in Spiritual & Religious Care: Change, Challenge and Transformation*, edited by Mohamed Taher (Canadian Multifaith Federation, 2020; pp. 250–58). He has served as guest editor to the international journal *Religions*, which did a special issue on "Catholic Youth & Young Adult Ministry," which became an edited book (2021).

Dr. Canales has also authored or coauthored four books: coauthor of *Keeping the Cup Full: Financial Stewardship for Teens and Young Adults* (Cornerstone, 2008; 2009); *A Noble Quest: Cultivating Spirituality in Catholic Adolescents* (PCG Legacy, 2011); *Ceasel the Weasel* (Tate, 2014); *Models*

& Methods for Youth & Young Adult Ministry: Ecumenical Examples and Pastoral Approaches for the Christian Church (Cascade, 2018).

Dr. Canales is a member of National Catholic Youth Ministry Leaders Association (USA), Association of Youth Ministry Educators (USA), and International Association for the Study of Youth Ministry (UK), National Association of Lay Ministry (USA), and the American Association of Pastoral Counselors (USA). He is involved with the National Initiative on Adolescent Catechesis (USA) and is a consultant for *Fe y Vida* (USA). Dr. Canales is a contributing editor to a joint USCCB and NFCYM document titled *The Joy of Adolescent Catechesis: A Letter to Those Who Minister with Catholic Teenagers in the United States* (2017). He is also part of the National Dialogue on Youth & Young Adults (USA) that will produce a new ecclesial document for the Catholic Church on youth and young adult ministry. Moreover, Dr. Canales is a peer-referee/reviewer for *New Theology Review, Religious Education* and *Journal of Youth Ministry*.

Dr. Canales has presented over twenty-five keynote speeches and over one hundred workshops, seminars, and academic papers in over forty dioceses in the United States and abroad. He is a sought-after keynote speaker and popular workshop presenter on areas of Christian discipleship, pastoral theology, youth and young adult ministry, and LGBTQ ministry. Dr. Canales also provides ministry mentoring with undergraduate and graduate ministry students and pastoral supervision with youth and young adult ministers throughout the city of Indianapolis and online/virtually around the country.

Bibliography

Each source that I read, I would look through the bibliography and the footnotes, and use that as a map for the next thing I would read.

—ALEXANDER CHEE

Achtemeier, Mark. *The Bible's Yes to Same-Sex Marriage: An Evangelical's Change of Heart.* Louisville: Westminster John Knox, 2014.

Alison, James. *Faith beyond Resentment: Catholic and Gay.* New York: Crossroad, 2002.

Althaus-Reid, Marcella. *Indecent Theology: Theological Perversions in Sex, Gender, and Politics.* London: Routledge, 2000.

———. *The Queer God.* London: Routledge, 2003.

Aquinas, Thomas. "Of Right." In *The Summa Theologica of Saint Thomas Aquinas: Complete English Edition.* Westminster, MD: Christian Classics, 1981.

Arzola, Fernando, Jr. *Toward a Prophetic Youth Ministry: Theory and Praxis in Urban Context.* Downers Grove: IVP Academic, 2008.

Bagemihl, Bruce. *Biological Exuberance: Animal Homosexuality and Natural Diversity.* New York: St. Martin's, 1999.

Bailey, Derrick Sherwin. *Homosexuality and the Western Christian Tradition.* London: Longmans, Green, 1955.

Bayly, Michael J. *Creating Environments for LGBTQ Students: A Catholic Schools Perspective.* New York: Harrington Park, 2007.

Bergant, Dianne. "Reading the Signs of the Times." *America* 187 (2003) 38–39. https://www.americamagazine.org/faith/2003/11/24/reading-signs-times.

Bevans, Stephen B. *Models of Contextual Theology: Faith and Cultures.* Maryknoll: Orbis, 2011.

Bhabha, Homi K. *The Location of Culture.* New York: Routledge, 1994.

Bibliography

Bonino, José Míguez. *Toward a Christian Political Ethic*. Philadelphia: Fortress, 1993.

Boswell, John. *Christianity, Social Tolerance, and Homosexuality: Gay People in Western Europe from the Beginning of the Christian Era to the Fourteenth Century*. Chicago: University of Chicago Press, 1980.

Brill, Stephanie, and Lisa Kenny. *The Transgender Teen: A Handbook for Parents and Professionals Supporting Transgender and Non-binary Teens*. Jersey City: Cleis, 2016.

Brooten, Bernadette J. *Love between Women: Early Christian Responses to Female Homoeroticism*. Chicago: University of Chicago Press, 1996.

Burgess, Christian. "Internal and External Stress Factors Associated with the Identity Development of Transgender and Gender Variant Youth." In *Social Work Practice with Transgendered and Gender Variant Youth*, edited by Gerald P. Mallon, 39–51. London: Routledge, 2009.

Burke, Kevin F. "Thinking about the Church: The Gift of Cultural Diversity." In *Many Faces, One Church: Cultural Diversity and the American Catholic Experience*, edited by Peter C. Phan and Diana Hayes, 27–47. Lanham, MD: Sheed & Ward, 2005.

Burns, Virginia. *The Sex Lives of Saints: An Erotic of Ancient Hagiography*. Philadelphia: University of Pennsylvania Press, 2004.

Campbell, Colleen and Thomas Carani, *The Art of Accompaniment: Theological, Spiritual, and Pastoral Elements of Building a More Relational Church*. Washington, DC: Catholic Apostolate Center, 2019.

Canales, Arthur David. "The Biblical-Hermeneutical Model for Youth Ministry: Four Scriptural and Pedagogical Approaches for Youth Workers." *Bible Today* 51 (2013) 237–47.

———. "Christian Discipleship: The Primordial Model for Comprehensive Catholic Youth Ministry." *Journal of Religious Education* 60 (2012) 35–45.

———. "Ministry to Catholic LGBTQ Youth: A Call for Openness and Affirmation." *New Theology Review* 28 (March 2016) 60–71.

———. "Ministry to Transgender Teenagers (Part One): Pursuing Awareness and Understanding about Trans Youth." *Journal of Pastoral Care & Counseling* 72 (2018) 195–201.

———. "Ministry to Transgender Teenagers (Part Two): Providing Pastoral Care, Support, and Advocacy to Trans Youth." *Journal of Pastoral Care & Counseling* 72 (2018) 251–56.

———. *Models & Methods for Youth & Young Adult Ministry: Ecumenical Examples and Pastoral Approaches for the Christian Church*. Eugene, OR: Cascade, 2018.

———. "Models of Christian Leadership in Youth Ministry." *Religious Education* 109 (2014) 24–44.

———. *A Noble Quest: Cultivating Spirituality in Catholic Adolescents*. Waco, TX: Pilot, 2011.

———. "Pastoral & Spiritual Care to Transgender People." In *Multifaith Perspectives in Canadian Spiritual & Religious Care*, edited by Mohamed Taher, 250–56. Toronto: Canadian Multifaith Federation, 2020.

———. "Pope Francis' Theology of Young People: The Impact It Will Have for Catholic Youth and Young Adult Ministry in the United States." *Journal of Youth Ministry* 19 (2021) 90–110.

———. "The Ten-Year Anniversary of *Renewing the Vision*: Reflection on Its Impact for Catholic Youth Ministry." *New Theology Review* 20 (2007) 58–69.

Bibliography

―――. "Transforming Teenagers: Integrating Social Justice into Catholic Youth Ministry or Catholic Education." *Verbum Incarnatum* 4 (2010) 69–91.

Canales, Arthur David, and Matthew Sherman. "Franciscan Campus Ministries and LGBTQ Emerging Adults: Providing Moral Guidance and a Pastoral Plan." *AFCU Journal: A Franciscan Perspective on Higher Education* 13 (May 2016) 36–52.

Chee, Alexander. *How to Write an Autobiographical Novel.* Boston: Mariner, 2018.

Cheng, Patrick S. *Radical Love: An Introduction to Queer Theology.* New York: Seabury, 2011.

Coleman, Gerald D. *Homosexuality: Catholic Teaching and Pastoral Practice.* Mahwah, NJ: Paulist, 1996.

Congregation for Catholic Education. *Male and Female He Created Them: Towards a Path of Dialogue on the Question of Gender Theory in Education.* Vatican City: Libreria Editrice Vaticana, 2019.

Congregation for the Doctrine of Faith. *Considerations regarding Proposals to Give Legal Recognition to Unions between Homosexual Persons.* Vatican City: Libreria Editrice Vaticana, 2003.

―――. *Homosexualitas Problema.* Letter to All Catholic Bishops on the Pastoral Care of Homosexual Persons. Vatican City: Vatican Press, 1986.

Copeland, M. Shawn. *Enfleshing Freedom: Body, Race, and Being.* Minneapolis: Fortress, 2010.

Copper-White, Pamela. *Shared Wisdom: Use of Self in Pastoral Care and Counseling.* Minneapolis: Fortress, 2004.

Cottrell, Susan. *"Mom, I'm Gay": Loving Your LGBTQ Child and Strengthening Your Faith.* Louisville: Westminster John Knox, 2016.

Crowley, Paul G. "Homosexuality and the Counsel of the Cross." *Theological Studies* 65 (2004) 500–529.

DeFranza, Megan K. *Sex Difference in Christian Theology: Male, Female, and Intersex in the Image of God.* Grand Rapids: Eerdmans, 2015.

De La Torre, Miguel A. "Confessions of a Latino Macho: From Gay Basher to Gay Ally." In *Out of the Shadows into the Light: Christianity and Homosexuality,* edited by Miguel A. De La Torre, 59–75. St. Louis: Chalice, 2009.

―――. *Doing Christian Ethics from the Margins.* Maryknoll: Orbis, 2015.

―――. *Liberating Sexuality: Justice between the Sheets.* St. Louis: Chalice, 2016.

―――. *Reading the Bible from the Margins.* Maryknoll: Orbis, 2002.

Delio, Ilia. *Franciscan Prayer.* Cincinnati: St. Anthony Messenger, 2004.

Department of Catholic Education. *A Vision of Youth Ministry.* Washington, DC: United States Catholic Conference, 1976.

DeYoung, Kevin. *What Does the Bible Really Teach about Homosexuality?* Wheaton, IL: Crossway, 2015.

Dickey, Lore M., et al. "Non-Suicidal Self-Injury in a Large Online Sample of Transgender Adults." *Professional Psychology—Research and Practice* 46 (2015) 3–11.

Doehring, Carrie. *The Practice of Pastoral Care: A Postmodern Approach.* Rev. ed. Louisville: Westminster John Knox, 2015.

Doyle, Dennis M. *The Church Emerging from Vatican II: A Popular Approach to Contemporary Catholicism.* New London, CT: Twenty-Third, 2008.

―――. *What Is Christianity? A Dynamic Introduction.* Mahwah, NJ: Paulist, 2016.

Dunning, Gemma. "Integrity and *Imago Dei.*" In *4 Views on Pastoring LGBTQ Teenagers: Effective Ministry to Lesbian, Gay, Bi, Trans, Queer, and Questioning Students among Us,* edited by Mark Oesteicher, 11–32. San Diego: Youth Cartel, 2018.

Bibliography

Durso, Earnest, and G. J. Gates. "Serving Our Youth: Findings from a National Survey of Service Providers Working with Lesbian, Gay, Bisexual, and Transgender Youth Who Are Homeless or At Risk of Becoming Homeless." Los Angeles: Williams Institute and True Colors Fund and the Palette Fund, 2012.

Dykstra, Craig, and Dorothy C. Bass. "A Theological Understanding of Christian Practices." In *Practicing Theology: Beliefs and Practices in Christian Life*, edited by Miroslav Volf and Dorothy C. Bass, 13–32. Grand Rapids: Eerdmans, 2002.

Ellacuría, Ignacio. "Los Pobres, 'Lugar Teologico' en America Latina." In *Escritos Teológicos*, volume 1. San Salvador: UCA Editores, 2000.

Ellison, Marvin M. "Practicing Safer Spirituality: Changing the Subject and Focusing on Justice." In *Out of the Shadows into the Light: Christianity and Homosexuality*, edited by Miguel A. De La Torre, 1–18. St. Louis: Chalice, 2009.

Ellison, Marvin M., and Kelly Brown-Douglas. Introduction to *Sexuality and the Sacred: Sources for Theological Reflection*, xv–xxii. 2nd ed. Louisville: Westminster John Knox, 2010.

Fanor, Frantz. *The Wretched of the Earth*. Translated by Constance Farrington. New York: Grove, 1963.

Farley, Margaret A. *Just Love: A Framework for Christian Sexual Ethics*. New York: Continuum, 2006.

Feely, Katherine. "The Principle of Human Dignity." https://www.caritas.org.au/media/kjokhdon/education-for-justice-dignity.pdf?sfvrsn=dd1f90aa_0.

Feray, Jean-Claude. "Homosexual Studies and Politics in the 19th Century: Karl Maria Kertbeny." *Journal of Homosexuality* 19 (1990) 23–48.

Fischer, Kathleen, and Thomas Hart, *Christian Foundations: An Introduction to Faith in Our Time*. Mahwah, NJ: Paulist, 1997.

Foucault, Michael. *Religion and Culture*. New York: Routledge, 1999.

Francis, Leslie J., et al. "The Sexual Attitudes of Religiosity Committed Canadian Youth within the Convention of Atlantic Baptist Churches." *Journal of Youth & Theology* 12 (2013) 7–23.

Francis of Assisi. *Francis of Assisi Early Documents* (cited as *FAED*). Vol. 1, *The Saint*; vol. 2, *The Founder*; vol. 3, *The Prophet*. New York: New City, 2001.

Fulkerson, Mary McClintock. "The Imago Dei and a Reformed Logic for Feminist/Womanist Critique." In *Feminist and Womanist Essays in Reformed Dogmatics*, edited by Amy Plantinga-Pauw and Serene L. Jones, 95–106. Louisville: Westminster John Knox, 2006.

Funk, Tim. "Was She Denied Communion Because She'd Been Chewing Gum—or, Because She's Transgender?" *Charlotte Observer*, August 8, 2018.

Gagnon, Robert A. J. *The Bible and Homosexual Practice: Texts and Hermeneutics*. Nashville: Abingdon, 2001.

Gearhart, Sally. "The Miracle of Lesbianism." In *Loving Women / Loving Men: Gay Liberation and the Church*, edited by Sally Gearhart and William R. Johnson, 119–52. San Francisco: Glide, 1974.

Genovesi, Vincent J. *In Pursuit of Love: Catholic Morality and Human Sexuality*. 2nd ed. Collegeville: Liturgical, 1996.

Gilson, Etienne. *The Spirit of Mediaeval Philosophy*. Notre Dame: University of Notre Dame Press, 1991.

Gittings, Barbara B. "The Homosexual and the Church." In *The Same Sex: An Appraisal of Homosexuality*, edited by Ralph W. Weltge, 146–55. Philadelphia: Pilgrim, 1969.

Bibliography

Goss, Robert E. "Christian Homo-Devotion to Jesus." In *Queering Christ: Beyond Jesus Acted Up*, edited by Robert E. Gross edits, 113–39. Cleveland: Pilgrim, 2002.

Graham, Larry Kent. "The Role of Straight Allies in the Pastoral Care of Lesbians and Gays." In *Out of the Shadows into the Light: Christianity and Homosexuality*, edited by Miguel A. De La Torre, 104–20. St. Louis: Chalice, 2009.

Greenough, Chris. *Queer Theologies: The Basics*. New York: Routledge, 2020.

Greytak, Emily A., et al. "Putting the 'T' in 'Resource': The Benefits of LGBT-Related School Resources for Transgender Youth." *Journal of LGBT Youth* 10 (2013) 45–63.

Gridley, Samantha J., et al. "Youth and Caregiver Perspectives on Barriers to Gender-Affirming Health Care for Transgender Youth." *Journal of Adolescent Health* 59 (2016) 254–61.

Grossman, Arnold H., and Anthony R. D'Augelli. "Transgender Youth." *Journal of Homosexuality* 51 (2006) 111–28.

———. "Transgender Youth and Life-Threatening Behaviors." *Suicide and Life-Threatening Behavior* 37 (2007) 527–37.

Guest, Deryn. *When Deborah Met Jael: Lesbian Biblical Hermeneutics*. London: SCM, 2005.

Guest, Deryn, et al. *The Queer Bible Commentary*. London: SCM, 2006.

Haas, Ann P., et al. *Suicide Attempts among Transgender and Non-conforming Adults: Findings of the National Transgender Discrimination Survey*. Los Angeles: Williams Institute and American Foundation for Suicide Prevention, 2014.

Hallman, Janelle. "Do No Harm: Considerations in Supporting Youth with Same-Sex Attraction." In *Living the Truth in Love: Pastoral Approaches to Same-Sex Attraction*, edited by Janet E. Smith and Paul Check, 233–41. San Francisco: Ignatius, 2015.

Harvey, John F. *Homosexuality and the Catholic Church: Clear Answers to Difficult Questions*. West Chester, PA: Ascension, 2007.

Healy, Mary. *Scripture, Mercy, and Homosexuality*. El Cajon, CA: Catholic Answers, 2016.

Herman, Jody L., et al. *Age of Individuals Who Identify As Transgender in the United States*. Los Angeles: Williams Institute, 2017.

Heyward, Carter. *Touching Our Strength: The Erotic as Power and Love of God*. San Francisco: HarperSanFrancisco, 1989.

Higa, Darrel, et al. "Negative and Positive Factors Associated with the Well-Being of Lesbian, Gay, Bisexual, Transgender, Queer, and Questioning Youth." *Youth & Society* 20 (2012) 1–26.

Himbaza, Innocent, et al. *The Bible on the Question of Homosexuality*. Washington, DC: Catholic University of America Press, 2012.

Holland, Joseph, and Peter Henriot. *Social Analysis: Linking Faith and Justice*. Rev. ed. Maryknoll: Orbis, 2000.

Hornsby, Teresa J., and Deryn Guest. *Transgender, Intersex, and Biblical Interpretation*. Atlanta: SBL, 2016.

Huegel, Kelly. *GLBTQ: The Survival Guide for Gay, Lesbian, Bisexual, Transgender, and Questioning Teens*. Minneapolis: Free Spirit, 2011.

Ingham, Mary Beth, and Thomas A. Shannon. *The Ethical Method of John Duns Scotus*. Bonaventure, NY: Franciscan Institute, 1993.

International Theological Commission. *Communion and Stewardship: Human Persons Created in the Image of God*. Vatican City: International Theological Commission, 2002.

Bibliography

Jacober, Amy E. *The Adolescent Journey: An Interdisciplinary Approach*. Downers Grove: InterVarsity, 2011.

James, Sandy E., et al. *The Report of the 2015 U.S. Transgender Survey*. Washington, DC: National Center for Transgender Equality, 2016. https://transequality.org/sites/default/files/docs/usts/USTS-Full-Report-Dec17.pdf.

Johnson, Bill. "The Good News of Gay Liberation." In *Loving Women / Loving Men: Gay Liberation and the Church*, edited by Sally Gearhart and William R. Johnson, 91–117. San Francisco: Glide, 1974.

Jones, Kimbell H. *Toward a Christian Understanding of Homosexuality*. New York: Association, 1966.

Kellogg, Elizabeth A. "Transvestism, Transgenderism, and Deuteronomy 22:5." *Whosoever.org*, November 1, 1998. http://www.whosoever.org/v3i3/deut.html.

Kelly, Kevin. *New Directions in Sexual Ethics: Moral Theology and the Challenge of AIDS*. New York: Continuum, 1998.

Kim-Kort, Mihee. *Outside the Lines: How Embracing Queerness Will Transform Your Faith*. Minneapolis: Fortress, 2018.

King, Martin Luther, Jr. *Strength to Love*. Philadelphia: Fortress, 1963.

———. *Why We Can't Wait*. New York: New American Library, 1964.

Kinnaman, David, and Gabe Lyons. *Un-Christian: What a New Generation Really Thinks about Christianity and Why It Matters*. Grand Rapids: Baker, 2007.

Kolakowski, Victoria S. "Towards a Christian Ethical Response to Transsexual Persons." *Theology and Sexuality* 6 (1997) 10–31.

Kreeft, Peter. *Summa of the Summa: The Essential Philosophical Passages of St. Thomas Aquinas' Summa Theologica, Edited and Explained for Beginners*. San Francisco: Ignatius, 1990.

Krietemeyer, Ronald. *Leaven for the Modern World: Catholic Social Teaching and Catholic Education*. Washington, DC: National Catholic Education Association, 2000.

Kristeva, Julia. *Powers of Horror: An Essay on Abjection*. Translated by Leon S. Roudiez. New York: Columbia University Press, 1982.

Kundtz, David J., and Bernard S. Schlager. *Ministry among God's Queer Folk*. Cleveland: Pilgrim, 2007.

LaCugna, Catherine Mowry. *God for Us: The Trinity & Christian Life*. San Francisco: HarperCollins, 1991.

Legge, Dominic. "Do Thomists Have Rights?" *Nova et Vetera* 17 (2019) 127–47.

Leone, Katie. *The Transsexual and the Cross: Disproving the Myth that Transsexuality Is a Sin*. Lexington, KY: CreateSpace, 2013.

Levine, David A., et al. "Office-Based Care for Lesbian, Gay, Bisexual, Transgender, and Questioning Youth." *Pediatrics* 132 (2013) 198–203.

Loughlin, Gerard. "Introduction: The End of Sex." In *Queer Theology: Rethinking the Western Body*, edited by in Gerard Loughlin, 1–34. Malden, MA: Blackwell, 2007.

Lu, Rachel. "Eros Divided: Is There Such a Thing as Healthy Homoerotic Love?" In *Living the Truth in Love: Pastoral Approaches to Same-Sex Attractions*, edited by Janet E. Smith and Paul Check. San Francisco: Ignatius, 2015.

Maher, Michael J., and Linda M. Sever. "What Educators in Catholic Schools Might Expect When Addressing Gay and Lesbian Issues: A Study of Needs and Barriers." *Journal of Gay & Lesbian Issues in Education* 4 (2007) 79–111.

Martin, Del, and Phyllis Lyon. "A Lesbian Approach to Theology." In *Is Gay Good? Ethics, Theology, and Homosexuality,* edited by W. Dwight Oberholtzer, 213–20. Philadelphia: Westminster, 1971.

McGuine, Jennifer K., et al. "School Climate for Transgender Youth: A Mixed Method Investigation of Student Experiences and School Responses." *Journal of Adolescence* 39 (2010) 1175–88.

McNeil, John J. *The Church and the Homosexual.* Boston: Beacon, 1993.

Melina, Livio. "Homosexual Inclination as an 'Objective Disorder': Reflections of Theological Anthropology." In *Living the Truth in Love: Pastoral Approaches to Same-Sex Attractions,* edited by Janet E. Smith and Paul Check, 129–40. San Francisco: Ignatius, 2015.

Mizzoni, John. *Catholic and Franciscan Ethics: The Essentials.* Philadelphia: Cognella Academic, 2016.

Mollenkott, Virginia R. *Omnigender: A Trans-Religious Approach.* Cleveland: Pilgrim, 2001.

Montefiore, Huge William. "Jesus, the Revelation of God." In *Christ for Us Today,* edited by Norman Pittenger, 109–16. London: SMC, 1968.

Moore, Gareth. *A Question of Truth: Christianity and Homosexuality.* London: Continuum, 2003.

Myers, David G., and Letha Dawson Scanzoni. *What God Has Joined Together: The Christian Case for Gay Marriage.* San Francisco: HarperSanFrancisco, 2006.

National Center for Transgender Equality. "Transgender People and Bathroom Access." July 10, 2016. http://www.transequality.org/issues/resources/transgender-people-and-bathroom-access.

Nothwehr, Dawn M. *The Franciscan View of the Human Person.* Bonaventure, NY: Franciscan Institute, 2005.

Oord, Thomas Jay. "What Is Relational Theology?" In *Relational Theology: A Contemporary Introduction,* edited by Brint Montgomery et al., 1–6. Eugene, OR: Wipf & Stock, 2012.

Oraker, James R., and Janis Hahn. "The Church in Action: Asking Hard Questions." In *Out of the Shadows into the Light: Christianity and Homosexuality,* edited by Miguel A. De La Torre, 121–35. St. Louis: Chalice, 2009.

Owen, Gabrielle. "Adolescence." *Transgender Studies Quarterly* 1 (2014) 22–24.

Perry, Tony. *The Lord Is My Shepherd and He Knows I'm Gay.* Los Angeles: Nash, 1972.

Peterson, Claire M., et al. "Suicidality, Self-Harm, and Body Dissatisfaction in Transgender Adolescents and Emerging Adults with Gender Dysphoria." *Suicide and Life-Threatening Behavior* 47 (2017) 475–82.

Pew Research Center. "Most American Catholics Say Pope Francis Has Done at Least a Little to Make the Church More Accepting of Homosexuality, Divorce, and Remarriage." https://religiondocbox.com/Christianity/75803147-For-release-march-6-2018.html.

———. "Pope Francis Still Highly Regarded in U.S., but Signs of Disenchantment Emerge." https://www.pewforum.org/2018/03/06/pope-francis-still-highly-regarded-in-u-s-but-signs-of-disenchantment-emerge/.

Phillips, Robert. "Abjection." *Transgender Studies Quarterly* 1 (2014) 19–21.

Pitchford, Susan. *Following Francis: The Franciscan Way for Everyone.* Harrisburg, PA: Morehouse, 2006.

Pittenger, Norman. *Time for Consent? A Christian's Approach to Homosexuality.* London: SCM, 1976.

Placher, William C. *Jesus the Savior: The Meaning of Jesus Christ for Christian Faith.* Louisville: Westminster John Knox, 2001.

Pope Francis. *Christus Vivit.* Vatican City: Libreria Editrice Vaticana, 2019.

———. *Evangelii Gaudium.* Vatican City: Libreria Editrice Vaticana, 2015.

Pope John Paul II. *Catechism of the Catholic Church.* 2nd ed. Vatican City: Libreria Editrice Vaticana, 1997.

Pope Paul VI. *Gaudium et Spes* (Joy and Hope). Pastoral Constitution on the Church in the Modern World. December 7, 1965. https://www.vatican.va/archive/hist_councils/ ii_vatican_council/documents/vat-ii_const_19651207_gaudium-et-spes_en.html.

———. *Octogesima Adveniens* (The Eightieth Anniversary of *Rerum Novarum*). Vatican City: Libreria Editrice Vaticana, 1971.

Pope, Stephen J. "The Magisterium's Arguments Against 'Same Sex Marriage': An Ethical Analysis and Critique." *Theological Studies* 65 (2004) 530–65.

Reasoner, Mark. *Five Models of Scripture.* Grand Rapids, MI: William B. Eerdmans Publishing Company, 2021.

Reicherzer, Stacee, et al. "Counseling in the Periphery of Queer Discourse: Transgender Children, Adolescents, Women, and Men." In *Counseling Gay Men, Adolescents, and Boys: A Strength-Based Guide for Helping Professionals and Educators*, edited by Michael M. Kocet, 178–93. New York: Routledge, 2014.

Rejón, Francisco M. "Fundamental Moral Theology in the Theology of Liberation." In *Mysterium Liberationis: Fundamental Concepts of Liberation Theology*, edited by Ignacio Ellacuría and Jon Sobrino, 210–21. Maryknoll: Orbis, 1993.

Riggle, Ellen D. B., and Sharon S. Rostosky. *A Positive View of LGBTQ: Embracing Identity and Cultivating Well-Being.* Lanham, MD: Rowman & Littlefield, 2013.

Roberts, Vaughan. *Transgender.* Auckland, New Zealand: Good Book, 2016.

Root, Andrew, and Kenda Creasy Dean. *The Theological Turn in Youth Ministry.* Downers Grove: InterVarsity, 2011.

Sanabria, Samuel, and Joffrey S. Suprina. "Addressing Spirituality when Counseling Gay Boys, Adolescents, and Men." In *Counseling Gay Men, Adolescents, and Boys: A Strength-Based Guide for Helping Professionals and Educators*, edited by Michael M. Kocet, 52–65. New York: Routledge Group, 2014.

Sanders, Cody J. *A Brief Guide to Ministry with LGBTQIA Youth.* Louisville: Westminster John Knox, 2017.

———. "LGBTQ Pastoral Counseling: Setting a New Scholarly Agenda." *Sacred Spaces: E-Journal of the American Association of Pastoral Counselors* 8 (2016) 1–5.

Scanlon, Michael. "Postmodernism and Theology." *Ecumenist* 37 (2018) 15–24.

Scanzon, Letha Dawson, and Virginia Ramey Mollenkott. *Is the Homosexual My Neighbor? A Positive Christian Response.* San Francisco: HarperSanFrancisco, 1994.

Schneider, Laurel C., and Stephen G. Ray Jr. *Awake to the Moment: An Introduction to Theology.* Louisville: Westminster John Knox, 2016.

Scroggs, Robin. *The New Testament and Homosexuality Contextual Background for Contemporary Debate.* Minneapolis: Fortress, 1984.

Seubert, Xavier John. "But Do Not Use the 'Rotten Names': Theological Adequacy and Homosexuality." *Heythrop Journal* 40 (2002) 60–75.

Shore, John. *Unfair: Christians and the LGBT Question.* Miami: CPSIA, 2013.

Bibliography

Stuart, Elizabeth. *Just Good Friends: Towards a Lesbian and Gay Theology of Relationships.* London: Mowbray, 1995.

Sullivan, Michael K. *Sexual Minorities: Discrimination, Challenges, Development in America.* New York: Haworth, 2004.

Swindal, James. "Faith and Reason." *Internet Encyclopedia of Philosophy.* 2019. https://www.iep.utm.edu/faith-re/.

Tanis, Justin E. *Transgendered: Theology, Ministry, and Communities of Faith.* Cleveland: Pilgrim, 2003.

Taslim, Najla, et al. "Gender Dysphoria: A Medical and Ethical Perplexity as Distinct from Reality and the Rational Approach for Muslim Young People." *Psychiatria Danubina* 33 (2021) 475–84.

Thomas, Calvin. *Straight with a Twist: Queer Theory and the Subject of Heterosexuality.* Urbana: University of Illinois Press, 2000.

Tolbert, Mary Ann. Foreword to *Take Back the Word: A Queer Reading of the Bible*, edited by Robert Goss and Mona West, i–xv. Cleveland: Pilgrim, 2000.

Tonstad, Linn Marie. *Queer Theology.* Eugene, OR: Cascade, 2018.

Trible, Phyllis. *Texts of Terror: Literary-Feminist Readings of Biblical Narratives.* Philadelphia: Fortress, 1984.

Tutu, Desmond. "South Africa's Blacks: Aliens in Their Own Land." In *Ethics in the Present Tense: Readings from Christianity and Crisis, 1966–1991*, edited by Leon Howell and Vivian Lindermayer. New York: Friendship, 1991.

United States Conference of Catholic Bishops. *Always Our Children: A Pastoral Message to Parents of Homosexual Children and Suggestions for Pastoral Ministers.* Washington, DC: USCCB Publishing, 1997.

———. *Economic Justice for All: A Pastoral Letter on Catholic Social Teaching and the U.S. Economy.* Washington, DC: USCCB Publishing, 1986.

———. *Ministry to Persons with Homosexual Inclination: Guidelines for Pastoral Care.* Washington, DC: USCCB Publishing, 2006.

———. *Renewing the Vision: A Framework for Catholic Youth Ministry.* Washington, DC: USCCB Publishing, 1997.

———. *Sharing Catholic Social Teaching: Challenges and Directions.* Washington, DC: USCCB Publishing, 1998.

———. *Sons and Daughters of the Light: A Pastoral Plan for Ministry with Young Adults, Second & Revised Edition.* Washington, DC: USCCB Communications, 2012.

Vines, Matthew. *God and the Gay Christian.* New York: Convergent, 2014.

Volf, Miroslav. *Exclusion and Embrace: A Theological Exploration of Identity, Otherness, and Reconciliation.* Nashville: Abingdon, 1996.

Waltz, Alan K. *A Dictionary for United Methodists.* Nashville: Abingdon, 1991.

Wells, Kristopher, et al. *Being Safe, Being Me in Alberta: Results of the Canadian Trans Youth Health Survey.* Vancouver, BC: Stigma and Resilience among Vulnerable Youth Centre, School of Nursing, University of British Columbia, 2017.

Whitehead, James D., and Evelyn Eaton Whitehead. *Method in Ministry: Theological Reflection and Christian Ministry.* San Francisco: HarperSanFrancisco, 1980.

Williams, Robert. *Just As I Am: A Practical Guide to Being Out, Proud, and Christian.* New York: Harper Perennial, 1992.

Wilson, Nancy. *Our Tribe: Queer Folks, God, Jesus, and the Bible.* San Francisco: HarperSanFrancisco, 1995.

Bibliography

Wolter, Allan B., and Blane O'Neill. *John Duns Scotus: Mary's Architect*. Quincy, IL: Franciscan, 1993.

Wood, Robert W. *Christ and the Homosexual*. New York: Vantage, 1960.

Woods, Eric. "Belonging and Transformation." In *4 Views on Pastoring LGBTQ Teenagers: Effective Ministry to Lesbian, Gay, Bi, Trans, Queer, and Questioning Students among Us*, edited by Mark Oesteicher, 65–90. San Diego: Youth Cartel, 2018.

Yarhouse, Mark A. *Understanding Gender Dysphoria: Navigating Transgender Issues in a Changing Culture*. Downers Grove: IVP Academic, 2015.

Young, Iris Marion. *Justice and the Politics of Difference*. Princeton: Princeton University Press, 1990.

Zalot, Jozef D., and Benedict Guevin. *Catholic Ethics in Today's World*. Winona, MN: Anselm Academic, 2011.

Index

abjection, 5, 116

abominations, in the Holiness Code, 39

abstinence, 58, 59, 95

academic literature, queer understood in, 136–37

accompaniment, with LGBTQ young people, 172–73

Achtemeier, Mark, 48

acting, as a component of the hermeneutical circle, 17, 24–25

action plan, for ministry with trans youth, 125

action-prayer, called contemplative action, 22

addiction, treating homosexual activity as, 59

adolescence, for transgender teenagers, 112–14

adolescents, teaching to cope, 105

adult role models, for transgender young people, 130–31

adults, young people needing love and acceptance from, 108

advice, trans youth and young adults and, 126

advocacy, 2, 100–101, 105, 122, 130–33

affectional orientation, defined, 5

affectionate orientation, toward young people, 131

affirming, 65n32

African American men, presenting as straight (heterosexual) in public, 8

agape, 23

agender, defined, 5

alienation, creating, 98

Alison, James, 60

"allies," in unity and solidarity with queer people, 12

ally. *See* LGBTQ ally

Althaus-Reid, Marcella, 78–79, 138, 139, 150

Always Our Children: A Pastoral Message to Parents of Homosexual Children and Suggestions for Pastoral Ministers (United States Conference of Catholic Bishops), 55n1, 96, 97–98

Always Our Children (USCCB), discussing, 156

American Foundation for Suicide Prevention, on suicide attempts among trans, 120

Amos, 36

analyzing, observing as a form of, 18

androgynes/androgynous, defined, 5

189

Index

angels, 49–50
anti-homosexual feelings, 68
anti-homosexual groups, 69
apologetic theology, influence on queer
    theology, 144–45
Aquinas, Thomas, 84–85, 141, 142
Arbelo, Max, 74
arsenokoitai, 43, 46, 47
arsenokoitēs, 43
Arzola, Fernando, 105
asexual
    defined, 5
    transgender as, 109
assigned sex at birth, defined, 5–6
assumptions, pastoral ministers
    examining, 125–26
Atticus Finch, in the movie *To Kill a
    Mockingbird* (1962), 35
attitudes
    changing on homosexuality and
        transgender rights, 89–91
    negative harming transgender
        teenagers and young adults, 123
    on the primacy of heterosexualism, 16
Augustine of Hippo, 141
authentic self, finding in sexuality and
    gender, 145

Bailey, Derrick Sherwin, 66n37
bathroom, 24, 163–64
behavioral counseling, 73
behavioral therapies, 112
Bergant, Dianne, 87
Bevans, Stephen B., 143
Bhabha, Homi K., 19
Bible
    Christians comprehension of, 29
    as a collection of books, 32
    as God's truth, 35–36
    homosexuality as a misnomer in, 32
    loving and committed relationships
        not renounced in, 48
    narrow-minded, fundamentalist, and
        literalist approach to, 46n46
    on same-sex relations between
        women, 42
    on sexual confirmation surgery, 112
    weekly study of, 168

*The Bible and Homosexual Practice: Texts
    and Hermeneutics*, 44
Bible studies, weekly, 168
biblical narratives, reading, interpreting,
    and researching all, 140
biblical passages, addressing
    homosexuality, 31–33
bigender, defined, 6
binaries, as categories of organization,
    64n29
binary gender, queer theory challenging
    ideas of, 147
binary system, as the correct and
    orthodox position, 68
binary thinking and presumptions,
    removing, 147
birth, ambiguous at, 11
bisexual, defined, 6
bloggers, rhetoric toward LGBTQ folks, 69
body
    as an element of gender, 8
    as a temple, 57, 57n8
body/self-image discomfort, 128
Bonino, José Miguez, 25
book club, creating an LGBTQ, 162–63
Book of Sirach, 36
Book of Wisdom, 36
books, listing of LGBTQ, 162–63
"Born This Way" (song), 77
"born-again" Christians, on
    homosexuality, 69
Boys Don't Cry (1999), 114
Brief Guide (Sanders), 127n66
*A Brief Guide to Ministry with LGBTQIA
    Youth* (Sanders), 160
Brill, Stephanie, 117, 127
Brooten, Bernadette J., 44
Burgess, Christian, 113
Burke, Kevin F., 87
butch, defined, 6

Catechism of the Catholic Church (CCC)
    on homosexuality, 55, 60–62
    on repercussions for "not following,"
        104
catechizing, about transgender, 123
categorization, resisting ideas of, 147

Index

Index

Index

Index

Index

South American liberation theologians, 17
speaker series, for LGBTQ youth and/or
    young adults, 154–55
spiritual and pastoral care, providing
    ongoing to LGBTQ young people,
    165–66
spirituality
    assisting youth and young adults in
        exploring as a trans person, 132
    sexuality connected with, 30–31, 79,
        81, 102
"Stand Up!" walk/run, 164–65
status quo, subverting or disturbing, 78
"Stop the Hate Campaign," sponsoring,
    157
stories, 131–32, 165
straight, defined, 12
straight folks, on what is sinful for
    LGBTQ folks, 145
strategies, for youth and young adult
    ministers, 154–68
stressors, for trans young people, 117
student ministry, creating LGBTQ peer-
    led, 157
subjective rights, Aquinas on the
    contemporary notion of, 85n29
suicide, among transgender young
    people, 120–21
Summa Theologica (Aquinas), 84
support, for transgender young people,
    126–30
"syntax of forgetting," not remembering
    the defeated Other, 19
systemic change, bringing about real, 25

T, in LGBTQ representing transgender
    persons, 109
Tanis, Justin E., 50, 112–13, 123–24
teachings
    challenging denominational and
        magisterial, 94
    critiquing current, 54–75
teenagers, advocacy section on the rights
    of, 100
temple homosexual prostitution, texts
    against, 39
tenderness, revolution of, 82

terminology, LGBTQ, 3–14
texts of terror, 31, 140
theologians, viewing lesbian and gay
    people as disordered, 63
theological challenges, of the
    Catholic Church's position on
    homosexuality, 62–68
theological convictions, harming
    transgender teenagers and young
    adults, 123
theological points, envisioning the
    dignity of the LGBTQ person, 84
theological quandary, regarding LGBTQ
    youth and young adults, 94–106
theology
    in dialogue with the dominant
        intellectual categories, 21
    doing outside the dominant culture,
        77
    on faith and reason as sources of
        authority, 141
    of imago Dei, 77–78, 79
    queer theory and, 147–48
    reflecting on, 87
    on sensus fidelium and the signs of
        the times, 91
theósis, Russian Orthodox concept of, 80
thinking, deconstruction of old patterns
    of, 78
"third way," defined, 6
To Kill a Mockingbird (1962), 35
Tom Robinson, innocent black man, 35
Tonstad, Linn Marie, 63
tools for ministry, social sciences
    providing, 21
town hall meeting, holding an LGBTQ,
    164
traditional and conservative view, on
    sexual relations as abstinence and
    chastity, 95
traditional or conservative camp, of
    theological thought, 94
traditional or totalitarian theology
    (T-theology)
    deconstruction of, 137
    defined, 13
    experiencing un-shaping, 138

Printed in the USA
CPSIA information can be obtained
at www.ICGtesting.com
LVHW010301230823
755964LV00002B/108